THE LEAST WORST PLACE

THE

LEAST

WORST

PLACE

Guantanamo's First 100 Days

KAREN GREENBERG

UNIVERSITY PRESS

2009

OXFORD
UNIVERSITY PRESS

Oxford University Press, Inc., publishes works that further
Oxford University's objective of excellence
in research, scholarship, and education.

Oxford New York
Auckland Cape Town Dar es Salaam Hong Kong Karachi
Kuala Lumpur Madrid Melbourne Mexico City Nairobi
New Delhi Shanghai Taipei Toronto

With offices in
Argentina Austria Brazil Chile Czech Republic France Greece
Guatemala Hungary Italy Japan Poland Portugal Singapore
South Korea Switzerland Thailand Turkey Ukraine Vietnam

Copyright © 2009 by Karen Greenberg

Published by Oxford University Press, Inc.
198 Madison Avenue, New York, New York 10016

www.oup.com

Oxford is a registered trademark of Oxford University Press

Library of Congress Cataloging-in-Publication Data
Greenberg, Karen J.
The least worst place : Guantanamo's first 100 days / Karen J. Greenberg.
p. cm.
Includes bibliographical references and index.
ISBN 978-0-19-537188-8
1. War on Terrorism, 2001—Prisoners and prisons, American.
2. Guantanamo Bay Naval Base (Cuba)
3. Prisoners of war—Cuba—Guantanamo Bay Naval Base.
4. Prisoners of war—United States. I. Title.
HV6432.G7345 2009
355.1'29609729167—dc22   2008043258

3 5 7 9 8 6 4 2

Printed in the United States of America
on acid-free paper

For Adam
and
for Katie

I would characterize Guantanamo Bay, Cuba, as the least worst place we could have selected. It has disadvantages, as you suggest. Its disadvantages, however, seem to be modest relative to the alternatives.
—Secretary of State Donald Rumsfeld,
December 27, 2001

Contents

Acknowledgments   ix

Guide to People   xi

Guide to Acronyms   xiii

Preface   xv

1   **World Gone Wrong**   1

2   **The First Team**   23

3   **The Void**   41

4   **Filling the Void**   50

5   **The Bad Guys First**   68

6   **The Petting Zoo**   87

7   **The Caribbean Hilton**   105

8   **The General and the Chaplain**   126

9   **Missing Pieces**   143

10 **A Political Animal**   163

11 **Towels into Turbans**   176

12 **Bowing Out**   198

Postscript   213

Notes   223

Bibliography   247

Index   253

Photos follow page 104

Acknowledgments

This book was a learning experience, requiring me to enter not only unknown legal and military turf but the profession of journalism itself. As a result, the lessons provided by my friends and colleagues were as invaluable as the material itself.

It perhaps goes without saying that the individuals who agreed to be interviewed deserve most of the credit for this book. They not only prodded their memories at busy times in their lives, but they went into their own archives, discovering photographs, journal entries, letters, and e-mails that helped identify the cast of characters, nail down the timeline, and flesh out the issues. To them, I owe the most gratitude.

A handful of journalists, lawyers, and friends who have followed the war on terror since its inception educated me with great patience along the way. Matthew Waxman brought me into the story with his ingeniously subtle suggestions. Larry Wright's generous guidance was invaluable in the final stages of the manuscript. Peter Bergen, Bart Gellman, Jane Mayer, Amos Elon, Sidney Blumenthal, Craig Unger, Tara McKelvey, Henry Schuster, and Dana Priest taught me how to ask the right questions—and how to hear the answers. Paul Cruickshank helped me find the seemingly unfindable. Daniel Freifeld pitched in with his knowledge and his determination to help get things right. Jan Elster guided the translations from the French. Marty Lederman, Scott Horton, Phillippe Sands, David Golove, David Bowker, and Andy Peterson made it their business to educate me over and over again about all the things they know that were once terra incognita to me. Carol Gilligan and Jim Gilligan gave much-needed advice at a crucial time in London. Elliott Millenson brought his critical eye to questions of context. Michael Sheehan set me an example and then stood by my side for this as for so much else. Danny Goldberg coaxed me into thinking the bigger thoughts. Joshua Dratel's friendship, exuberance, and counsel were, as always, one-of-a-kind and much appreciated.

The staff at the Center on Law and Security—Nicole Bruno, Maggie McQuade, Colleen Larkin, and David Tucker—caringly nurtured the Center during the writing process, kindly overlooking the many distractions that a book demands. Francesca Laguardia's passion for research and accuracy and her searing intellect accompanied me every step of the way, keeping me true to myself as well as to the facts. Jeffrey Grossman cast his laserlike intelligence and never-tiring enthusiasm over every page. This book could not have been done without the help of Rush Atkinson, my research assistant who has not only a talent for finding facts but a love of the story itself. Cara Manket, Susan MacDougall, and Angela Zhu worked painstakingly through the final fact-checking with the dedication of true scholars. Zachary Stern helped me assemble the names of the detainees. Joan Dim read early proposals and later drafts with her unerring eye.

Sydelle Kramer, my agent, developed an interest in the story even when the general media had turned away from Guantanamo. David MacBride and Christopher Wheeler at Oxford were always there to guide me.

As with any creative piece, one's close friends can make all the difference. Margaret Benners kept the end in sight for me even in the darkest moments. Beth Elon and Karma Kreizenbeck banished ghosts along the way. Pat Bernard accompanied me to many distant interviews.

Above all, there was my family. My brother Gary Greenberg, whom I once taught to read, now shared with me the lessons of his special brilliance— writing. My brother Richard Greenberg, one of the last standing investigative journalists in television news, brought me wisdom and rules of integrity from the field. My dad Larry Greenberg stood by supportively, always full of questions. My mother Ruth Savin Greenberg saved the day, as only mothers can, in the last moment of revisions. Katie Sticklor, with her exquisite judgment, helped me sort fiction from fact, worked tirelessly on the early drafts of the manuscript, and kept my spirits up from start to finish. Adam Sticklor, with his unerring sense of fairness, guided me through the more difficult stories of character and context, all the while building his own new world. Jessica and Addison Sticklor kept my real life alive and flourishing. Stephen Holmes brought the universe to my story, giving me not only the Tuscan hills but the marvelous insights of his own special genius.

To all these friends and colleagues, and many more, I am incredibly indebted.

Guide to People

David Addington: Legal Counsel to Vice President Dick Cheney

Captain Samuel Patrick Alford, USMC: Medical Officer, JTF 160

Brigadier General Rick Baccus, U.S. Army, Rhode Island National Guard: Commanding General, JTF 160 after Brigadier Gen. Michael Lehnert

John B. Bellinger III: Senior Associate Counsel to the President and Legal Advisor to the National Security Council

Debra W. (Debi) Buehn: Commanding Officer Robert Buehn's wife, often referred to as the "First Lady" of the naval base

Captain Robert Buehn, USN: Commanding Officer, Naval Base Guantanamo Bay Cuba; Deputy Commander, JTF 160

Brigadier General Ronald Burgess, U.S. Army: Director of Intelligence (J2), U.S. Southern Command

Colonel Terry Carrico, U.S. Army: Commanding Officer, Joint Detention Operations Group, JTF 160

Major Steven Cox, USMC: Public Affairs Officer, JTF 160

Major General Michael Dunlavey, U.S. Army: Commanding General, JTF 170; Commanding General, JTF GTMO

Timothy Flanigan: Deputy White House Counsel

Rear Admiral Jan Gaudio, USN: Navy Regional Commander for the Southeast

Alberto Gonzales: White House Counsel

William "Jim" Haynes, II: General Counsel, Department of Defense

Brigadier General Galen Jackman, U.S. Army: Director of Operations, (J3) U.S. Southern Command

Brigadier General Michael Lehnert, USMC: Commanding General, JTF 160

Colonel William Meier, USMC: Chief of Staff, JTF 160

Major Timothy Nichols, USMC: Director of Intelligence (J2), JTF 160

Ambassador Pierre-Richard Prosper: Ambassador at Large for War Crimes Issues, State Department

Donald Rumsfeld: Secretary of Defense

Lieutenant Abuhena Saifulislam, USN: Chaplain, JTF 160

Captain Albert Shimkus, USN: Commanding Officer, Naval Hospital, Naval Base Guantanamo Bay; Joint Task Force Surgeon, JTF GTMO

Major General Gary Speer, U.S. Army: Acting Commander in Chief (ACINC), U.S. Southern Command

Colonel Manuel Supervielle, U.S. Army: Staff Judge Advocate, U.S. Southern Command

William H. Taft, IV: Legal Adviser, State Department

John Yoo: Deputy Assistant Attorney General, Office of Legal Counsel, Department of Justice

Guide to Acronyms

CENTCOM	U.S. Central Command
CIA	Central Intelligence Agency
CINC	Commander in Chief
CO	Commanding Officer
DIA	Defense Intelligence Agency
DOD	Department of Defense
DOJ	Department of Justice
EPW	Enemy Prisoner of War
FBI	Federal Bureau of Investigation
FORSCOM	U.S. Army Forces Command
FSSG	Force Service Support Group
GBC	Guantanamo Bay, Cuba
GPW	Geneva Convention relative to the Treatment of Prisoners of War
ICRC	International Committee of the Red Cross
IRF	Immediate Reaction Force
J-2	Joint Chiefs of Staff Directorate for Intelligence
JAG	Judge Advocate General
JTF	Joint Task Force
MP	Military Police
NEX	Navy Exchange
NSC	National Security Council
OLC	Office of Legal Counsel
OSD	Office of the Secretary of Defense
PAO	Public Affairs Office/Public Affairs Officer
POW	Prisoner of War
QDR	Quadrennial Defense Review
SECDEF	Secretary of Defense
SOUTHCOM	U.S. Southern Command

Preface

The beginning is thought to be more than half of the whole.

—Aristotle, *Nicomachean Ethics*, Book I

The prisoner's cry pierced through the hot Caribbean air. It was not the first time that such a shriek had roused the rest of the detainees from their daily lethargy. But this time it brought them to their feet and unleashed a flurry of noise, as they pounded the cement floors and rattled the wire mesh of their cells. An invisible force unsettled the stillness of the island. Despite slights against the prisoners' religious practices, insults muttered by angry guards, and accusations from interrogators, prior to this moment, life at Guantanamo had appeared under control.

Until one prisoner saw his Koran kicked. Until his wail became a call to action.

Several evenings later, the prisoners still in revolt, another man, his hat in hand, walked through the camp as he had done many times before. This time, he paused before a row of cages that had direct sight lines into the cage of the one who shrieked. Bending forward, the general sat on the hardened, dry earth, his legs crossed and his head bare, and looked through the mesh and into the eyes of the prisoner before him, one of many who had elected to go on a hunger strike after the incident with the Koran. "Talk to me," he said. "Please talk to me."

With this, the commanding general of Camp X-Ray detention facility, Guantanamo Bay, Cuba, began yet another chapter in a story that has yet to be told.

The Least Worst Place: Guantanamo's First 100 Days describes a three-month-long episode in which a group of military men and women received the vaguest of orders from the Pentagon and responded as they saw fit. Their names will be new to you and so will their experiences, but their story stands as a piece of history that tested ordinary people, individuals who were far from exceptional but who tried their best to rise to the occasion. Law-abiding, self-respecting Americans, they confronted their mission—tending to 300 captives from the war on terror—with little guidance and even less approbation, making up their own rules and regulations along the way.

The period covered in this book—December 21, 2001, through March 31, 2002—predates the coercive interrogation regimes that were set up in the second half of 2002. It predates the now famous August 1, 2002, torture memo and subsequent Department of Justice legal opinions authorizing previously banned techniques for extracting information from detainees. It predates Rumsfeld's authorization of coercive interrogation techniques. It predates the abuses at Abu Ghraib that took place in 2003. And it predates most of the stories of abuse and torture that have been told about Guantanamo.[1]

Seen through the eyes of the officers on the ground, these 100 days shed light on later crimes that were ordered and committed at Guantanamo, making us wonder: Could those subsequent circumstances have been avoided? Though fleeting, these early days suggest as much by showing us the human condition when it tends toward dignity rather than disgrace.

THE LEAST WORST PLACE

1

World Gone Wrong

If it doesn't go easy, force it.

—Rumsfeld's Rules

Naval Captain Robert Buehn, Bee Bee or Skipper to his friends, gazed out the window of his seaside office at Guantanamo Bay Naval Base and observed the sailboats rocking gently from side to side, balancing effortlessly. Fit, muscular, and of medium height, his clear, blue eyes emitting boundless energy, Buehn was feeling good these days. He had run the Pentagon's Marine Marathon earlier that fall, just weeks after the lingering fires of 9/11 had died down. He could still feel the rush of running before a crowd that was openly weeping as the national anthem played at the starting line.[1] Now Buehn was savoring the first idyllic days of a sunny Caribbean winter, blessed by unseasonable summer rains and an unexpected burst of new foliage from the fall. He was looking forward to going fishing with his sons over the upcoming Christmas break, when the phone rang.

Buehn lifted the receiver that day in mid-December 2001, unaware that life as he knew it at Guantanamo Bay was about to change.

On the line was Rear Admiral Jan Gaudio, Navy Regional Commander for the Southeast United States, an area of responsibility that encompasses Puerto Rico and Guantanamo Bay, Cuba.

"Three hundred in three weeks," the admiral said excitedly. "What do you think? Can you do it?"

At 50, nearing the end of a 30-year career in the Navy, Buehn knew that he wasn't being asked a question; he was being told to find a credible way to answer "Yes."

Rumors had been trickling down the chain of command for weeks. Launched in early October in response to the September 11 attacks, the U.S. invasion of Afghanistan had led to the capture and improvised internment of hundreds of prisoners.[2] Now, it seemed, the Secretary and his general in the field, General Tommy Franks, Commander of CENTCOM, the regional U.S. military command that includes Afghanistan, wanted to remove battlefield captives from Franks's area of responsibility. They were looking for a new location for the detention effort.

Two weeks earlier, on Thanksgiving weekend, Pierre-Richard Prosper, the State Department's Ambassador at Large for War Crimes Issues, had been enjoying the holiday with his parents in Saratoga, New York. That Friday, he had received his own phone call about prisoners from the Afghan battlefield. The State Department and the Joint Chiefs of Staff wanted to inform him about the battle of Mazar-e Sharif, in which the Northern Alliance had just captured 300 Taliban and were in the process of turning many of them over to the United States. Normally, prisoners are held in the rear of a war zone, accessible to intelligence officers seeking tactical information that can be used on the battlefield. But General Franks was worried about the security issue. Keeping the prisoners there could drain his support services as well as provide a vulnerable target. Prosper was needed back in Washington immediately to help address the issue of where to put these prisoners.[3]

A Haitian-American known for his expertise in prosecuting war crimes and especially for his successful prosecution of crimes of genocide before the UN's International Criminal Tribunal for Rwanda, Prosper's fame came largely from his success at convincing the War Crimes Tribunal that rape in time of conflict constituted an act of genocide and a crime against humanity. Now he was being asked to address another tribal war situation, this one connected to his own country.

The Thanksgiving call was one of many Prosper had received that fall about the detention of suspected terrorists outside of the United States. Within 24 hours of the September 11 attacks, Deputy Secretary of State Richard Armitage had contacted Prosper to discuss the likelihood of prisoners in U.S. custody as part of the response to the attacks of the day before. At the White House, unbeknownst to Prosper and Armitage, a group with a similar sense of urgency about possible prisoners had been convened by White House Counsel Alberto Gonzales.[4] Only when a story about the White House group was leaked by the *Washington Post* did Prosper realize that he should make his way to the White House to see what they were doing—which he did.

On September 19, Gonzales called a meeting that included Prosper and appointed him head of an interagency group whose task was to consider and make recommendations on the legal parameters that would apply to prisoners the United States apprehended in retaliating against al Qaeda and the Taliban.[5] For the next couple of months, Prosper's group, consisting of lawyers and staffers from across the executive branch, continued to meet to discuss the legal context in which prisoners might be detained and tried.[6]

Yet two months later, unbeknownst to Prosper, President Bush issued the first official statement of the policy that would come to define his administration's detention of prisoners. Titled "Detention, Treatment, and Trial of Certain Non-Citizens in the War Against Terrorism," the Military Order of November 13, 2001, established the framework that would govern the detention of prisoners in the war on terror throughout the Bush presidency.[7]

The order was groundbreaking. In contrast to the document on which it was modeled—Roosevelt's Proclamation #2561, "Denying Certain Enemies Access to the Courts"—the Bush Military Order was broad and ambiguous and recognized no legal or procedural checks on the president's proclaimed powers. The Bush Order failed to take into consideration the fact that much had changed in international law since FDR's order, including new, post-1949 Geneva Conventions and a new U.S. Uniform Code of Military Justice (UCMJ), not to mention the major developments in human rights law and civil rights law.[8] Bush's order enabled the secretary of defense not only to oversee the detention of alleged noncitizens who "aided or abetted, or conspired" or planned or threatened to commit acts of violence against the United States or its citizens, but also to wield authority over the tribunals under which they would be tried. Empowering the Department of Defense over other possible players, such as the Department of Justice, it pushed domestic courts as well as international ones out of the picture.[9]

Uninformed ahead of time about the Military Order, Prosper was astonished when the Order was publicly announced. Nor was he not the only high-ranking official to be blindsided by the Order's release. The general counsels for the secretary of state and the national security advisor were stunned, as were their bosses, Colin Powell and Condoleezza Rice.[10] Even the Joint Chiefs were left out of the loop—a notable absence when it came to a so-called Military Order.

The exclusion of principal players from a discussion that was unprecedented in its aggrandizement of presidential powers was the first hint that there was another team at work within the executive, one that was willing to cast aside the previously accepted interagency process. The issuance of the Military Order sent a signal—exclusionary, secretive meetings that resulted in national policy could and would take place under this president.

With one blow, then, the Department of State, long-standing members of the national security team, had been put on notice, both by the secretive manner in which the Military Order was produced and by its contents. This was not going to be their war. But only in the weeks to come would it become clear just whose war it would be.

Despite the previous disempowerment of his interagency group on the matter of detention and military commissions, Prosper responded to his Thanksgiving phone call by heading back dutifully to Washington, where he turned the interagency group's attention to the newest issue: where to put the detained prisoners who were uncomfortably close to Tommy Franks's theater of battle.

Although the impetus to remove the captives was based largely on a determination to keep the captives from impeding the war effort, the reality was that a human rights disaster was in the making on the ground in Afghanistan. The United States had not made adequate preparations for the capture of large numbers of prisoners. Lack of planning meant that manpower, space, and materials were all in short supply. An old Soviet prison 10 kilometers northeast of Kabul, Pol-e-Charkhi, proved uninhabitable, nor could it be easily refurbished to meet minimally acceptable standards. As a stopgap, the captured soldiers and others were being held primarily at several locations—some initially put in Sheberghan prison and then moved to Kandahar—while work on a detention facility at Bagram Air Base was under way.[11]

At Kandahar, prisoners were living without sufficient protection from the cold, and with the notoriously harsh Afghan winter approaching, illnesses such as pneumonia and tuberculosis and even contagious malaria threatened the detainee population. Many had gunshot and shrapnel wounds that threatened to fester, but the immediate medical attention that they needed was not readily available. And the 300 that Prosper would make preparations for had suffered at the hands of General Abdul Rashid Dostum, who, as head of the Northern Alliance, had kept many of them locked in airtight metal containers, suffocating beside their fellow combatants, licking moisture off the walls in the effort to stay alive.[12]

Under Prosper's leadership, the interagency group now considered the question of where to put the prisoners, those from Mazar-e Sharif plus the ones who were certain to accumulate as the war went on. To clarify their choices, the group gathered before a map of the world. Together, they digested information that Ambassador Prosper had collected from embassies around the globe, including venues in Eastern Europe as well as in Germany, and bases in the Pacific, such as those in the Marshall Islands, Guam, Tinian, and American Samoa. Pakistan and ships at sea were also under consideration.[13]

For each of the foreign sites, Prosper elicited the following information: Are the sites under consideration on U.S. or U.S.-controlled territory? Are they secure? Are they big enough? Could they be made big enough?

Almost no place, it seemed, was on sovereign U.S. or U.S.-controlled territory. Germany, the group reasoned, would insist on having a say on detention at U.S. military bases within that country. So, too, with Guam, Tinian, and American Samoa. Any arrangement at one of these places would have necessitated a treaty, or more precisely, in most cases, a status of force agreement that would include details and agreements about the detention mission.

Prosper's group thus recognized that using facilities located in foreign countries, such as Germany or the Marshall Islands, would require onerous negotiations at the diplomatic level. The law of war, international treaties, and the laws of the countries in question would no doubt have obstructed, or at least complicated, the American plan to move battlefield prisoners out of the theater of war. Poland and the British island of Diego Garcia were also considered. But Europe posed a particular problem. Not only would the relocation of prisoners there require negotiations and the consent of the host country to conditions and practices, but the European Court of Human Rights would inevitably beome involved.[14] As for facilities in places like Tinian, Guam, Wake Island, and American Samoa, a different set of insurmountable problems presented themselves. For them, a status of forces agreement would be required. Because these were U.S. territories, prisoners detained there could arguably be subject to the protections of U.S. law, and that, too, from the earliest days, was considered a constraint to be avoided.[15]

The interagency group even considered the United States as a possible venue for the prisoners. Entertaining all possible options, they raised the possibility of using Manhattan for the relocation. After all, it was home to the U.S. Southern District Court, the court that had distinguished itself for terrorism trials, as for example against the perpetrators of the first World Trade Center attack in 1993 and of the U.S. embassy bombings in East Africa in 1998. There had also been some discussion about bringing the prisoners to the brig in South Carolina or to Fort Leavenworth in Kansas. In fact, there was a precedent for bringing captives from the battlefield to the United States. During the Second World War, nearly a half million Axis prisoners of war had been transferred to the United States for the duration of the war. Although this time around there would be only 300 prisoners, replicating the policy seemed unlikely.[16] "There was no way we were bringing the detainees to the United States. Or 300 al Qaeda to Manhattan," recalled Prosper. In fact, "America was out." It would be too tempting a target for a repeat attack, and too difficult a political move for the administration.[17]

In the midst of the discussions, as Prosper remembers it, one of the representatives from the Department of Justice blurted out, "What about Guantanamo? We have a 99-year lease there. We don't need Cuban permission." In fact, it was more than a 99-year lease. The actual terms of the treaty were such that it lasted until both parties consented to breaking the terms of the treaty. In essence, this meant that Cuba had no control over ending the treaty and the United States would hold to it for as long as possible.[18]

The suggestion came as a surprise to most in the interagency group. On the lists that were being generated, no one had yet mentioned Guantanamo. Now, as soon as the name surfaced, it seemed to fill the room, excluding other options. Could it work? Was it secure enough? Were there really no foreign-country constraints that applied there?

Almost from the moment the words were uttered, Guantanamo became the answer to the queries that the interagency group faced. Guantanamo Bay was outside the United States but not beholden to or under the control of another government. Thus, moving the detained population there would not require any treaty arrangement.

It is curious that the idea of a status of forces agreement was such an anathema to the working group. For places like Guam and other islands in the Pacific and Caribbean where the United States had bases, such a treaty might have been a rather simple affair. And as far as the balance of power in the war on terror, such a treaty would have directly involved the Department of State—a development that the White House and the Department of Defense would continually try to block as policy for Guantanamo took shape. Moreover, though one of the world's leading experts in international law, Prosper did not realize at the time what would later become apparent—that within the executive branch, some of his colleagues were opposed to international law on the grounds that it compromised the interests of the United States.

Prosper and his group, determined to be team players in this time of crisis, dutifully took diplomacy off the table in the name of expediency once the ready availability of Guantanamo Bay Naval Base became apparent. That the choice of a military base would empower the anti–international law bent of the administration and that it would ensure Secretary Rumsfeld's complete control over Guantanamo did not deter the interagency group from the goal of supporting the war effort in every way it could—in this instance, by recommending the choice of Guantanamo, a military base exempted from any civilian or extra-governmental protocols. There was no way to step off the base into civilian territory, no need to consider the opinions of a foreign government.

This assertion of legal limbo was a wedge. As such, it opened up the door to a much wider set of questions about the kinds of legal exceptions that might be acceptable on the island base. Simultaneously, the lawyers at the Department of Justice's Office of Legal Counsel were doing their very best to accede to what was rumored to be Secretary Rumsfeld's request for "the legal equivalent to outer space." It was the impression of some lawyers in the executive branch that this disturbing preference for a place where law didn't apply was particularly ardent among an emerging and small group of lawyers who would come to be known as the War Council.[19] This group included five lawyers from throughout the executive branch. Headed by David Addington, legal counsel to Vice President Cheney, and Alberto Gonzales, then White House Counsel, the group also included Gonzales's deputy Tim Flanigan, Office of Legal Counsel lawyer John Yoo, and William "Jim" Haynes II, General Counsel for the Department of Defense.

Over the course of the next several weeks, the legal parameters of Guantanamo's status would be fleshed out in discussions among the lawyers, but for now, the preference for Guantanamo had started to push other prospective sites aside.

Admiral Gaudio's December phone call to Buehn came as part of the due diligence that followed Washington's wholehearted embrace of the Guantanamo option. Personally familiar with the base, having been stationed there in 1974–75 as a search and rescue helicopter pilot and then as a systems administration officer, Gaudio was prepared to jump-start the process of answering questions for the Pentagon. He asked Buehn about the number of beds, the potential for expanding the facilities for an influx of troops, the general level at which the base was currently functioning. How often and in what quantities could supplies be delivered? What were the medical facilities and capacities? How fast could a buildup of the base be accomplished?

As Commander of the Naval Base at Guantanamo, Buehn dutifully promised to look into expanding the base along the suggested lines and to report back how rapidly and under what conditions the requested feat could be accomplished. For Buehn, the questions were not a complete surprise, as he sensed early on that Guantanamo had been selected as the site despite the evident continuing discussions in D.C. Buehn remembers a senior member of his staff summing it up this way: "I think there are two lists . . . one with all these exotic Pacific islands and other places. And then the list that just has Guantanamo on it."[20]

The easy answer didn't require much research. Despite the eagerness of the interagency group, the actual conditions at Guantanamo meant that the introduction to the base of even 300 prisoners posed a Herculean task.

In the fall of 2001, the base lay in a state of permanent hibernation. As part of the general downsizing of the U.S. military after the Cold War, Buehn had spent his 18 months at Guantanamo following orders "to keep the lights on" without "asking for a lot of money down there."[21] In military terminology, Guantanamo's 45 square miles, half of it water, stood at "minimum pillars," its footprint dwindling weekly as buildings were demolished and others emptied in preparation for demolition. The base, under Buehn, retained four basic functions: as a refueling station; as a forward presence for the United States in the Caribbean; as a place for aid and assistance when necessary, largely for the Coast Guard should refugees be picked up at sea in any large numbers; and as the caretaker for maintenance of the Bay and the upkeep of the leased land, as required by the treaty with Cuba. For those purposes, a skeletal military presence of 750 active duty personnel was all that was necessary. An additional 2,000 family members and contract laborers, mostly Jamaicans and Filipinos, completed the resident population.[22]

Life for the Americans on Guantanamo, a low priority for the U.S. military, was in many ways akin to being adrift at sea, though for some, including Buehn, the disconnectedness was part of the attraction of being there. Castro's relations with the United States made the isolation complete. The Cuban leader has never hidden his deep hostility to the treaty establishing American control over Guantanamo, which Teddy Roosevelt imposed on the Cubans in 1903 and which can be suspended only by the mutual consent of both parties. As the United States will never consent to revoking the treaty, Cuba is essentially tied to the unwelcome convenant in perpetuity. In 1964, Castro expressed his desire to end it by curtailing access to both the desalinization plant and the electricity on the island and by building a floating sea gate, a waterborne border crossing, for the Guantanamo River. Since then, Guantanamo has been forced to produce its own electricity and its own potable water.[23] Unable to purchase products from their Cuban neighbors, the servicemen and women and the civilians stationed at Guantanamo were entirely dependent on the household items and groceries that arrived around twice a month by barge from Jacksonville, Florida.

There may have been some charm in this for those who had left behind the pace and glitziness of American strip malls and shopping centers. But it meant that any rapid expansion of the base's resident population would likely drain its resources. The Navy Exchange (NEX)—a mini department store—and two convenience marts were the only shops in town. Once the eagerly awaited items were offloaded and placed on the shelves, residents had to hope that current stocks would suffice until the next barge haul. The first shoppers to arrive at the market on delivery day were also the first to snatch up the food and comfort items many others would have been equally eager to buy. On occasion, wives would find themselves improvising when the NEX ran out of milk or other staples. They could sometimes be seen walking the aisles with open cookbooks, making last-minute decisions based on the supplies in stock. And should the system become suddenly overtaxed for some reason—a run on cold medication or on hurricane-preparedness supplies such as flashlights and batteries—everyone would likely suffer.[24]

If Guantanamo was in no way ready, logistically speaking, to receive an influx of prisoners from Afghanistan, especially within a matter of weeks, there was one way in which the base was prepared, or so its residents thought, for the new operation—and that was emotionally. Just as Buehn had wanted to run in the Pentagon's marathon as a display of his patriotism, so the other officers and enlisted personnel at Guantanamo were eager to demonstrate a post-9/11 patriotism. As a group, they had been palpably frustrated during the three months since the attacks, repeatedly expressing their desire to be included in some mission, any mission, that would give them a part in America's retaliation for the deaths at the Twin Towers and the Pentagon. They felt marooned, in the Caribbean, working to downsize an obsolete base, the relic of an almost forgotten conflict, rather than engaging the current enemy. Now, when the possibility of making Guantanamo a detention facility arose, there was no doubt that the resident military would be ready to play their part.[25]

Buehn, like the community he represented, was excited by the seriously daunting task before him. This patriotic fervor, in part, reflected a professional reflex. When asked to do something, an officer in the U.S. military finds a way to say "Yes." The details—finding resources, identifying positions to be filled and filling them, breaking the assigned task down into its component activities—could be worked out later. Dutifully, Buehn looked into refitting the base's services, ready to report back how rapidly and under what conditions the requested feat could be accomplished. Thus, he continued to take the inventory of sheets, beds, available rooms, and supply schedules, doing everything it took, despite persistent doubts that Guantanamo would actually be chosen.[26]

Migdalia Hettler, his Deputy Supply Officer, described this circumstance—well known to the military—of working as hard at they could, even for something that most likely wouldn't happen. The potential futility of it all was beside the point. The mission was, in Hettler's words, that of "Getting ready for maybe," and doing so with all the passion that the real event would require.[27] This was the military way. Buehn of course knew that when and if the order to deploy *was* issued, funding would quickly be approved, and the arrival of prisoners would be dizzyingly sudden.[28]

With the general question of international standing and the more specific questions of logistics being readily handled, the military could focus on a second-level question—that of security. In particular, the brass wanted to know whether a facility there could be defended against an attack by al Qaeda. How vulnerable was Guantanamo to an attack by land, sea, or air? How would the location of a new detention facility in an isolated corner of one of the world's last Communist countries affect the base's potential vulnerability to attack?

For weeks, the military worked on an answer to the security question, beginning with external threats, and concluding that ground or water provided the most likely avenue of attack for terrorists and that in both cases the military could successfully counter any offensive. Air defense, though less secure, was less necessary, in the estimation of those reviewing the risk of attack against the base.[29]

All told, then, security of the base from an attack by al Qaeda did not set off any alarms, even where there were known vulnerabilities.

Significantly, Cuba itself posed few security concerns. In part, this was explained by the unusual course that U.S.-Cuban relations had taken in the decade following the Cold War. Unnoticed by most of the outside world, and despite the official standoff between Castro's Communist regime and the United States, a surprisingly congenial diplomatic relationship had sprung up between the United States and its alleged enemy. The general feeling of physical well-being that infused the island had seeped into day-to-day political interactions. Yet, there were still some evident dangers remaining. The Cubans continued to keep land mines on their side of the fence line, and Castro throughout his leadership stubbornly refused to cash the U.S. government's $4,200 annual rent checks.[30]

When Admiral Gaudio had been stationed in Guantanamo in the mid-1970s, it had been anything but the good old days. Back then, "we were still shooting at each other," training to take cover and even to return fire when necessary. The earlier generation had "thought the Cubans were going to come across the fence line any day." At times, when Gaudio was making routine nighttime helicopter flights along the perimeter of the base, the Cubans would fire off tracer rounds. "They didn't hit us, and I don't think they intended to hit us. It was harassing fire, [part of the] whole game."[31]

Even today, the Marines who man the base perimeter still point to the 30-foot-high portion of fence near the Northeast Gate and recount how it was built to keep the Cubans from hurling rocks onto the tin roof of their barracks, creating an unrelenting din at night and depriving the Marine guards of sleep.[32]

By the time Buehn assumed command, in June 2000, the "whole game" had become little more than a playful ritual. Neither side thought of winning because there was no longer anything to win. Several of the watchtowers were no longer even manned. In addition, the United States had long since exhumed the antitank land mines that had once sealed off their side of the fence line. Buehn's appointment reflected a desire to continue this state of détente. Never officious, Buehn had a subtle understanding of the role of amiable behavior in potentially antagonistic circumstances, preferring to share a joke, or offer a compliment, rather than look for signs, however subtle, of hostility.

Under Buehn's tenure, relations had become so congenial, in fact, that the two sides had even taken preliminary steps toward a medical exchange. In June of 2001, Buehn made an historic trip through the Northeast Gate and onward to Havana, the first officer in four decades to cross the line to visit the renowned burn unit of the hospital in Havana. Later that summer, he invited the Cubans to meet and observe the medical team at the U.S. base. The hope was to combine Cuban facilities and U.S. medical know-how to improve the treatment of burns.[33]

Rather than the hatred expected of enemies, the feeling of the Americans for Cuba and for the Cubans they knew personally had become by the year 2001 a mixture of curiosity and affection. Some, like Captain Buehn's wife, Debi, devoted their days to salvaging the Cuban heritage. The first lady of the base not only dug beneath her linoleum floors to discover the Cuban hardwood floors, but also organized an oral history of the 75 to 80 Cubans who had resided on the base among the Americans, refugees from Castro's revolution, unable to see their families ever again, who had chosen to stay on the island of Cuba rather than move to the United States.[34]

More formal relations with Cuba, though, still required constant tending. U.S. authorities—Captain Buehn accompanied by Tom Gerth from the State

Department's Office of Cuban Affairs as well as a translator from military intelligence and sometimes a specialist from one of Buehn's departments— would meet with the Cubans on the third Friday of every month, on alternating sides of the fence. Buehn's counterpart from the Cuban Border Brigade (also referred to as the Frontier Brigade) was Brigadier General José Solar Hernández, in charge of supervising the eastern part of Cuba and, like Buehn, a man inclined toward camaraderie.

Their meetings, essentially friendly affairs, focused on the nuts and bolts of coexistence, like managing the brush fires that cropped up along the fence line or maintaining the channel leading up to Cuban waters, a U.S. responsibility according to the treaty. Occasionally, the two officers discussed issues with relatively serious implications, like the procedures for repatriating Cubans who had fled to the base seeking asylum and who, under an agreement dating from May 1995, were to be returned to Cuba unless they had well-founded fears of persecution.

Both emissaries recognized that they weren't there to reignite the embers of an old conflict but simply to resolve ticklish problems as they arose according to mutually accepted if unspoken rules. When General Solar complained about the signal from the base radio station spilling into Cuban territory, for instance, Captain Buehn quickly promised to reduce the transmitter's power output. When the Americans were preparing for the Fourth of July, he would forewarn the Cubans that there would be guns firing, but only for celebration, nothing more. And when a serious issue arose—the need for U.S. Navy planes to fly into Cuban airspace to make their landings safer—he managed to get the Cubans to agree to limited air rights for the U.S. overflights. Buehn became a devout participant in Friendship Day, to celebrate in a formal way the growing tolerance, even arm's-length affection, between the two sides.

True, vague threats sometimes lurked beneath the sociable gamesmanship, a reminder of past Cold War tensions. The Cubans liked to make clear to their American counterparts that they could see just about everything on the U.S. side—and that they were watching. According to Buehn, when Debi Buehn went to the States to visit her mother, who was dying, General Solar greeted the captain at their next regular meeting with the question, "How is your wife's mother?" When planes flew deeper into Cuban space than allowed, Solar would likewise inform Buehn tersely that the Cubans were aware of it. Solar never sought compensation or redress, and Buehn merely informed the General that he would pass along the information; but neither side ever suggested that it was spoiling for a fight.[35]

Risks from Cuba proper were minimal, it was clear. But those who were vetting Guantanamo as a potential detention site in December 2001 also had to consider other potential security risks issues, ones that were internal to the base itself. Among the oddities of the Cuban-American relationship, none was stranger than the scene that unfolded each and every morning at the Northeast Gate. Promptly at 6:00 a.m., a handful of aging Cubans walked up the steep hill on the Cuban side of the gate. Some of Buehn's staff would meet them with a small bus, drive them to their jobs as shelf-stockers at the NEX or supply clerks or schedulers on public works projects, and return them to the gate at the end of the day.[36] In earlier days, the Cuban workers had been stripped for inspection each and every day and then forced to change into "Navy base" clothes and to march single file through the "cattle chute," where the grade was steep enough to force the group to rest along the way. The commuters crossed the fence line each day as part of a 1963 agreement that, although it prohibited new hires from Cuba, allowed those already employed to work there until retirement or death.

By the spring of 2000, this group of Cuban employees—at one time numbering in the many hundreds—had dwindled to 13. Today, only three workers, all of them in or near their 80s, continue to make the arduous commute. Mercifully, the strip-searching stopped years ago. These three workers, the remainder of the population termed *gusanos* or "worms" by the Cuban authorities, continue to show up each day in part for the good of their countrymen—because the Cuban government has refused to cash the checks the U.S. issues to retired commuters, the three remaining workers serve as remittance couriers, bringing ex-workers now living on the Cuban side the U.S. pensions that they live on. These old men obviously posed no security risk of any sort. They were too old, too necessary to the community of former commuters, and too close personally to the Americans to serve as Castro's spying eyes and ears, let alone to work for al Qaeda. In Debi Buehn's words, the "old Cubans" "were the first ones to stand up and say, 'God bless America.' "[37]

The only potential internal risk remaining involved the foreign contract laborers who inhabited the base. Guantanamo couldn't function efficiently if its labor force consisted exclusively of enlisted men and women. The military's version of downsizing—outsourcing routine tasks traditionally performed by enlisted personnel to private contractors—required an increased reliance on local and foreign labor at bases around the world. At Guantanamo, too, the labor force was largely made up of Filipino and Jamaican workers living rent-free in old Navy quarters in partial exchange for pay. These imported civilians, most employed by Burns and Roe, an American engineering firm, or the Norwegian company Kværner, accounted for over a third of the population living at the base in December 2001. They run and maintain the desalinization plant and other infrastructure, staff the port, service the airfields, and tend to the general needs of the population.

However necessary these workers were, in the heightened state of fear that dominated U.S. policy in the months after 9/11, these civilians could have been deemed a risk. But for some reason, their presence did not seem to raise concerns among those considering the detention effort.

The relative difficulty of attacking Guantanamo from land, sea, or air led Buehn, as well as the military strategists and policy makers at the State Department to give the thumbs-up when questioned about security at the base. But it wasn't just legal loopholes and security assurances that made Guantanamo an appealing location for the proposed detention facility. History, too, seemed to point at Guantanamo as a logical and viable choice.

If a detention facility were set up at Guantanamo, it wouldn't be for the first time. Twice before, the base had served as a holding facility for foreigners of indeterminate status.

In the early 1990s and again in the mid-1990s, the American base had been inundated by large waves of refugees, classified as "migrants" by the U.S. government. In the first of these "migrant crises," nearly 30,000 Cuban and Haitian "rafters"—men, women, and children—had lived under U.S. control on the island, most of them Haitians fearing persecution after the overthrow of Jean-Bertrand Aristide.[38] In the mid-1990s, a new wave of migrants arrived on the island. This later group of roughly 18,000 was predominantly Cuban. Another 150–175 were Haitians. Technically, the refugees lived in detention facilities, eventually referred to as migrant camps. And the Pentagon insisted that the detained individuals be referred to as migrants rather than refugees, so as not to assume their legal status as individuals eligible for entry to the United States.[39]

The possibility that Guantanamo might someday be hit by another migrant crisis had always hovered in the back of the minds of officers stationed there—and in the minds of military policy makers. Contingency plans had been drafted for such an event, specifying the chain of command, housing procedures, sources of additional personnel, and the like. According to Buehn, the likelihood that Guantanamo might end up serving a strategic purpose—as a bulwark against possible incursions of desperate boatpeople from Latin America and the Caribbean—was "always kind of looming in the background."

Occasionally, during Buehn's command, a boatload of Haitians did arrive; the refugees would be temporarily housed on the base until the INS made a decision about whether to repatriate them or send them to a third country, such as Canada, Australia, or Nicaragua. The Cuban refugees, fleeing Castro's punitive regime, arrived on homemade boats and rafts, scaled the fence, or, in some cases, simply swam ashore onto the base. Occasionally, single-family or even single-person boats, "onesie-twosies," from Haiti washed up on shore, at times with dozens of Haitians aboard, the sails made of patched-together T-shirts and jeans.[40]

To be sure, Guantanamo was not America's only former refugee camp. The U.S. base at Panama had housed Cubans during the migrant crises of the 1990s. The naval base at Guam had served as a holding facility for refugees from Vietnam in the 1970s. Guam had also provided a remote haven in the 1990s for more than 2,000 Kurds whose collaboration with U.S. authorities had brought them to the point of such deadly peril that they had to be airlifted out of southern Turkey, where they had fled from the murderous regime of Saddam Hussein, and brought to the tiny Pacific island for safety.[41]

But the combination of factors at Guantanamo was unbeatable. Historical experience combined with legal flexibility and a low-risk security environment, making Guantanamo an increasingly irresistible choice for the Bush administration, in its search for a detention facility. So, as the political and legal pieces fell into place in the discussions held in D.C., Buehn continued to collect detailed answers about logistics and capacity, and to deliver his reports up the chain of command. Until all the facts were in, both from the military side and from the bureaucracy in D.C., no firm decision could or would be announced.

Beyond the assessment of the facilities and the base's capacity, Buehn knew that he would have to provide some sort of motivational leadership. The existing community of military personnel would to his mind require help navigating through any transition that might occur. The change to the way of life for the naval base community would be radical, and presumably irreversible. Families with young children would now be living at close quarters with detainees presumably posing a grave threat to physical security. Meanwhile, the routines of the military families would be totally upended when the size of the military population doubled or even tripled in size, taxing supplies, roads, and facilities. How, some mothers wondered, would the changes affect traffic, getting to the stores, to school, and to the cinema at night?

Without waiting for a final decision, Buehn began immediately to reassure his community about continued personal safety and standards of living. To those fearful of change, he promised, as President Bush had at home, that life would for the most part continue as it had been. And to those who had complained repeatedly to him of feeling left out of America's newest war, he promised the kind of challenge any patriot would seek.

Finally, he could turn his attention to what he had an inkling would be a central part of any detention operation—namely, the medical facilities of the base.

Like everything else at Guantanamo in the fall of 2001, the hospital capacity stood at minimum pillars. The incoming captives, Buehn had been told, might very well be wounded or sick. Yet, by a sheer stroke of luck, a planned demolition of the hospital had not yet begun, and a relatively high proportion of medical personnel remained. But the hospital's surge capacity was small, as it was basically an outpatient care facility. Serious cases were routinely referred to the mainland. The local doctor medivaced emergency patients and those needing surgery to Jacksonville Memorial Hospital in Miami. With its six to eight beds, the Guantanamo base hospital rarely had more than one person at a time staying overnight, and its emergency services were slim.[42]

The Chief Medical Officer, Naval Captain Albert Shimkus, was an ambitious and exceptionally accomplished naval nurse whose skills had yet to be tapped in December of 2001. Small-boned, spry, a self-described "seat-of-the-pants anesthetist" with "a good clinical foundation," Shimkus had arrived in Guantanamo in August of 2000, several months after Buehn, and had quickly become a trusted confidant of the naval commander. After serving in Vietnam, he had spent most of his career on the surgical teams of aircraft carriers. But "my heart was in the operating forces," he admits, relishing the proximity of battle or tending to those on missions rather than training missions or ministering to those awaiting deployment.

In 1992, Shimkus rose to prominence when he attended the Naval War College, a prestigious opportunity, and wrote a paper on the use of chemical and biological weapons for future wars. His study had been selected as part of the military's global war game in 1993, a significant honor and one that made him eager to take on more challenges pertinent to current wars.[43]

By chance, Buehn had been enrolled at the Naval War College during this same period. Although the two men did not get to know each other in Newport, the bond of having both been selected for the elite program made them natural collaborators when, in the year leading up to September 2001, Buehn and Shimkus found themselves stationed together at Guantanamo. They became personally close, running on the beach in the mornings and going fishing when time allowed. They discussed endlessly the ins and outs of downsizing the now obsolete Cold War base.

Shimkus had run the Pentagon marathon along with Buehn that fall—a shared show of patriotism after the devastating attack of September 11. When it came to the possibility of hosting a detention operation at Guantanamo, the two were determined to find some way to accommodate their superiors, even if it meant downplaying the deficiencies of Guantanamo for housing and caring for the battlefield captives.

Underneath their eagerness, both Buehn and Shimkus recognized that the rural community in which they lived offered remarkably little by way of medical services to deal with the proposed arrival of a prisoner population and the military that would be needed to tend to those prisoners. The handful of beds on-site and the makeshift emergency operating facilities were not even serviceable as a starting point for the delivery of medical services for wounded or ill patients. And the use of the naval hospital was ill-advised, not only because of its small size and poor functionality but for security reasons. Using it to care for battle-hardened zealots would simply be too dangerous for other patients as well as for medical attendants. Buehn and Shimkus turned themselves into students of prison medicine, committed to accomplishing well beyond the capacity of the base.

By the third week of December, the cards were indeed stacking up in favor of Guantanamo as a feasible site for the new mission. Guantanamo had held thousands in detention in the recent past. It provided, or promised to provide, maximum exemption from legal regulation should such operational flexibility be needed. The base's Cuban neighbors posed only negligible concerns. And the military seemed willing and even eager to embrace the Guantanamo option. Together with U.S. Southern Command (SOUTHCOM), and to a smaller extent, Atlantic Command—where Gaudio reported to his superior Admiral Robert J. Natter—and aided by the advice of Buehn and others, the upper echelons of government bureaucracy had examined the pros and cons and gradually reached a consensus that the island base was the destination best suited to General Franks's captives. U.S. Southern Command would oversee the mission. A joint task force—a combination of all of the services—would mount the operation under SOUTHCOM's aegis. Among other things, the new effort would put into practice a theory of joint operations that had come to dominate the modern U.S. military—that joint doctrine coordinated resources, allowed for the best skills across the military to be called up, and generally provided for a lean, focused military effort.

The challenge of building a detention facility at Guantanamo was rapidly becoming viable from an operational as well as a legal point of view. And the most persuasive fact of all came to the fore—there already was a detention facility located at the naval base.

Camp X-Ray, as it was called, had been built in 1994 when the migrants were moved from Panama to the naval base at Guantanamo. The detention facility consisted of 40 or so open-air cages, called "dog cells" by some, with cement slab floors and tin roofing that could serve as a starting point for the kind of facility Gaudio and the other brass wanted.

Here, Guantanamo's past life cast another appropriate—if eerie—shadow. The cages at X-Ray had been built during the migrant crisis of the mid-1990s to house those refugees whose looting and random violence led them to be reclassified as criminals. The name of the camp reinforced its mission of segregating the bad guys. The existing migrant camps had been named in order from the beginning of the military alphabet onward. Camp Delta followed Camp Charlie, Charlie followed Bravo, and Bravo followed Camp Alpha. X-Ray seemed the perfect name, a proper antonym to Camp Alpha and Camp Beta, as far away, physically and symbolically, from them as could be.

The decision makers up the chain of command and into the Pentagon decided that the spot once occupied by the old Camp X-Ray, now overgrown by weeds, could be revived in function and even in spirit. Buehn had informed his superiors of the site's disarray and state of decay, but he also tried to accommodate their wishes, providing as positive an assessment as possible about military housing, medical facilities, and general resources. True, Buehn and his team could not disguise X-Ray's serious logistical shortcomings. The electricity could be reconnected without much foreseeable trouble, but water would be another matter entirely. Reconnecting the pipes would probably take longer than building the rest of the facility.

And then there was the matter of visibility. While some parts of the naval base were harder than others to observe from the Cuban side, X-Ray, nestled into a groove directly underneath the Cuban hills, was in clear sight of the Cuban watchtowers, as was most of the U.S. base. As Admiral Gaudio put it, "anybody that knows Guantanamo knew that [the Cubans] were going to see everything that happened. . . . They have the ability to watch us at night. They have the ability to watch us during the day. And that's their job."[44]

But concerns about Cuban surveillance did not deter the policy makers in Washington. And with this last caveat tossed aside, Guantanamo Bay, and specifically the defunct Camp X-Ray, became the Pentagon's first and only choice. Once a definitive voice from the executive weighed in, the deal could be closed.

Back in the United States, the War Council as well as Prosper's interagency group continued to meet regularly during December as Buehn and others in the chain of command marshaled their facts and presented them to the White House. None would have claimed that the legal situation of Guantanamo Bay Naval Station was clear. When jurisdiction, procedural concerns, and even treaty rights came up, more questions than answers defined the conversation. Three treaties, spanning four decades and two wars, defined the legal status of Guantanamo. All tended toward confusion rather than clarity. All illustrated the fact that Guantanamo was a unique legal entity. Even the exact borders of the land rights were unclear. According to some experts, though there are no official documents verifying this, Guantanamo's leased area has grown over the years, exceeding its original 45-square-mile tract.[45]

As Guantanamo's status rose to the center of the legal and policy discussions, the utter lack of legal clarity began to appear increasingly as an opportunity. Neither U.S. nor international law clearly applied. The U.S. presence in Cuba seemed to have one-of-a-kind status. In essence, this anomalous patch of territory was a no-man's-land for justice. The matter of sovereignty was unclear. There was no embassy, nor did rules governing embassies abroad apply. Even ships had clearer jurisdictional mandates than did Guantanamo.

Procedural precedents on the naval base itself offered little guidance as well. Civil and legal services at Guantanamo were minimal. No one had the authority to issue wedding licenses. Marriages had to take place on the mainland. Birth certificates and death certificates came from the U.S. embassy in Nassau, the capital of the Bahamas. A traffic court sat on the base.

The base's only policing and legal authority was that of the military. If a civilian got into trouble, no office or officer, other than the commanding officer (CO), was charged with handling the situation. There was no territory outside of the base with conflicting civil jurisdictions—Cuba was off-limits. The best the CO could do was to send civilian violators off the island and ban them from returning. Beyond petty infractions, which the skipper could handle, Buehn expected to send members of the military who violated the law to Florida to face justice. There, the U.S. Attorney for the Northern District of Florida could assert jurisdiction if need be. In theory, a foreign national—a Filipino, a Jamaican, or even a Cuban commuter—who committed a crime could be sent to the mainland as well. And, in a couple of instances in the 1990s, the Eastern District of Virginia had heard cases from Guantanamo.[46] In the one migrant (rather than criminal) case where the U.S. courts had intervened—the sequestering of HIV migrants whose quarantine had been successfully challenged by the Center for Constitutional Rights—the Supreme Court overruled a lower-court injunction and decided to repatriate the Haitians. This signaling of the U.S. government's determination not to have the courts get involved too deeply with decisions involving foreign populations offered a subtle but relevant precedent for any new detention of foreign prisoners at Guantanamo.

The pressure to make a decision by year's end persisted. The notorious cold of the Afghan winter was imminent, resources such as food and clothing were low, and medical facilities for treating the wounds and diseases of the prisoners were minimal to nonexistent—all of which carried the realistic threat of a humanitarian crisis breaking out at Kandahar. From a tactical point of view as well, the prisoners' position in the middle of battle was unacceptable to Tommy Franks, who was determined to stay focused on the war effort and not be distracted by concern for the prisoners in his area of responsibility. Meanwhile, the policy makers in Washington were putting the final pieces of their interagency due diligence into place.

Two days after Christmas, the decision was announced to the public. Donald Rumsfeld made it official. The new detention operation would be set up at Guantanamo Bay. SOUTHCOM would supervise the activities on the base. The 2nd Force Service Support Group, normally based at Marine Corps Base Camp Lejeune in Jacksonville, North Carolina, would run the effort. It would be a joint command, combining the efforts of the various branches of the U.S. military. The name of the joint task force would be JTF 160—the very same label that had been used for the task force during the migrant crisis.

Relying on the patriotism of the forces on the ground and their obedience to the chain of command, Secretary Rumsfeld anointed Guantanamo in defiance not just of warnings from the past, but of military professionalism.

True, the military men and women on the ground, their superiors at SOUTHCOM, the interagency group in Washington, and the Pentagon all seemed to agree with one another. In the shadow of 9/11, they all wanted to do the patriotic thing—which in this case was to help General Franks get rid of the prisoners under his command. But the ready assent was the beginning of a long, slow slide into an untenable and, as it would turn out, extralegal situation that would be more and more difficult to end with each phase of its existence.

But underneath the narrative of agreement lay missteps and warning signs that would come to plague Guantanamo going forward and that were apparent even before the operation was up and running. Chief among these exceptions to the norm had been the subversion of process that had been illustrated in the exclusionary and secretive way in which the Military Order of November 13 had been drafted and turned into policy, a habit that would come to define the Bush administration throughout its eight years.

This bureacratic exclusivity would grow in its destructive impact as Guantanamo came into being, But for the moment, there was a more pressing danger, one that lay outside of the usurpation of powers in Washington or the extralegal premises of Guantanamo, and one that was overlooked by those making policy in D.C. This was the danger posed by the fact that the United States military was not quite equipped to handle the mission that was about to be handed them—that of detaining prisoners of war. It wasn't just that the naval base itself was being asked to perform well above its capacity in terms of resources. It was also a matter of professional expertise. The nation's military did not have the requisite expertise in prisoner of war detention, as the United States had not had to deal with prisoners of war on its own since World War II.

Nor was it helpful that the military was to conduct the operation on the blueprint of migrant detention operations. The task at hand and the professional skills readily available to the Pentagon did not match up. The plan for the detention effort that JTF 160 was given stood on the books as a migrant crisis operation, a template that ironically had itself struggled with definitional terms when it forbade the use of the term "refugee" for the camp's residents. Now, in the year 2001, the definition of terms was intentionally obfuscated once again. No matter what words were used, prisoner incarceration was not equivalent to migrant detention. Captives were neither refugees nor migrants; they demanded a whole other kind of treatment and a separate set of policies. This lack of expertise was further hindered by the fact that the job of SOUTHCOM was to deal with the countries of the Caribbean and Latin America and the issues germane to that geographical part of the globe. Thus, its knowledge base was largely irrelevant when it came to Middle Eastern and South Asian culture.

Though Guantanamo may have provided a legal godsend and a logistically manageable environment, deeper realities suggested that trouble lay ahead for the new detention facility. It stood not just on historical precedent and legal opportunism but also on the unstable ground of secrecy, disregard for professionalism and expertise, and legal flexibility. The deployment of JTF 160 to Guantanamo was an emergency act, done in lieu of a better option—the least worst choice for the least worst place.

No one understood better the treacherous pragmatic—and moral—implications of sidestepping established law and policy than the man chosen to command the detention operation there.

2

The First Team

The Marine Corps will prove that it is up to any task, no matter how humanitarian.

—Lt. Martin Nevshemal[1]

Walking the perimeter of the camp, Marine Colonel Michael Lehnert squinted in the sun before entering the enclosure surrounded by concertina wire. Ordinary looking, of average height and weight, with medium brown hair and eyes, yet identifiable by bushy eyebrows and a square jaw, Lehnert tried to take it all in with one glance. There they were, hundreds of them, clustered in groups of twos and threes and more, talking and waving their light-brown arms, animated and, to the naked eye, innocuous. He was coming in on the heels of a few rough months. There had been two rapes, numerous instances of arson, and periodic rioting. The rate of attempted suicides was on the rise.[2]

It was 1995 in Guantanamo Bay, Cuba, and Lehnert was responsible for the care and custody of the 8,000 men, women, and children who, having fled Cuba, were awaiting admittance to the United States, and the approximately 150 from Haiti, most of whom were expecting to be repatriated.

Six years later, on December 21, 2001, Michael Lehnert was called again to Guantanamo. This time he was a brigadier general. This time he was to watch over not several thousand refugees but several hundred al Qaeda and Taliban terrorists. He would, of course, do his best. But he was worried about this repeat performance. He had an uneasy feeling that Commander, JTF 160, at Guantanamo Bay was not going to be an enviable deployment. How unenviable he still had no idea.

Quiet-spoken, a religious Catholic, disarmingly unpolished and deeply patriotic, Lehnert had served for 25 years in the U.S. Marine Corps as an engineer and logistician. Now, his reputation for professionalism and his prior experience at Guantanamo and elsewhere made him seem an optimal choice to the brass, clearly the right man for this politically sensitive job. His reputation for decency was another matter. That it might rudely collide with the plans for the Guantanamo Bay detention facility that were developing inside

Donald Rumsfeld's Pentagon would have seemed likely, were anyone paying attention.

By experience and training, General Lehnert is not easy to push around. Physically fit but with no particular heft or muscular bearing, he relies upon his character rather than an overpowering physical presence to exert control. Growing up in rural Michigan, Lehnert lost his mother in a car accident when he was seven. Adapting and surviving thereafter became Michael Lehnert's inadvertent philosophy. Working odd jobs through high school, he eventually enrolled in a community college and then, through ROTC, was admitted to Central Michigan University, following in the footsteps of his father, who had been an enlisted Marine. The young Lehnert was hired, largely out of compassion for the hardworking student by Dr. Dan Dean, a family practitioner with a number of bizarre hobbies, including raising cougars. Soon after engaging the boy, Dean received a phone call from an acquaintance who worked in a nearby clinic.

"Hi Dan," the caller said, "I just wanted to let you know about something. You know that young fellow you hired? Did you know he is coming here weekly to sell his blood serum?" The cells extracted from this blood were given, by transfusion, to seriously ill patients, including those who were suffering from various forms of cancer or undergoing bone marrow transplants. "He apparently needs it to make ends meet. Thought you'd like to know." At 25 dollars a pop, weekly bloodlettings allowed the impecunious young man to support himself in college. But selling one's blood did not strike the doctor as a healthy way to earn one's keep. On the spot, Dean decided to hire Lehnert full-time, bringing him into his home, trusting him to share the responsibility for household chores as well as for the care of his children.[3] Dr. Dean even encouraged Lehnert to share in his eccentric hobby of raising the pet cougars, a task well suited to the young man who seemed attracted to things outside the norm.

As an adult, the honing of survival skills persisted. On Saturday mornings, he would sometimes gather his two sons and announce, "You have two hours. Scour the neighborhood and come back with whatever you can find that could even by a stretch be called food. Ready, set, go! Best meal wins." Because Lehnert joined this contest himself, everyone knew the outcome before the competitive foraging began. Lehnert would always win. "He would find roots and nuts, berries of all sorts. He knew how to scavenge. And he was proud of it," one Marine colleague says. As Lehnert likes to say, "You part with the skill of survival at your own risk."[4]

Joining the Marines in 1970 honored the allegiance to survival and adaptation. And it promised to keep order in his life. According to Dr. Dean, Lehnert "chose the Marines because it was so regimented. Everything had its place, everything was in order."

The Marine Corps is famous for providing young men—as it did Michael Lehnert—with the opportunity to expand their abilities by compelling them to face difficult challenges. Joining the Platoon Leaders Class, the primary commissioning source for officers in the Marine Corps, Lehnert soon learned the ways of this almost cultlike organization, dedicated, as its motto—emblazoned on everything from doormats to flags—announces, to Honor, Courage, and Commitment. As the Corps's preeminent historian puts it, "In a century and a half, they evolved an elite, almost mystical institutional personality."[5] Emblematic of its ethos—its official slogan is "The Few, The Proud"—is the rite of passage that concludes the training for enlisted men, an excruciatingly difficult 54-hour trial that tests recruits physically, mentally, and morally. When Lehnert attended Marine Officer Candidates School, the officers' training template for this institutionalized hazing, which promised to turn "self-discipline into selflessness," was already in place. The ascetic and self-denying principles of this code appealed to Lehnert, as did the fact that he was following in part in his father's footsteps. It was a chance to jump-start the entry into responsible adulthood.[6]

The U.S. Marines is not an independent branch of the services. Rather, it is a stepchild of sorts. The Marines are officially part of the Navy, just as the Air Force was once part of the Army. The Corps cannot boast its own Secretary, as can the other branches. Instead, the Corps has a Commandant. Budgetarily and institutionally, its status falls below that of the other services. However, prestige and morale are another matter. As one historian puts it, "The Air Force has its planes, the Navy its ships, the Army its obsessively written and obeyed 'doctrine' that dictates how to act. Culture—that is, the values and assumptions that shape its members—is all the Marines have. It is what holds them together. They are the smallest of the U.S. military services, and in many ways the most interesting. Theirs is the richest culture: formalistic, insular, elitist, with a deep anchor in their own history and mythology."[7] The Marines like to say that a Marine is recognizable even out of uniform anywhere in the world. "It's the way he stands, the way he holds himself, you just know. In any size crowd, we recognize each other."[8] As part of its ethos, the Corps prides itself, as Lehnert often does, on taking on unpleasant tasks.

"We're the third world of the U.S. military," Lehnert says, referring to the fact that the Marines present themselves as the most willing and able of their country's men-at-arms to do what it takes, to make any sacrifice, to pay any cost.

Originally planning to remain in the Corps for three or four years, Lehnert has never strayed from his Marine Corps home. From time to time he considered accepting a private sector position, but he never took the leap. True, just a year before the call to Guantanamo, he had made the decision to retire. But at the very last moment, he had been tapped to be a brigadier general, a one-star. To explain his decision not to leave the Corps, he simply says, "You don't turn down a generalship. You just don't."

And once a general, you don't think twice about a deployment order.

On December 21, the definitive word came to General Lehnert. He had been appointed commander of the new detention mission taking shape at Guantanamo Bay. Both the Marine Corps division that would head the mission and he himself were, so they thought, ready for anything.

As commander of the 2nd Force Service Support Group, Lehnert was deployed to Guantanamo, technically, because the contingency plans for a new migrant crisis—the blueprint for the Afghan detainee operation—called for the commander of the 2nd FSSG to lead the mission. His experience made the bureaucratic reality acceptable for this new mission. To begin with, Lehnert had worked closely with U.S. Southern Command in his assignments over the years in Panama, Honduras, and other places in Central America. He had gotten to know this particular combatant command, its bureaucracy, its main players, its way of doing business. And as the new mission was bound to be littered with pitfalls and stumbling blocks, a good working relationship with SOUTHCOM was imperative.

Secondly, Michael Lehnert knew Guantanamo. As a colonel, he had run the detention piece of Operation Sea Signal, the migrant crisis operation of the mid-1990s. As a result, he understood the logistical problems of the island base, the nuanced relationship with the Cubans, and the potentially sensitive relationship between a task force and a host base.

Operation Sea Signal, in which he had taken part, was best described as a humanitarian operation. For the first year of Lehnert's deployment, the migrants continued to reside at the base in a state of limbo, uncertain about their futures and hoping for the best. U.S. policy at the time was to make sure that the frustration of the migrants did not turn into anger, that the group did not become a mob.

"If they are hopeless, they will strike out. We need to make hope the center of the operation," one commander of the camp explained.[9] Yet such attempts were only partially successful. Two rapes, 67 suicides, and numerous instances of "rock-throwing melees" occurred over the course of the operation, as did several riots and a few fires lit in protest inside their own dwellings.[10]

Lehnert's job at the time had been as head of the detention (i.e., the care and custody) part of the overall migrant operation. It was nonpenal detention except for the existence of a small camp for the few dozen who became violent or otherwise unruly. Working alongside the logistics team and under the direction of an overall commander, his role, as he saw it, had been to counter these destructive impulses and ensure that things didn't spin out of control, to foster "good morale," and to give the Cubans and Haitians "opportunities to perform meaningful work."

Lehnert earned a reputation for bringing a philosophy of community outreach to the mission. Making lethargy and boredom among migrants his personal nemesis, he devised and encouraged recreational activities of all kinds. Together with his operations counterpart, Lehnert included schools, chapels, libraries, and day care facilities in his detention program. Jobs were posted and individuals employed to work around the camps. Residents were encouraged to prepare the camp food in keeping with their customary cuisine. The inmates tended the place, weeded and mowed the lawn, created gardens and cooked and cleaned for themselves. Other activities included sports, arts and crafts, and theater groups. At one camp, stand-up comedians mocked Castro and his "henchmen," and musicians, young and old, performed. Both vegetable and flower gardens abounded, as did citizens' leagues that would represent different interest groups in parlays with Lehnert's management team. Sports, primarily soccer, became so popular that leagues eventually developed. Camp newspapers were published and radio programs broadcast in both Spanish and Creole.[11]

When the Clinton administration announced its decision to allow the Cubans to migrate to the United States, Lehnert arranged a civics curriculum and the creation of elected committees tasked with making recommendations on all aspects of life at the camp as an exercise in democratic participation. For Lehnert, the civics regimen was a sign of strength. "I ran a tough ship" when it came to the immigrants. "I would say, you're going to a land of freedom. So you need to learn how to exercise self-discipline."[12]

But when the Haitians as a group were refused asylum, Lehnert learned another lesson: that despair could undermine any amount of good intentions.

The Haitian camps, which from the early days had been "permeated with despair,"[13] spiraled further into hopelessness in the wake of the decision to repatriate them, leading to threats of suicide and erratic outbreaks of violence.

That there would be civics lessons, painting workshops, and concerts at the new Guantanamo of 2002 was improbable. More likely, despair and hopelessness would be everpresent. But in either case, what even a distant regard for Lehnert's prior work at Guantanamo and his character would have shown was that he was intent on countering despair among those in his charge—a worrisome precedent for what was to develop under his command.

Lehnert valued his dedication to outreach in Operation Sea Signal, but the highest echelons of the Marine Corps did not judge the operation to be altogether satisfactory. In the post-mission evaluation, the Marine Corps leaders questioned particularly those aspects of the mission where Lehnert's personal achievements had been most palpable.

True, the official executive summary and lessons learned reflected a pride in the demonstration of the combatant commander's ability to exercise "unity of command" over all four services and over every aspect of the operation. "Interagency cooperation" and proof of the military's professionalism and flexibility were also seen as successes of Sea Signal. And according to Colonel John McKay, one of the Commanders of the Sea Signal JTF, and John Shalikashvili, then Chairman of the Joint Chiefs, "The operation has reshaped the role of the military."[14]

But the official report cast considerable doubt on the wisdom of using the armed forces for humanitarian rescue efforts, concluding that "Operation SEA SIGNAL had an adverse impact on force readiness and operation tempo. In the future, consideration should be given to using contractors or reserve forces following the crisis response stage once the situation has stabilized." The use of active military for humanitarian operations was considered a waste of time and money and had significant opportunity costs—namely, the ability to mobilize elsewhere, if needed, for combat missions.[15]

Therefore, as with the choice of Guantanamo itself, a superficially logical decision—to send Michael Lehnert to organize the detention facility at Guantanamo after 9/11—when examined more closely, was anything but logical. Lehnert believed that principled humanitarianism was not only compatible with, but essential to, the Marines' sacred code. Resurrecting JTF 160 from the Haitian and Cuban migrant days and restoring Lehnert to Guantanamo, this time as the commander in charge, was like erecting a building on a fault line. It brought a man with a reputation for tending to the spirit as well as the physical health of those in his custody to the task of incarcerating men said to be criminals whose goal was to destroy the United States. The gap between migrant detention and penal incarceration threatened to widen into a profound policy disconnect in the person of Michael Lehnert. It wasn't that he did not know how to supervise a prison; he had done so as a young officer at Subic Bay and then again at the prison that serviced the migrant crises. It was that he insisted on thinking about the treatment of those in his custody and assuming that it should be fair, just, legal, and, if possible, even rehabilitative. Thus, the appointment of Lehnert carried into the new mission of terrorist detention the grave risk that clashing sensibilities would breed incompatible agendas. This would turn out to be particularly true under the stewardship of Donald Rumsfeld.

In the wake of the Cold War, questions were raised inside the branches of the armed services and in Washington policy and budget discussions about the future direction of the U.S. military. What kind of defenses and weapons were needed in the new age, and what, if any, major structural changes were required to exploit new capabilities and to meet new threats? The tension between active combat forces and developmental, humanitarian aid agendas reflected these larger considerations.

Among the individuals who had been most involved in questions about the future of the U.S. armed services was Secretary of Defense Donald Rumsfeld, the man who ultimately would be controlling the new state of affairs at Guantanamo. And while he was not there to weigh in on Sea Signal, he was, from 2001 onward, more influential than any other individual over the direction the U.S. military would take going forward.

In and out of the defense department since 1975, Donald Rumsfeld had given a great deal of thought to the direction he preferred. Early in his assumption of the secretaryship, Rumsfeld had announced his plan to transform the military. He was appalled, he wrote, by the imbalance between combat forces and support services, the latter being a costly deadweight to a military that needed to be able to respond quickly and with flexibility to the challenges of the 21st century.[16] In this, he was following a path identified by George W. Bush, who while running for the presidency announced in a speech given at the Citadel, "I will begin creating the military of the next century." Promising to "defend the American people against missiles and terror," the then president-to-be touted "lighter... more lethal forces" and a change in military structure. In his speech accepting the nomination for president, George W. Bush reiterated his interest in transforming the military, which was "low on parts, pay and morale."[17]

Donald Rumsfeld was just the man to turn Bush's stated intentions into policy. In the 2001 Quadrennial Defense Review (QDR), he pledged himself and his department to the creation of a military of speed, not mass; of high-tech weaponry, not bureaucratic paralysis and cost overruns. His capsule summary of the new approach emphasized replacing a "threat-based strategy" with a "capabilities-based approach." Essentially, Secretary Rumsfeld wanted to focus on increasing investment in high-tech weaponry and on enhancing the role played by the military in shaping the foreign policy of the United States.[18]

But for the rush to action, the mismatch between the choice of commander for Guantanamo and the philosophy of Rumsfeld's Pentagon might have been eminently clear. In a military that was being slimmed down to concentrate on fighting wars, humanitarian rescue operations such as Sea Signal seemed wholly beside the point. Because the operation's initial phase was considered a temporary stopgap, pending an Army command, no one paid any regard to the potential risks of, for the time being, putting an officer with humanitarian leanings in charge. In normal circumstances, the particular philosophy of Lehnert, a one-star general several layers removed from the Pentagon, would have been considered irrelevant. His job was to implement orders. And Lehnert would have been the first to say, "I'm not a policy guy."

But policy guy or not, he was not going to be the flexible instrument that Rumsfeld's Pentagon was seeking at the time. The pieces were now in place for a radical disconnect, inside the chain of command, regarding the aim and parameters of the new mission. In addition to potential disagreements over Marine Corps philosophy, serious confusions about who was responsible for what tasks had arisen. This was true within the civilian leadership at the Pentagon, between the civilian leadership and the top brass, and within the military chain of command itself.

These confusions about responsibility, jurisdiction, and authority contributed to the still poorly defined nature of the mission to bring prisoners to Guantanamo. The intermediaries between Rumsfeld and Lehnert had been severely compromised by the time Lehnert was deployed. For one thing, Rumsfeld had made it crystal clear, publicly and privately, that he had little or no use for the Joint Chiefs. During the drafting of the QDR, in fact, the Secretary displayed what can only be called a lack of respect for the uniformed military.[19] The report is customarily written from reports submitted by individuals in each branch of the armed services. Since 1999, therefore, the Joint Chiefs had overseen the process of producing the QDR. Embracing the reputation he had earned among business associates as a bull in a china shop, Rumsfeld pushed tradition aside, hired consultants from outside the Joint Chiefs' staff, and produced a report that denigrated the breadth and depth of the military in favor of bureaucratic streamlining and the purchase of advanced weaponry. Thus by the time the new Guantanamo mission began to take shape, the influence of the Joint Chiefs had already been considerably diminished.

So, too, under Rumsfeld, SOUTHCOM stood to exercise less power than it had traditionally wielded as one of the Unified Combatant Commands. In August 2001, the Secretary of Defense had removed the four-star general Peter Pace from his position as combatant commander for SOUTHCOM, and as of September 30, 2001, promoted Pace to the position of vice chairman of the Joint Chiefs. While the process of nomination and confirmation for a replacement went on, the deputy commander of SOUTHCOM, Gary Speer, stepped in for Pace as acting commander. Whatever his skills may have been, as a two-star instead of the four-star required to hold the post of combatant commander, Speer's authority was severely compromised, something of which the entire staff of SOUTHCOM was acutely aware at the time. In addition, no deputy was appointed to assist him. At the top, then, there was an unmistakable, debilitating void. This was most likely not an intentional attack on the military structure, but a mere side effect arising from the normal course that promotions and confirmations take. But the effect was nonetheless to reduce the authority of a key link in the chain of command that went from Guantanamo to the Pentagon.

Rumsfeld's appointments and preferences meant, in essence, that Lehnert was on his own, a state of affairs evident during his first post-9/11 trip to Guantanamo on December 22, 2001. Departing within 24 hours of his official deployment, Lehnert left for his one-day site visit on a jet rather than the customary prop plane used for trips to Guantanamo. Everything signified the hurried nature of the new mission. Once the Joint Task Force (JTF) landed in force, they would have 96 hours to construct an entire world ready to receive 100 or so detainees.

The purpose of this initial visit was to discuss in detail the logistics of building the proposed internment camp and to assess what would be needed to mount, staff, and support such a mission.[20] But a further point to this visit was the establishment of the working team that would create the new Guantanamo.

Joining Lehnert on the trip was a whole crew of higher-ups,[21] but more central to his immediate purposes was the inclusion of two individuals he had selected from the 2nd Force Service Support Group to be part of his inner council.

Lehnert knew that, practical realities aside, it was his command staff that would make all the difference. By his side were two Marines from Camp Lejeune, Colonel William Meier, whom he had selected as his Chief of Staff for the new mission, and Major Timothy Nichols, his intelligence officer, tasked at the outset with providing security for 2nd FSSG operations. Meier was Lehnert's "make it happen guy,"[22] a combat engineer who had become a masterful logistician. Meier would be Bob Buehn's partner on the island. Together they would coordinate available resources in personnel and materials to make the new mission run efficiently. A physical education major, originally from Yuma, Arizona, Meier had little experience of the world, yet he had a reputation for flexibility, adaptability, and a trait Lehnert focused on—a seeming ability to be at ease with different cultures and habits.

Tim Nichols was another story altogether, a yin to Meier's yang. Educated, thoughtful, worldly, and smart as a whip, he was a perfect counterpart to the nose-to-the-grindstone logistician. Today an associate professor of naval science at the Piedmont Consortium[23] in North Carolina, where he teaches leadership and ethics as part of the Naval ROTC program, he was as devoted to learning as he was to the life of military discipline and camaraderie. This made him an apt companion for Lehnert, able to offer pointed counsel on a wide range of things, from his specific duties as an information officer tasked with the logistics of security to political and even philosophical questions about the nature and purposes of the mission.

Nichols had joined the military after he graduated from college at the University of Virginia on an ROTC scholarship. Once in, he reveled in the opportunity to explore the world, which he did for 10 years while working in military logistics intelligence. Thereafter, he returned to the States, earned a master's degree in American Studies at the University of South Florida while still in the service, and was then deployed to Camp Lejeune. Fortunately, Nichols had just completed a tour for CENTCOM during which he had come to know the region, including Afghanistan and even Kandahar, where many of the prisoners who would soon be en route to Guantanamo were now detained.

Confident in the professionalism and judgment of Meier and Nichols, Lehnert turned his focus to the island itself.

The rough ground, the cactus, the dried brush, all resembled a deserted isle rather than a Caribbean haven. The difficult landing on the leeward side of the bay, which even highly skilled pilots dreaded, reminded him of all the strange Cuban directives he'd seen in his time at Guantanamo. The inviting hills and the murmur of the desalinization plant, built on the spot where Columbus landed in 1492, not to mention the intense January heat, were immediately recognizable.

But the familiarity of the landscape did not disguise the deep and serious changes that had taken place during his five years away. Although the cliffs overlooking the sea and the winding hills taking him toward Naval Base Headquarters were obviously unchanged, the feel of the place was almost wholly unrecognizable. When he had pulled out in March of 1996, the grounds were still littered with the refuse of tens of thousands of lives. Not only were the men, women, and children gone—now there was nothing to remind anyone that they had once been there. No tents, no facilities, not a trace. It was a veritable ghost town. Radio Range and McCalla Airfield, where most of the migrants had been housed, stood as naked terrain. The once bustling Bachelor Officers' Quarters had been mothballed. Dwellings that were still standing, but were now vacated, languished in disrepair. Ominously, what was once boisterous was now hushed.

In this familiar yet newly strange setting, Lehnert was relieved to meet two old acquaintances again: Captains Bob Buehn and Al Shimkus. Both were eager to work with their old classmate. Both, Lehnert knew, would attend with care and consideration to the needs of the mission and do whatever jobs they were assigned with professionalism and discretion. The goal of this preliminary site visit was to consider firsthand the island's possibilities, to look into logistics, operations, security, and coordination between the Naval Base and the JTF.

With Major Nichols and Colonel Meier by his side, and reassured by the support and professional expertise he knew Al Shimkus and Bob Buehn could deliver, Michael Lehnert was feeling at least a modicum of confidence. He had the beginnings of a reliable team of advisors to help him navigate the daunting logistical challenges that were sure to follow.

The group was there to assess and listen, to designate buildings for specific tasks, to get to know some of the personnel on the ground, to gauge their capacity, and in general to design and refine the logistical plan for getting the new detention facility up and running. For one day, the core team walked the island grounds. They surveyed the place where the migrants had been housed, examined abandoned quarters such as the old dental facility and an abandoned building known as the Pink Palace, and evaluated the former airfield, a large flat patch of land that could be used for specialty buildings such as medical facilities.

They toured the hospital and the former sites of the migrant camps. They surveyed the empty officers' quarters, hoping that these could perhaps be refurbished to house the JTF officers. They noted the scarcity of amenities for service personnel, which included the NEX and the modest eatery that specialized in ribs. But whatever information they collected and stored away from this walking tour, the heart of their trip was the visit to Camp X-Ray, the abandoned former facility for "bad guys."

Approaching Camp X-Ray, Lehnert's team could spot the Cuban watchtowers overlooking various points of the base. Lehnert and Buehn would attempt to alert their superiors to the potential risks of Cuban surveillance of Camp X-Ray, but they never received any response. Here, on location, the camp's vulnerabilities to Cuban eyes and ears, not to mention weaponry, were evident without words. True, the towers atop the hills were now customarily unmanned, but they could still be used at any moment to surveil activities on the American side. The proximity of the recycling plant adjacent to Camp X-Ray's gate would mean the daily passage of local traffic. It was just another reminder that, despite all this empty land, little could take place here that would go unnoticed.

As head of the migrant detention camp for the Cubans and Haitians in Operation Sea Signal, Lehnert had walked through X-Ray numerous times. He had regularly visited the prisoners at X-Ray, most of whom were returned to Cuba within 45 days or so. One of his few memories was of thinking that the sooner the Cubans held there returned to Cuba, the better. Walking through Camp X-Ray now was a crash course in how remarkably things can change in a brief stretch of time. Beneath their boots, untended brown meadows greeted the visitors. The grass, more like toughened reeds, was knee-high. A couple of overgrown and half-effaced paths guided their footsteps. Twenty or so cement slabs lay exposed to the elements; old cell floors lay in various stages of decay and disrepair, thick with weeds; cement-cracked interiors were darkened by a forest of vines clambering over the decrepit wire walls. Toilets and electricity were nowhere to be found. Empty and lifeless, the collapsed state of X-Ray made it difficult to imagine that within weeks this patch of ground could be transformed into a functioning detention center, housing up to 300 prisoners, guarded and supported by several thousand American military personnel.

In a few short hours, Lehnert and his small team absorbed the magnitude of the challenges facing them in the days and weeks ahead. Yet each was aware in his own way that logistics, however pressing and however essential, would be the smaller part of the difficulties before them. For each of them knew that their task, as the first military unit to receive prisoners at Guantanamo, would cast a spotlight not just on their professional skills but on their patriotism. What they may not have intuited at the time was that they were about to confront a moral challenge for which neither the peaceful life at Guantanamo nor the logistics-focused training at Camp Lejeune had prepared them.

For the moment, however, perhaps sensing how important a united team would be for the mission ahead, Lehnert had a discrete task on his mind, one that may have seemed perfunctory but would have significant consequences for the nature of the detention mission: the structure of the command itself. At a quiet moment, he took Buehn aside. To Lehnert, defining Bob Buehn's role was critical to the new mission.

As commander of the naval base on Guantanamo, Buehn would continue to oversee the basic functioning of the community there. Any task that arose having to do with migrants or drug smuggling fell under his purview. But when it came to JTF 160, his role remained undefined. He was expected to advise and to be always available to help. However, from Lehnert's point of view, Buehn's informal advisory role was far from optimal. For one thing, it disrupted the chain of command, leaving two separate operating units on the base. As such it would disrupt a sacrosanct doctrine of military organization—unity of effort, a concept that had philosophical as well as structural implications. Lehnert shared the conviction that the theory of unity of effort and its sister concept, unity of command, could make the difference between the success or failure of a military mission, and of this particular mission above all.

The U.S. military of the late 20th century had refined the notion of unity of command. Given the dwindling resources, the manpower decrements, and the expansion of potential global commitments, the new military was dependent on streamlined coordinated efforts among services, professional skills, and geographic specializations. In July 2001, the Joint Chiefs formally articulated the necessity of integration for future activities. Going forward, the military would rely increasingly upon joint task forces and unified commands. Unity of effort and unity of command would be the twin drivers of the 21st-century doctrine. Unity of effort referred to the idea that the president and the Washington agencies needed to be coordinated so as to work together toward a common goal. Unity of command constituted the military part of this agenda. But the basic idea of unity of command remained what it had been for centuries—the lockstep coordination of distinct military units working in tandem toward one common goal.[24] The Joint Task Force was one manifestation of joint doctrine.

Essential to unity of command was the notion of the inviolable chain of command. To verify and strengthen the notion of unity of command, the commander's authority was essential. However many branches, divisions, and specializations were combined in any one operation, the commander was charged with unifying the mission by virtue of his presence. He was responsible for ensuring that the disparate pieces meshed seamlessly, cognizant of the same goal and aware that the mission had a centralized point of reference around which coordination took precedence over individual agendas.

Facing the task of building and overseeing a detention facility for alleged terrorists, Lehnert sought a single direct line of responsibility running from top to bottom, without semiautonomous units that reported elsewhere and were accountable outside the JTF structure for what was JTF activity. With this in mind, he approached Buehn.

"What do you think of making this a single command? Of bringing you directly and officially onto the JTF team, provided I can get approval for this?"

Buehn understood the question. He knew that it was standard military doctrine as well as good common sense to have a single chain of command. He also knew that his status was about to change noticeably and for the worse; he was about to go from being, essentially, the mayor of a small town to being a minor official of a subcommunity in a neighborhood that was minuscule in size and in significance compared to what was coming in. Although he didn't care to verbalize it, Michael Lehnert understood Buehn's fear of receiving a de facto demotion as well. "What do you think," Lehnert continued, getting specific about the offer, "of you serving as my Deputy Commander?"[25] Eagerly, Buehn assented.

It was a logical offer, and one that satisfied Lehnert's desire for unity of command as well as Buehn's preference not to be diminished in his position and importance. Most important, it established a tone at the beginning of the operation that would seep down layer by layer through the entire command. Lehnert intended to unify his team on the ground, across reporting streams, across the branches of the services, across a wide swathe of military bases. Buehn would be the first of those whom Lehnert would invite into his inner circle. Captain Shimkus, too, would soon come to be included in this small group of trusted advisors—like Buehn, an individual with two sets of command structures, that of Atlantic Command and that of JTF 160. But the pattern of one dominant command for the mission was set here, before even the earliest troops landed. This was not to be a mission in which divisiveness would play a part, at least not as long as General Lehnert had control of the command.

It was a fairly auspicious beginning for JTF 160. Pivotal choices had been made about where to locate offices, a temporary medical facility, and a tent city for the military units that would be coming in to support the mission. But most important, the core team had been identified, assembled, and jump-started in their work. Lehnert's focus, beyond choosing the best patches of earth for building and the easiest routes for electric cables, had been on the personalities, and thus the character, that would drive his new mission.

His team as a group shared an unmistakable—and unusual—ability to make judgments that required a mixture of professionalism and flexibility. With Buehn's dedication to making things easy for his superiors and counterparts, Meier's reputation for a wide-ranging tolerance of issues and personalities, Nichols's persistently critical eye, and Shimkus's continual desire to exceed what was expected, Lehnert had drafted a team equal to an unprecedented task. His plan was for one team, one mission, and one goal—that of success.

Little had been discussed about the prisoners themselves, but the serious nature of the mission had hovered over each of these appointments to his inner circle.

Flying back later that day to Cherry Point, an airfield that services major deployments from Camp Lejeune, Lehnert celebrated a brief Christmas at home. The next day, preparations got under way with startling rapidity. Michael Lehnert immersed himself in meetings with a whole new cast of experts, including lawyers and technicians, in secured quarters, to detail the mission as it was now shaping up. Bill Meier prepared to move down to Guantanamo on December 28 along with a small team. Bob Buehn began to amass Seabees, the construction battalions of the U.S. Navy, and others for the building effort. In addition, Buehn began to prepare the population on the base. Al Shimkus began to think through the ways in which prisoners would require different procedures than military men and women. And Tim Nichols began to assess the new security concerns that would occur once the prisoners had landed.

On the day after Christmas, even before Rumsfeld had made the choice of Guantanamo public, Buehn issued an invitation for a town meeting to be held the next day. The families of the servicemen and women were invited to

Bulkeley Hall Auditorium. The auditorium's walls are lined with bright orange, red, and yellow canvases. Numbering just under 500, the red-upholstered chairs that night were almost all filled. The meeting was held on the night of Thursday, December 27, the day the Pentagon finally decided to inform the press that Guantanamo had been selected to serve as a temporary holding facility for al Qaeda, Taliban, and other terrorist personnel who would come under U.S. control as a result of the ongoing global war on terrorism.[26] Beyond that, neither the newspapers nor the commanders were providing any information about the nature and purpose of the mission.

Thus, when Bob Buehn faced the community assembled before him that evening, he was to some extent operating in a vacuum. It is not unusual for a mission to have a classified status and for the military community to trust that those in command are making the correct decisions. Skipping over the obvious haziness of the mission, Buehn focused on what he did know. It was true, he informed his audience, that prisoners from the war on terror would be arriving at the base and would be kept there in detention. He assured his listeners that the prisoners would be handled in such a manner that they would pose no risk to the community, that the military had plans to contain them. For that reason, the mission was expected to have little impact on the life of the community. Moving on to logistics, Buehn answered confidently a series of questions from the floor. How will this affect traffic? We don't have enough supplies as it is. How will there be enough food for our families at the exchange? Where will we put all these new people? As President Bush had assured citizens at home, so Buehn reassured those at Guantanamo. The life of shoppers would go on pretty much as it had before.

But the biggest fear arising from the list of unknowns affecting the community was not about the detainees. It was, as Buehn had anticipated, about whether or not the families, haunted by memories of the refugee emergencies of the 1990s, would be dispatched home. That evening, the importance of this concern pushed matters of security and logistics into the background as family members reiterated their fears about being ousted from the base. From the audience came the anxious question, "Are we going to be sent home? Can you tell us what decisions have been made about us?"

In Operation Sea Signal, the families had been forced to leave the island for security reasons. The schools had been closed, the commissary restocked accordingly, the civilian community activities truncated. It was a bitter memory for those who had experienced the transfer firsthand and a painful prospect for the families for which Buehn was responsible.

Buehn had already discussed the community's fears about relocation with Lehnert, who had reassured Buehn as best he could that he would make it his business to try to keep the families there on the island—though none of the JTF staff would be allowed to bring their own families. For Lehnert and Buehn both, removing the families would harm morale and create more problems than it was worth. Of course, they agreed, if the families wanted to leave, given the high security risk associated with this new mission, that would be a different story.

Debi Buehn sat there, watching her husband, admiring his ability to relax those around him. Suddenly, she realized that the audience, far from being eased by his efforts at reassurance, was now animated. Someone had inserted into the discussion the question of whether or not, for security reasons, the families should just volunteer to leave the island.

For Debi, this was an even less acceptable solution than remaining in limbo. She had made it a key principle over the years to keep her family together and to give them a home base, no matter what. As often as she could, she took the family to Jacksonville, where she and Bob had bought a home, one they planned to keep wherever they were stationed. Confronting the prospect of separation, she balanced the desire for her boys to be safe against her personal pledge to preserve the togetherness of the family at all costs.

As she sat there, listening and considering her choices, a voice from the crowd called out, "Well, if Debi's staying, then I'm staying." After all, she was the CO's wife, the First Lady of Guantanamo, so what she did mattered. "Me, too," said another voice. And then another. And so the decision was made. If they were to have a say, then the community as a whole would stay. As for the mission itself, Debi and her friends concurred. In the absence of an official policy, they would decree their own. They were staying. Certainly, as military families accustomed to being uprooted at a moment's notice and sometimes transferred farther away than they might have liked, they knew that their decision was somewhat chimerical. But it was psychologically comforting. And it made them feel less on the receiving end, less victimized by uncertainty.

Refusing to be passive, the Guantanamo community turned an absence of formulated policy into an opportunity to take matters into their own hands. Ironically, deciding how to behave in a policy vacuum would become imperative—and in a much more significant way—for Lehnert's team as well.

While administration lawyers were busy refashioning the nation's legal principles and policies, and while the prisoners in Afghanistan awaited their fate, the logistical readying of Guantanamo proceeded with workmanlike efficiency. The war in Afghanistan was worlds away. The captives had not yet arrived. The thorny problems surrounding the legally allowable treatment of detainees did not fall within the purview of any of the officers working to prepare Guantanamo for the sketchily defined mission. As a result, practical problems were front and center.

As military professionals, everyone involved took personal satisfaction from swinging into action, solving immediate problems, assembling equipment, and mobilizing know-how. But there was something disturbing about the operation, even on the drawing board.

To an uncomfortable extent, those tasked with constructing and running the new holding facility were being forced to operate in the dark. This lack of direction pervaded the entire operation. For starters, a mission could not be launched without a planning order. But the proposed Guantanamo operation had only a working order, and one that the Pentagon continued to rework and rework.[27] The higher-ups seemed unwilling or unable to commit a definitive plan to paper.

In addition, the nature of the mission had not been spelled out in any detail. Lehnert had been told that he would be at Guantanamo for roughly 60 days, but he still had not learned the exact purpose of the mission. He knew that the new facility would be holding battlefield captives. Beyond that, he knew almost nothing. What was the purpose of the detention camp? Was the refurbished and reorganized facility to serve primarily as a rear holding area for CENTCOM's war, used to provide tactical guidance if necessary? Were the Taliban and al Qaeda captives to be tried by military commissions, as Rumsfeld had suggested early in December?

Lehnert had no idea.

There was, in fact, a reason he had been left in the dark. Back in Washington, discussions over Guantanamo, inside the larger policy group and legal group, were at an impasse in the latter days of December and the first days of January. The detainees, it seemed, were going to be en route before even a modicum of mission clarity began to guide the work of JTF 160.

Abandoned and essentially left to his own judgment, Lehnert behaved more or less as did the assembled community of civilians at the town meeting. He and his team took matters into their own hands. In the absence of policy, they looked to training and experience for guidance. The Marine code of honor, Lehnert's prior detention command—albeit with migrants rather than imprisoned enemies—and the professionalism of his newly assembled team would have to suffice.

3

The Void

Get mad, then get over it.

—Colin Powell

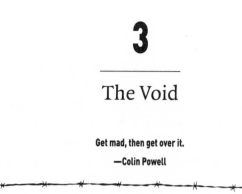

On December 26, Colonel William Meier greeted a group of Marines—gunnery sergeants, lance corporals, and others, all returning in haste from a prematurely interrupted Christmas break and time with their families. Together they boarded the bus at Camp Lejeune and headed out to an airfield in the middle of nowhere. Among them was Master Gunnery Sergeant Marc Coudriet, who had hastily packed when the callback order arrived for a "secret mission." His luggage bulged with extra-warm clothes meant to fend off the bitter Afghan winter. Once everyone was seated, Meier asked, "Okay, everyone ready? You ready to go to Gitmo?" Coudriet's woolens were not going to be useful after all.[1]

Once the Marines were assembled and informed about their destination, the confusion did not abate, either for them or for the larger JTF unit of 1,700 men and women on their way to Guantanamo.

The marks of confusion were everywhere apparent. When the group that Meier had picked up by bus boarded the outbound plane, they did so in an atmosphere of secrecy and uncertainty about the details of their mission. Lieutenant Colonel Tim Miller, a lawyer, grabbed the law books he thought might be relevant.[2] Gunnery Sergeant Robert Farabee, a corrections specialist, put together a notebook on the detention practices and procedures that he guessed would be relevant to whatever mission he eventually found himself assigned.[3]

En route, the confusion continued. Excited and energized although not yet adequately briefed, Meier's group landed at a stopover in Miami, only to discover that they were among the few still left out of the loop. The rest of the country, including their girlfriends and wives, who were now calling them, already knew what the Marines now learned. The secret had been reluctantly disclosed on television by the secretary of defense. Rumsfeld believed that his hand had been forced by the media, which had ferreted out the decision and was on the verge of making it public: Guantanamo Bay had been chosen as the holding facility for the "worst of the worst" captured in the war on terror. Coudriet's first thought about the decision to announce was: "Now we have an additional security risk."[4] Announced to the world as the holding facility for the captives from the war, Guantanamo, even before it was set up, could now be considered a terrorist target. Clearly, the communication between Washington and the Guantanamo mission was weak, bordering on dysfunctional.

At the staff level, and even among the officers, few seemed to have a clear sense of the mission's policy directives. Neither the lawyers nor the engineers, neither the commanders at SOUTHCOM nor the hospital administrators, understood the contours of the detention program or the purpose it was intended to serve.

Casting about for guidance, the members of the task force turned to their own superior officers, to Brigadier General Lehnert and his team at Lejeune and to SOUTHCOM for some sense of direction.[5]

Ensconced in a secured facility at Lejeune, the Second Marine Expeditionary Force Headquarters Building, Lehnert had convened teams of experts during the last days of December 2001 and the first days of January 2002. (Eerily, these meetings took place in the very same building in which the general himself had been born half a century earlier.) As the experts in logistics, operations, the law, and public affairs began to discuss the various pieces of the operation, it quickly became apparent that their collective knowledge about how to create a detention facility was of only limited value. No matter how experienced they were, the appalling lack of mission clarity from their higher-ups meant that they were mostly guessing. Above all, they were hearing that these prisoners might not be prisoners but would belong to another legal category, one that had not yet been determined by lawyers in Washington.

At Lejeune, as on the ground at Guantanamo, these first days were, by all accounts, "chaotic," "frantic," and exhausting. The planning meetings were being held without an official "execute order" in place, one which would have specified the policy details that had been ordered from above.[6]

With written guidelines for the detention operation virtually nonexistent, formal military protocol was compromised from the start. At this point, two short weeks before the first prisoners would arrive, nobody had any answer to such basic questions as what equipment—shackles, locks, jumpsuits, and the like—would be needed on the ground. As one senior official recalled, "We never saw an operations plan."[7] All told, the Pentagon's storeroom of ideas about detention was even less well stocked than the warehouses containing standard construction materials at Guantanamo—knowing how and with what restrictions to train their guards, whether or not there were specific codes to follow for the size and conditions of the cells, what kinds of walls and ceilings would be permissible, and what supplies would be needed for restraining the detainees. Above all, knowing whether the prisoners were covered under international law was a necessary baseline for answering the questions.

Fortunately, logistical improvisation is a particular strength of the U.S. military, and the Pentagon has reliable and expeditious procurement facilities.[8] But the speed with which the operation needed to be accomplished required additional innovation on the ground. Although the naval Seabees, Marines, and others involved in construction bemoaned the absence of Home Depot, they confronted the material shortages with the spirit of castaways, scouring the base for wood, wire, cement, and corrugated tin. An abandoned air base, McCalla Field, provided runway lights, steel poles that could be cut down and rewelded, and bits of wire mesh. Wood was in short supply, but the troops found enough to build observation towers. SEA huts,[9] quick-assembly structures, became the medical facility.[10]

"The Taliban are already in the air," became the daily rumor as teams of workers labored around the clock in 12-, 14-, even 18-hour shifts.[11] Meanwhile, estimates of how many prisoners would be arriving increased day by day. "Originally," Sergeant Marc Coudriet recalls, "it was just going to be 200 detainees. And I had three weeks to get it done in. And then it jumped up to 500 detainees, and I only had two weeks to get it done."[12] Buehn heard estimates of up to 1,000, if over a longer period of time. Lehnert, refusing to panic, advised Meier, "We will receive prisoners when we say that we're ready." "Okay," replied Meier. "But don't make it too long," the General added.[13]

Michael Lehnert himself, at this stage and even into the first week of January 2002, had no idea how many prisoners would be detained at the base, nor did he know precisely when they would be arriving. But number and timing were only two of the many things he didn't know about the operation he was now charged with running.

Of much greater importance was the fact that he wasn't quite sure what laws, and therefore what standards of treatment, would apply to the arriving captives. Nowhere was the sense of limbo and lack of direction more acute than in the legal arena.

Was this a mission designed to keep enemies off of the battlefield, or was it aimed at organizing military tribunals? Or were there other purposes in mind?

Would these captives be prisoners of war? Would they have lawyers assigned to them? The answers to these questions would have everything to do with the policies followed. What Lehnert's team needed to know was simply which legal codes they should abide by. The type of holding facility that would be built, the size and conditions of the cells, the nature of the food and medical care, the daily regiments of the prisoners and their guards, the treatment of the prisoners—all of these specifics were contingent upon the legal regime under which they would incarcerate these men.

And while they could build resourcefully, they couldn't plan the operation without substantial legal guidance from Washington—or so they thought.

The legal cloud hanging over the Guantanamo mission in these early days was not due to a deficit of lawyers or legal analysis. On the contrary. Arguably, U.S. government lawyers had never had as much impact on policy as they did during the first two or three years of the war on terror. By December, the implications of the Military Order of November 13 had set in, and lawyers inside and out of the administration were engaged in a fierce battle over interpretations of the law that would apply to the new detention mission.

The debate played out in a public forum in a series of legislative hearings before Senator Patrick Leahy's Judiciary Committee and Senator Carl Levin's Armed Services Committee. In both settings, legal experts lodged protests against the expansion of presidential power and the denial of rights to prisoners.[14] In defense, the administration lawyers tried to calm the fears of their opponents.

The Leahy committee brought the administration's legal heavyweights to the table: Michael Chertoff, then head of the Department of Justice's Criminal Division and as such responsible for overseeing domestic terrorism trials; and Ambassador Prosper, whose human rights credentials were impeccable. Chertoff and Prosper championed the military commissions. Chertoff assured the committee that "the right to an attorney...a full and fair trial...[and] humane conditions of pretrial detention" would be given.[15] (Two days later, Alberto Gonzales repeated these same assurances in an op-ed piece for the *New York Times*. He insisted that the commissions were "not secret," would be "full and fair," and would preserve "judicial review in civilian courts."[16]) Prosper praised the order for "add[ing] additional arrows to the President's quiver," pointing out that "we are at war" and under the laws of war, "unlawful combatants...are subject to trial and punishment by military tribunals for acts which render their belligerency unlawful."[17]

Ashcroft, testifying later that week for the Judiciary Committee, supported the idea of military commissions. Speaking generally about the continued threat of terrorism and the need for domestic law enforcement reforms such as the USA PATRIOT Act,[18] he deferred to the president to whom he gave "privileged and confidential" advice. "I cannot and will not divulge the contents, the context, or even the existence of such advice to anyone—including Congress—unless the President instructs me to do so," Ashcroft said.

For the Levin committee, which met the following week, the secretary of defense issued his own defense.[19] His prepared statement claimed the war on terror to be "not a law enforcement action; it is war." DOD's general counsel, Jim Haynes, assured the committee that the administration's intention was not to sidestep the domestic court system.[20] Not quite satisfied, Levin asked whether there would be any authority other than the president that could review the commission's decisions. Senator Warner specifically wondered whether the attorney general and the Department of Justice would have a say in the military trials.[21] But ultimately, neither committee made much substantive headway, other than creating a forum for the expression of dismay and doubts about the possible ramifications of the Military Order and at the same time providing the administration with a chance to justify it. Congress, in theory, had its chance to step in and push back on the Military Order and its implications for the future but chose not to. "Essentially, they got Congress's blessing," Prosper would reflect years later.[22]

Other agencies inside the executive branch were similarly passive. The Joint Chiefs said nothing publicly, or even confidentially, never indicating in any memo that has been uncovered their opposition to either the legal premises of the Military Order or the secretive process that brought it into being. Nor did Colin Powell raise any warning signals. As a general and the former Chairman of the Joint Chiefs, he could have publicly enumerated the ways in which the use of military commissions to skirt due process restraints violated the spirit of the Uniform Code of Military Justice. But he did not, and the silence spoke volumes.

Within the context of executive politics under Bush, the continued rationale for the empowerment of the president and the Department of Defense was jarring for many. But it would take time for those who had been excluded to respond. Colin Powell, for example, waited nearly two months to take overt action against the arbitrary exclusion of his legal team, which he would do in a memo dated January 26,[23] reflecting his good-soldier style, not the Department's acquiescence in such behavior.[24] Elsewhere, the various

interagency principles of the executive branch were rethinking and reformu-
lating their approaches.

Tinkering aside, the message was becoming increasingly clear. A concerted
group of administration lawyers would say precisely what they needed to in
order to proceed with the premises of the Military Order, the basis on which
the new detention policy would be built.

Over time, the group of lawyers known as the War Council drafted a series
of memos that fleshed out the details for implementing the Military Order.[25]
Essential to their progress was the close alliance between the vice president's
office and that of the secretary of defense. The Cheney/Rumsfeld partnership
had been forged in 1969, during the Nixon administration, when Rumsfeld
first employed the younger Cheney as his special assistant, subsequently hir-
ing him in other capacities in the Ford administration.

Now, the Rumsfeld/Cheney relationship was extended by proxy to the relationship between David Addington at the Office of the Vice President and Jim
Haynes at the Office of the Secretary of Defense. Addington had been Cheney's
special assistant and then general counsel when Cheney had been secretary of
defense under George H.W. Bush. Addington, considered the "invisible hand"
behind the emerging Cheney powerbase in 2001,[26] had hired Haynes to be his
special assistant in 1989, when Addington was special assistant to Secretary of
Defense Cheney. Later, Addington appointed Haynes to be general counsel to
the Department of the Army.

Said by one reporter to "mirror" Donald Rumsfeld "with a dash of Pierce
Brosnan's good looks,"[27] Haynes's experience was only moderately helpful for
someone charged with thinking through the legal dilemmas associated with
prisoners of war. Working in the private sector for General Dynamics and then
for the law firm of Jenner & Block, Haynes had developed a strong expertise in
military contractors and the law that pertained to them. Additionally, Haynes
was someone the administration could trust. According to John Yoo, Haynes
saw his role at the Pentagon as that of "preserving the Defense Department's
legal and policy options and the prerogatives of his boss, Secretary Donald
Rumsfeld."[28]

Haynes's position as the Pentagon's lawyer would turn out to be pivotal to
the Guantanamo mission.

The rationale for the war on terror had found its legal team: the War Council
and their allies within the administration. It was a team wedded to the concept of strong presidential authority and to the insistence that the nation was

at war and that therefore its legal policy should fall within the purview of the Pentagon. As Timothy Flanigan would later write, "The presidency will not concede any of its constitutional prerogatives while George W. Bush holds the office."[29] And for President Bush, in matters of detention policy, the point man was to be Donald Rumsfeld.

As Congress debated and held hearings, as lawyers wrangled over the potential ramifications of the Military Order, and as Michael Lehnert built cell block after cell block, reconnecting electricity and water cables, the influence of this group's ideas began to manifest itself in the necessary paperwork for policy, internal legal memoranda. In late December, with the hearings behind them, the Office of Legal Counsel produced a document that began the process of clarifying, within the secretive corridors of the executive branch, just what was intended by the detention operation that was scheduled to begin within days.

The December 28 Office of Legal Counsel memo, signed by John Yoo and fellow OLC lawyer Patrick Philbin, picked up where the congressional hearings had left off. It addressed the issue of whether or not the detainees at Guantanamo would be entitled to the writ of habeas corpus, and thus have access to U.S. courts to challenge their detention. The memo argued that "a federal district court could not properly exercise habeas jurisdiction over an alien detained at GBC" (Guantanamo Bay, Cuba), though, the authors admitted, some litigation risk did in fact exist. Still, they made their argument as strongly as they could. The reach of the U.S. courts did not in their opinion extend to Guantanamo. Their reasoning was that Guantanamo was sovereign territory of Cuba. U.S. rights there existed under treaty, so U.S. courts could not have jurisdiction without infringing upon Cuban sovereignty.[30]

In this memo, which appeared two weeks after the hearings on the Hill, the reassurances and denials issued by Chertoff, Haynes, and others now fell flat. The suspicions of Senator Levin seemed confirmed. Legally, according to the OLC memo, Guantanamo was simply out of reach for domestic, not to mention international, courts.

Meanwhile, beyond the matter of trials and the processes that would or would not pertain to the prisoners about to arrive at Guantanamo, there were other pressing legal questions hovering in the air. At issue was just what legal status these captives would have, an important matter for the terms of confinement that JTF 160 would have to implement and oversee.

As the year wound to a close, the civilian leadership at the Pentagon continued to display a strange indifference to the needs of the detention facility that would open officially in a very few days. As administration officials had explained at the Senate hearings, the direction the policy should follow was still unclear at the very top. It was hard to answer questions about the nature and purpose of Guantanamo, not just because of internal disagreements but because the president had not yet "designated anyone to be tried by" a military commission. "He may do so. He may not," Haynes had stated before the Senate Armed Services Committee, stressing the inchoate nature of the Pentagon's plans. "[N]either the president nor the secretary has indicated a deadline for when he or they want these rules to be put into effect."[31] Surprisingly, there was little anxiety or embarrassment over this lack of clarity and direction in the legal realm. It was as if the legal premises of the Guantanamo operation could hang in limbo even as the pressure to get the prisoners out of Afghanistan mounted.

But this wasn't all. Washington still had not come to any conclusions about what rights—beyond those directly related to judicial processes—the prisoners would have. Word had trickled down that there was intense debate going on over the matter, but that any firm decisions were still pending.

For General Lehnert, this meant that he would be greeting the incoming "guests" at Guantanamo—as military e-mails at Guantanamo now surreptitiously referred to the unknown category of prisoners who would soon arrive—without much that was concrete in the way of rules or even guidelines. There was, put bluntly, no directive setting forth the scope and purpose of his new mission—an operation that was already well under way.

There was, however, a clear sense of how things were going.

Michael Lehnert isn't sure where or how he first heard about it. But early in his command, around the time he landed at Guantanamo on January 6 and well before the detainees arrived, he understood that the Geneva Conventions were under discussion in Washington. He had heard from up the chain of command that the lawyers in Washington were rethinking the applicability of the Conventions to the current situation—i.e., to prisoners in the war on terror, and specifically to those on their way to Guantanamo. What was he to do, given the fact that the legal grounding for the mission had yet to be established? What he was told gave him considerable food for thought. He was to be consistent with the Geneva Conventions, but should not feel bound by them. For example, his own troops, who under the Conventions would need to be housed in conditions similar to that of the detained, did not have to be housed in what the early JTF troops on the grounds acknowledged to be cages. But there was more.

Traces of this studiously vague terminology and diplomatically unprecedented idea had already appeared up and down the chain of command. It had found its way most prominently in the remarks made by high-ranking civilians in the Department of Defense. As early as December 18, Paul Wolfowitz had explained that the American citizen John Walker Lindh, the so-called American Taliban who had been captured in Afghanistan and was now in U.S. custody, was "being treated consistent with the Geneva protections for prisoner of war. So he enjoys all the protections that would go with prisoner of war status, but he is not a legal combatant."[32]

The directive confused everyone.

Telling individuals in the military that the rules—in this case, the Geneva Conventions—do not apply is tantamount to saying: You have entered a place in which you are not trained to function. Without rules—the Geneva Conventions, the Uniform Code of Military Justice, or the routine sequence for carrying out a mission described in one of the innumerable manuals for operations—the military has no sense of direction. By definition, the military is a hierarchical system in which following orders becomes second nature. The basic rationale behind this operational code is that disobeying or improvising orders will lead to losses in wartime, and therefore stands to compromise national security.

Military theory and protocol aside, Lehnert knew that he had little choice but to develop an understanding of just what this negatively worded policy directive meant. One thing it signified for certain was that the operation that General Lehnert now commanded belonged to uncharted terrain. And from the first moments of hearing that Geneva need not apply at Guantanamo, it was clear that of all the challenges facing Lehnert—including the scarcity of resources, the novelty of an incoming prisoner population, and the demand for SOUTHCOM to have immediate expertise in Muslim and Afghan regional matters—the policy directive that cast international law and military practice to the winds without offering a replacement was by far the most daunting challenge of all.

4

Filling the Void

We thought they were POWs. We always did. We were overruled...essentially
by the President of the United States.
—Col. Manuel Supervielle (Retired)

Since the end of the Second World War, few have doubted the authority of the Geneva Conventions. Originating in 1864 and updated throughout the 20th century with the intent of protecting the wounded and sick and the medical teams that attended to them, the Geneva Conventions have been amended and supplemented over time to cover "prisoners of war, civilians, children, even cultural property." The First Convention (from 1864) is aimed at enabling the International Committee of the Red Cross to have access to the wounded and sick. The Second Convention (1906) adds the shipwrecked to those who can safely be attended to by medical personnel, namely the Red Cross (the ICRC). The Third Convention (1929) includes prisoners of war among protected persons. The Fourth Convention (1949) protects civilians in times of war.[1]

Though violators have existed, even among the 194 signatories, to renege upon the Conventions is seen as a gross violation of international norms and standards. The law of war, of which the Conventions are a subset, is incorporated in the U.S. Uniform Code of Military Justice (UCMJ), which, along with customary and common laws of war, defines lawful behavior for the U.S. armed services.[2] Under this shared code, the ICRC works with the U.S. military to train its troops. Commonly, men in uniform in combat situations have been known to carry the Geneva Conventions in their pockets for reference. Central to all of four of the Conventions is Common Article 3, which prohibits, among other things, "violence to life and person, in particular murder of all kinds, mutilation, cruel treatment and torture," as well as "outrages upon personal dignity, in particular humiliating and degrading treatment."

The Conventions have been followed as a sacred trust even in taxing situations. Despite the fact that the Japanese were known to torture and maim their Allied prisoners, U.S. authorities in World War II insisted that Allied forces refrain from any violations of the Geneva Conventions. In the Korean War, camps for prisoners were established in South Korea, under the jurisdictional control of both U.S. and Korean forces. Provided the protections of the Geneva Conventions, they were housed, fed, often allowed to work for pay, and, at the end of hostilities, repatriated. In South Vietnam as well, where U.S. forces and the South Vietnamese army had shared responsibility for the treatment of captured Viet Cong, the Geneva Conventions remained in force. In fact, in the face of known Viet Cong use of torture, the U.S. government had overruled protests on the part of the South Vietnamese, who claimed there was insufficient reciprocity to warrant adhering to the Geneva standards.[3]

American violations of the Conventions have seldom been discussed. Instead, the issue of prisoner treatment that has dominated American minds, military and otherwise, has related to abusive treatment at the hands of the enemy. In the American Civil War, approximately 400,000 prisoners of war were taken. One in seven, historian Charles W. Sanders has pointed out, "perished at the hands of their captors," both Union and Confederate.[4] Most notoriously, 41,000 Union Army prisoners were kept under deplorable conditions at the infamous Andersonville prison in southwest Georgia, where nearly 13,000 prisoners died owing to shortages of food, spoiled food, unclean water, exposure to the heat, and poor sanitation.[5]

In Marine lore, the impact of violations of the Geneva Conventions on Americans was common knowledge because of the stories from Wake Island, where the beatings, starvation, and decapitations of captured American troops at the hands of the Japanese was a story not readily forgotten. And American POWs in Vietnam are known to have been tortured frequently.

In retrospect, not only was the directive startling, but so too was its timing. By the time Lehnert landed at Guantanamo, he had already heard rumblings of the mantra that would become stated policy in the immediate days to come: the operation would be "guided by Geneva but not bound by it."

The lack of a legal opinion from Washington on the matter was not from want of trying. In fact, the lawyers were doing their best to come to some sort of decision about the incoming prisoners and the applicability of Geneva to the detention effort.

On January 8, the legal advisor to the secretary of state, William H. Taft IV—elegant, gray-haired, and every bit the patrician-style great-grandson of his namesake, President William Howard Taft—had been called to a meeting at the White House. Alberto Gonzales, a number of OLC lawyers, Jim Haynes, and others were present.

After the meeting, Taft, according to one of his staff attorneys, told his legal team, "We've got trouble." He was determined to set things on a more legally defensible footing. The next morning, he and his lawyers at the State Department were faxed a 40-page memo and told that they had one day to respond to it with any comments or advice. The reason, they were told in a cover letter, was that "Jim Haynes needs comments back tomorrow because events on the ground are moving faster than anticipated."[6]

The memo, a draft memo signed by John Yoo and fellow OLC lawyer Robert Delahunty, shocked Taft's team. David Bowker, whose expertise was in international law, was a young, exceptionally bright and articulate recent graduate of Boalt Hall, the University of California at Berkeley School of Law. He found it hard to digest Yoo's sudden, and to his mind insufficiently knowledgeable, foray into this new and complex area of the law.

The memo concluded that the Taliban and al Qaeda captives had no legal status. "[N]either the federal War Crimes Act nor the Geneva Conventions would apply to the detention conditions in Guantanamo Bay, Cuba . . . " According to this view of things, the captives would not be prisoners of war, or in technical terminology, EPWs (enemy prisoners of war). They therefore, as a strictly legal matter, did not qualify for the protections that the Geneva Conventions assigned to prisoners of war. The OLC memo basically set the groundwork for the United States to renege on its obligations under international law as a signatory to the Geneva Conventions.

Whether or not the Geneva Convention relative to the Treatment of Prisoners of War (GPW) would apply had vast implications for the international reputation of the United States. It was one thing to declare that the detainees did not have the right to habeas corpus—as in the Military Order of November 13—but another thing to draft a legal document formalizing what Lehnert had been privately told even before he landed with his troops at Guantanamo: that the prisoners in his custody were not going to be protected by Geneva.

The memo's reasoning had many dimensions, among them that Afghanistan under the Taliban was considered a failed state, that al Qaeda operatives were nonstate actors, and that "customary international law has no binding legal effect on either the President or the military because it is not federal law, as recognized by the Constitution."[7]

For the next 24-plus hours, the lawyers at State scrambled without sleep to develop a legal riposte to the lengthy memo, which had obviously been improvised in haste.

For their part, Yoo and his group showed no interest in initiating a discussion with State Department lawyers, whom they treated as sticklers for the rule of law. They were seeking—even demanding—a rubber stamp, as their request for an immediate response indicated. It seemed that the Office of Legal Counsel lawyer, John Yoo, and his associates had already decided that the future demanded a radically new legal paradigm. Those who held a different opinion or who obstructed the process of making new law were, to their minds, standing in the way of national security.

But the desired acquiescence was not forthcoming.

Requesting a second day for their response, Taft and his staff were determined to deliver a thorough and comprehensive reply. They divided up the memo into different points of law and then sorted themselves into groups to address discrete legal points. Over the course of these two days, the State Department's legal team agreed that, on multiple counts, they could not support the conclusions of the memo that they had been expected to endorse uncritically.

Motivating their disagreement were numerous concerns, chief among them the War Council's reading of the phrase "non-international armed conflict," the concept spelled out in the Geneva Conventions' 1977 Protocol II Relating to the Protection of Victims of Non-International Armed Conflicts. For Taft's lawyers, it meant any armed conflicts except those "between nations" or high contracting parties, and therefore could include conflicts in which al Qaeda was a party.[8] For the War Council lawyers intent on justifying the new policy on military commissions and detentions going forward, the phrase could be applied only to civil wars. This implied that the Protocol did not apply to the current conflict. It was an interpretive divide the dueling lawyers would never be able to cross.

Taft's team reasoned that there was, in theory, no category of captive that is not identified under these Conventions, whether regular soldiers, civilians, or irregular unlawful combatants such as spies and saboteurs. Irregular combatants have been declared protected persons under the Convention precisely because labels such as saboteur, spy, bandit, and terrorist can be arbitrarily applied and would thus, if treated as exceptions, effectively make compliance with Geneva purely voluntary.[9]

Nor were there any solid logistical reasons for refusing to observe Geneva. For Taft and his group, the Conventions were flexible enough to cover any situation. They argued that the rule of thumb regarding the Conventions is that the detaining authority must do its best to follow the rules, and that where the specifics cannot be met, given conditions and circumstances, then and only then could the detaining authority bend the rules to accommodate reality.

The importance of adhering to Geneva could not be overemphasized, according to Taft's team. Violating them was tantamount to stepping outside the international comity of nations. Not to mention that it would allow for mistreatment of prisoners in U.S. custody, which few if any saw at the time to be a factor in the War Council's reasoning about Geneva.

The response document issued by Taft's group did not stand on politeness or ceremony. The State Department lawyers submitted their answer, titled "Your Draft Memorandum of January 9," on January 11, the very day that the detainees were arriving at Guantanamo. Their memo was anything but a rubber stamp. In barely restrained disbelief, Taft's memo and its cover letter, referred to the Draft Memorandum as "seriously flawed," "incorrect," "incomplete," and "fundamentally inaccurate" in both its analyses and conclusions. The OLC memo was also "procedurally impossible," "unsound," at points based on arguments that were "completely irrelevant," and ignorant about political concepts such as "failed states" and even about the Taliban, as well as about legal protocols such as reciprocity and treaty suspension.[10]

The memo was a persuasive rebuttal on substantive grounds of the January 9 memo. Taft's team appealed to the history of U.S. detainee treatment. It made the elementary point that "In previous conflicts, the United States has dealt with tens of thousands of detainees without repudiating its obligations under the Conventions." The State Department lawyers also set the record straight on failed states, reciprocity, and the permissibility of U.S. suspension of the Geneva Conventions in Afghanistan. The memo forcefully argued that in each case, OLC had distorted the historical record as well as misstated legal precedents and applicable rules.[11] Its ending was pointed: "Your draft acknowledges that several of its conclusions are close questions," Taft explained. "The attached draft comments will, I expect, show you that they are actually incorrect as well as incomplete. We should talk."[12]

As the lawyers in Washington continued to spar, and as Taft's team refused to be steamrollered, JTF 160, unaware of the discussion in Washington, began to look within for its own answers. With the detainees in the air, the military lawyers at the level of SOUTHCOM and JTF 160 had no choice but to try to figure out their own default instructions for the way prisoners were to be treated.

Beginning at Lejeune, and continuing at Guantanamo, these lawyers worked with Lehnert to begin to understand what it meant not to be bound by

the Geneva Conventions. Lieutenant Colonel Tim Miller from Lejeune struggled to figure things out as best he could, reading and rereading the suitcase
full of law books he had brought along for the operation. But, in large part,
Lehnert looked to SOUTHCOM for guidance.

At the top of the SOUTHCOM legal chain was Manuel Supervielle, the combatant command's Staff Judge Advocate. His staff lawyer, Wendy Stafford,
traveled down to Guantanamo to work with the troops, initially on the rules of
engagement—for example, when to use force and when to use deadly force—
but not on prisoner of war issues.

Pondering the order to be "guided by Geneva but not bound by it," Michael
Lehnert decided to do some thinking about this on his own. Downloading the
Geneva Convention's 143 articles to refresh his memory on codes that had been
instilled in him at an early stage of his career, he jotted down those aspects of
the Conventions that most likely could not be implemented at Guantanamo,
at least not in its first days. He focused on tangible issues tied to living conditions. Rights that would likely fall by the wayside, he surmised, included the
right to physical exercise and the right to have musical instruments, ironicalli-
cally among the opportunities that Lehnert, half a decade earlier, had enthusiastically offered the detainees in the migrant camps.

For Lehnert, it was not a matter of principle but of feasibility. It was simply
impossible to build a recreation facility in the time available for refurbishing
Camp X-Ray. Nor would there be musical instruments available, he guessed.
And there were other requirements—like the offer of pay to the prisoners and
the right to elect representatives—that he suspected would not be fulfilled
in the current circumstances. But Lehnert knew not to be overly concerned
about these deviations. What worried him was not that the old rules had been
swept aside but that no new rules had replaced them. In the military, this no-
man's-land between legal regimes was not a comfortable place to be. In fact,
it contradicted the very essence of military code.

Not surprisingly, when confronted with the unhelpful directive to act
"in conformity" with Geneva, Lehnert's legal advisors were at a loss. From
Lejeune, JAG lawyer Tim Miller was deeply unsettled by the directive's lack of
clarity. "One of the things that we have to do as Marines and as lawyers...is
to determine what these conventions mean, what is humane. And what is consistent with military necessity."[13] And without guidance from above, this was
difficult, if not impossible, for a lawyer who respected his profession, both
its military aspects and legal aspects. As Miller explained, "Really the problem that we have here is that those protections, the exact protections they are

entitled to are not written down... [W]e've had to determine what is humane, what is humane treatment and of course... this is a problem for the judge advocates..."[14]

At SOUTHCOM, the legal cloudiness was equally disturbing. When the prisoners boarded the plane in Kandahar, there had still been no formal order to execute or legal determination from the Pentagon or elsewhere in Washington as to what the status of the captives would be. To what category, under Geneva, would they belong? While Tim Miller's confusion left him feeling quite helpless, this was not the case for the lead JAG at SOUTHCOM, a man who was not accustomed to being put on hold when it came to protocol or the law, a man with a reputation for decisive action and a clear commitment to professionalism.

Manuel Supervielle had been a JAG for 20 years. As a military lawyer, he had experience with both criminal and international law, having begun his career as a criminal defense attorney, largely involved with drug cases. Since that time, he had served as the chief prosecutor in Korea, as an international and operational lawyer in Hawaii, as a negotiating lawyer in the Philippines and Thailand, as a specialist in the turnover of bases in Panama and the Philippines, and as an expert on humanitarian missions in Western Samoa and Bangladesh. With SOUTHCOM, he had extended his expertise to Latin America. As part of his ever-broadening career, he had gotten an MA in international law at the University of Miami.

And it was a good thing, given the task that lay ahead of him. In the first week of the Gitmo mission, Supervielle was on vacation, having sent his staff home for the period between Christmas and New Year's. He heard about the mission in the same way as several others who would be on the frontlines— via television. As the senior JAG for SOUTHCOM—a sleepy combatant command rumored at times to be on its way out, focused primarily on Operation Colombia, a drug interdiction program for the Caribbean—Supervielle had been Peter Pace's deputy. As best as Supervielle could tell, in the case of Guantanamo he was being asked to create a policy that was essentially unconstrained by standing law, but still largely consistent with it. The only possible interpretation was that some principles would not be adhered to, and that some violations would therefore be tolerated.

Supervielle had learned early on, for example, that there was going to be an unusual degree of deviation from the norm in regard to prisoners. He had drafted a document regarding prisoners with explicit reference to Article 5 hearings—those mandated by Article 5 of GPW—which are used to determine prisoner of war status when the status of a prisoner is in doubt. Supervielle was told to take the reference to Article 5 out of his document. Apparently, there weren't going to be Article V hearings for these prisoners.[15]

Wiry, intense, and energetic, Supervielle enjoyed getting things done. Cuban-born and raised in the United States, he liked to focus on a problem and cut through the confusions to arrive at a clean, clear answer, in this case perhaps more than ever. Given Supervielle's dedication to clarity and precision, he found the confused legal environment in which he had been placed at best unsettling and at worst compromising.

At first, he waited for direction, thinking that the evident impasse in D.C. would quickly be resolved. He read and reread the warning order that had come down the chain of command and the amendments to it that followed, but saw no signposts pointing in the direction of legal clarity.

The question being evaded by the confusing "consistent with" formula was this: Are the detainees prisoners of war? And if not, what are they and how should they be treated? Supervielle and his colleagues at SOUTHCOM argued that there should at least be Article V hearings on the battlefield that would determine whether or not the prisoners were prisoners of war. But the argument fell on deaf ears. They were left on their own to ponder the obscure command: Geneva does not apply, but its spirit should be a guide.

Somewhat baffled, the lawyers at SOUTHCOM turned to a specific question. What was to be the role of the International Committee of the Red Cross?

According to military protocol, the very first requirement for detaining captives in a time of war is alerting the ICRC, which oversees implementation of the Geneva Conventions. Each Convention addresses what the ICRC is allowed and expected to do. It would be a shocking surprise to be told that the ICRC was not to be contacted about Guantanamo. But without a go-ahead, Supervielle felt obliged to wait for a directive from above.

Thinking along the same lines, and acutely conscious of his personal responsibility for what was about to transpire on his watch, Lehnert had put in an official request for the ICRC to be invited to Guantanamo. The request, which went through General Jackman up the chain of command, had been summarily dismissed by the Pentagon.

But now, with the prospect of the prisoners arriving within days, Lehnert and Supervielle confided in each other about their shared sense of the difficulties—and dangers—of mounting this mission without an ICRC presence on site. Although the ICRC had not been part of Sea Signal during his time there, Lehnert understood that the Geneva Conventions and the ICRC were inextricably tied to one another. Even at Camp Lejeune, the ICRC was a frequent visitor, there to advise on humanitarianism and international law. Now, Lehnert and Supervielle agreed. They needed to have present an authority that could attest to their compliance with the law. Lehnert, concerned about transparency in his command, was insistent.

The ICRC could help supply an answer to one of the pressing problems faced by those in charge at Guantanamo. Were these particular captives members of an enemy army? Did they belong to an organized resistance movement? Or did they belong to another category of POW?

And there were other problems that the ICRC could help resolve, thereby taking up the slack produced by the Pentagon's virtual silence. Between themselves, Supervielle and Lehnert could enumerate several reasons for involving the ICRC—beyond its professional knowledge of international law. In addition to the obvious policy guidance on detention that the organization could offer, there were other benefits to having it involved. SOUTHCOM, they both knew, was not prepared to handle visitors from the Muslim world. The Muslim world was virtually opaque to the staff at SOUTHCOM, where the officers and staff had been trained to know Venezuela and Panama, Bolivia and the Caribbean Islands—not Afghanistan. Ignorance of Afghanistan was neither a sign of incompetence nor negligence on the part of SOUTHCOM. This was not their territory—they knew about drug trafficking and military coups and refugee matters. As a result, they were starting out with a severe handicap.

The Red Cross, by contrast, an organization with global reach, knew the population that was about to arrive, and included representatives who spoke many detainee languages, including Farsi, Arabic, and Pashto. The organization could be of immense value at Guantanamo, not just to help the military avoid violating international law as they had been trained to do, but also for advising on Muslim culture. Supervielle's intention was to protect the military from its own vulnerabilities, from some glaring, if perhaps excusable, deficiencies in its training. And there was another factor, besides the ICRC's experience in Afghanistan, to keep in mind. With the ICRC present, the U.S. military could fend off what would undoubtedly be innumerable requests from human rights groups to be present at Guantanamo. With one stroke, they could free themselves from the human rights noose that would be not only time-consuming, but also potentially dangerous. At least with the ICRC, confidentiality was ensured. The ICRC would make its recommendations to Washington, not to the press or the public. Amnesty International and Human Rights Watch, by contrast, served the public and would announce any infractions they detected with great fanfare to the press. At SOUTHCOM the argument that the ICRC would keep out other human rights groups seemed a more persuasive argument than the one that really mattered to Lehnert and Supervielle—using the ICRC to keep them from breaking the law.

General Galen Jackman listened to the rationale of Lehnert and Supervielle and nodded in agreement, despite the fact that an initial request for the ICRC had already been turned down. He decided to give it another try. Gary Speer, the acting commander of SOUTHCOM, had the same reaction, according to Jackman. It made sense to invite the ICRC to Guantanamo. After all, the planning order had approved voluntary "consistency" with the Geneva Conventions if not mandatory compliance.[16]

Time, however, was running out. And in the absence of legal and policy directives, Supervielle and Lehnert, independently, began to take things into their own hands. Supervielle did so with a series of questions posed within military circles—and then with one posed outside of the U.S. military. The first question addressed his counterpart at CENTCOM, the combatant command responsible for the prisoners while they remained in Afghanistan. He wondered how they were classified there. Surely his counterpart would know. Living up to his reputation as a man of decisive action, he picked up the phone and dialed the head JAG at CENTCOM headquarters in Qatr. "So," he asked, introducing himself and his new responsibilities, "What's the status of these guys?" Supervielle's main desire was for a quick answer so that he could launch himself into the development of a plan. His idea was to slice through the red tape with a simple phone call.[17]

"Hell if I know," came the response.

Frustrated and feeling somewhat derelict in his duty to set legal guidelines, Supervielle then turned to Washington. He put his question directly and in writing to the Joint Chiefs of Staff. "What," he asked, "is the status of the incoming prisoners?" Waiting for an answer that he feared might not come, Supervielle began to explore other, more active options.

Meanwhile, Lehnert, too, considered another approach. He was dismayed by the denial of his request to have the ICRC present at Guantanamo. What if he took another tack? What if, instead of the legal dimension, he focused on the military one? In military terms, he reasoned, this was a detention mission for captives from the battlefield. These captives were to be locked up in cells, and under no circumstances could they escape. Humanitarian issues aside, there was the issue of the mission itself—which, in essence, was amounting to what appeared to be a penal operation. Lehnert, like his superiors, recognized that the U.S. military really did not have a specialty in prisoner of war camps, as since the Second World War, foreign allies had usually taken on this responsibility. Accordingly, Washington had not only stretched the definition of detention from humanitarian (as in refugees and migrants) to penal (as in prisoners of war), but even in the latter realm was refusing the help of penal authorities and professionals. Lehnert reasoned that the military at least had the experience of its own brigs, prisons for members of the military who had been convicted of crimes.

Recognizing the discrepancy between the expertise on hand and the requirements of the maximum security detention facility he had been asked to set up, Lehnert originally tasked a unit of 10 gunnery sergeants out of Lejeune to come and advise on the setup of the new detention facility. They were an all-purpose group, there to create policies for perimeter security, prisoner transfers, and general guard detail. They would establish guidelines and train personnel in accord with those policies. But they could only be a stopgap measure. Although they were security experts with some knowledge of the brig system, they were not corrections experts. They knew the basics, not of maximum security prisons, but at least of holding individuals convicted on lesser offenses. But they didn't really know the first thing about shackling and feeding, transporting and caring for hardened criminals, as the arriving captives were expected to be.

So, as the New Year turned, the commander of JTF 160, Michael Lehnert—still at Camp Lejeune while Meier's team built up the facility at Guantanamo—put in a request through SOUTHCOM to the Joint Staff and the Office of the Secretary of Defense (OSD) for a corrections officer and a corrections unit. Once it went through the chain of approval, FORSCOM—the Army component of the U.S. Joint Forces Command at Norfolk—would do the staffing.

For the head position, they identified an army colonel out of Fort Hood, Texas. A military policeman, a devoted father and committed churchgoer, a vegetarian known for not drinking alcohol, Terry Carrico was proud of his by-the-book professionalism. To FORSCOM and the chain of command, he seemed to be the right person for the job.

As he was riding down the road to Fort Hood, the Army's largest installation, just after the New Year, Carrico had been summoned to headquarters. Thin, handsome, and well spoken, Carrico knew that such an unexpected call usually meant that he had done something wrong, and as he was ushered in immediately to the office of General Bell minus the usual half-hour wait, his sense of dread intensified. The seats at the conference table in Bell's office were full except for one that was waiting for Carrico—also a break with precedent, as Carrico's role was usually to stand by the General's side.

"Terry. You ever been to Cuba?"

Carrico shook his head.

"Well, you're going."

"What?" said Terry, as he listened to the rest of the description of the detention mission. He reminded himself that he was a brigade commander, not a corrections officer. "How many am I taking with me?"

"Just you," came the reply.

"I'm not the guy," he said. "I'm a military officer, not a corrections specialist. I would need to bring someone down there with me."

"That's not the plan."[18]

Over the course of the next few hours and days, Carrico worked hard to impress his superiors with the fact that a detention effort like the one they were describing necessitated the expertise of someone who had a familiarity with prisons. Unbeknownst to Carrico, this was acknowledged not only by General Lehnert but also at the level of the Joint Chiefs. Among the highest-ranking officers in the country, there was the distinct opinion that this was not a job for the military at all. This was a prison detail, and the United States military did not have well-developed professional prison expertise. They had guards and they had prison supervisors. But they were amateurs compared to officials at the Bureau of Prisons.

Eventually, Carrico won the argument about bringing along expertise, just as Lehnert had won his argument about adding a corrections professional to the team. Carrico, a military policeman but not a corrections specialist, boarded the plane with a 95-Charlie, the Army term for a corrections specialist. Carrico had had to talk his colleague into delaying his retirement for the effort, and had succeeded in doing so. In subsequent days, he garnered the services of others with a background in some form of detention. With the appointment of Carrico, a more responsible framework for erecting a prison began to take shape, the first of many steps that Michael Lehnert would seek to take in an effort to design and implement effective policy at Guantanamo.

Some risks, however, lay in inviting new players to the operation. Lehnert risked diluting his own command. His invitation to Buehn to be his deputy commander had demonstrated that he understood the importance of a unitary command. But his request for Carrico, motivated by his sense of the pressing needs of his mission, put this fragile unity at risk. Lehnert had no idea whether a corrections team would fit inside the JTF without friction.

Geneva, legally binding or not, would be the choice of any military person. But much still remained uncertain. For one thing, no official legal classification had been applied to the men about to arrive. The decision to refuse them prisoner-of-war status did not automatically classify them in another way. They were *not* prisoners of war, but what they *were* was not precisely clear. As a result, as Bob Buehn recalls, no one was sure what to call them. "We only knew that we were not to use the word 'prisoner.' Or for that matter 'prison,'" Buehn remembers with a grimace.[19]

Meanwhile, Manuel Supervielle, still awaiting word from Washington, was planning his own next step, given a Pentagon that was still effectively AWOL. Even as the hour of arrival edged closer, there was no policy directive forthcoming. The ground crews were performing miraculous feats, not only meeting the deadline they'd been given but beating it. And even as they put the finishing touches on the first group of cells at X-Ray, word came to Buehn that a more permanent facility for the prisoners had been authorized in Washington on the last day of the year. Construction on Radio Range, once the site of the migrant camps, would begin immediately with the help of the Halliburton subsidiary Kellogg, Brown & Root at a cost of $37 million.

As the need for money and men skyrocketed, Manuel Supervielle decided to take matters into his own hands, much as he had done earlier in calling CENTCOM and much as Lehnert had done with the request for a corrections unit. Communicating to one another their shared sense of the need for the ICRC to be present at Guantanamo, each continued to pursue the goal independently. Once again, the phone was Supervielle's weapon of choice. But this time, the stakes of his action were much greater. Now he chose a course of action that would force the administration out of its gridlock.

As the prisoners who weren't allowed to be called prisoners were prepared to board planes in Afghanistan and as the first corrections officers landed at Gitmo, Manuel Supervielle, Cuban-born, American-raised, and intolerant of being in limbo, single-handedly changed the future course of Guantanamo. This time, when he picked up the phone, it wasn't just for advice or to lobby or sway colleagues or superiors. This time, the phone call in and of itself was an action. For on the other end of his call was the ICRC in Geneva.

Supervielle spoke directly. "Would you be interested in coming to Guantanamo?" he asked the Geneva office.

And in the moment it took for the ICRC representative to answer, the legal context for Guantanamo was suddenly and irreversibly set. The call invited the eyes of the world to the new detention facility, regardless of the stalemate in D.C.

"Thank you," was the response from Geneva. "This is kind of you.... The answer is yes."

Supervielle insists that his call to the ICRC was not meant as a defiant act so much as a way of breaking through an impasse in order to solve an immediate and growing problem on the ground. Work could not proceed without knowing the rules.[20] It was that simple. Still, it is not an exaggeration to say that with this phone call, and with this question, Manuel Supervielle radically altered the Guantanamo story.

Among those he remembers telling about his call was his counterpart, the legal adviser to the Chairman of the Joint Chiefs of Staff and old friend, Jane Dalton. "Jane," he said, "I put in a call to the ICRC. They've agreed to come along." He thought that she would be as relieved as he was.

According to Supervielle, Dalton paused for a moment on the other end of the line. When her voice finally emerged from the unexpected silence, it was piqued. "What?" she cried out. "I think you should have asked us first." She promised to convey the news to her counterpart in OSD, Jim Haynes. Her expectation, according to Supervielle, was that he would not be pleased. "They are going to be really upset over there," Supervielle remembers her saying.

Maybe she was being hypercautious, Supervielle thought.[21]

But apparently, she was right. Supervielle was summoned immediately to Washington. He knew that he would be going straight to Gitmo from there. He wanted to make sure that he would arrive at the Pentagon prepped with arguments in favor of the Geneva Conventions. Carrying a copy of the Conventions in his briefcase, he called together a team of lawyers at SOUTHCOM. "We need to work and work quickly," he said, knowing they would be up through the night. "I want a bubble chart. Use the colors green, yellow, and red and code each of the 143 articles of the Conventions in terms of what we can allow with these prisoners, what we can't allow, and what we need to discuss." The color red would signify areas where security trumped the law: If a particular article might put a soldier at risk of bodily harm, or lead to a suicide or an escape, it would be coded red.

Supervielle instructed his staff not to underestimate the danger that al Qaeda could pose. When he was given the completed, color-coded chart, he placed it in his briefcase alongside the Conventions themselves, and headed up to Washington as he'd been ordered, unaware of the January 9 memo and the debate surrounding it. But unbeknownst to Manuel Supervielle, the War Council had finally come to a decision that they were willing to put on paper.

Debate in Washington became furiously intense in the days after the issuing of that draft. Technically labeled a draft, the January 9 Memo had important consequences for JTF 160. What had at first seemed to be a temporary lack of clarification now became standing policy. A sin of omission had become a sin of commission. Rather than a state of limbo being created out of a policy void, administration lawyers had formulated a policy embracing limbo as its primary characteristic. There was to be no policy. That was the policy. Henceforth, the gray area that had unsettled the lawyers became all-encompassing. There would be no black versus white, legal versus illegal, right versus wrong. It was a policy destined to spawn disaster both from the military and legal perspectives. Rumsfeld had not only circumvented the statutory process of interagency consultation in the legal sphere as in all others. He had also, intentionally or unintentionally, subverted the elementary premises of military management.

This, then, was the sand on which the Guantanamo operation was precariously built. It was ominously shifting ground on which no person, no code, and no precedent could weigh in with authority. It was not just a legal black hole, as it came to be called later. It was also a military black hole, a legally compromised operation whose premise would ultimately come to threaten the integrity of the military and those under its command.

If there was to be any clear direction forthcoming, it would depend not only on the command authority of Michael Lehnert and the professionalism of Terry Carrico, but on the ability of those in command to do as Lehnert and Supervielle had with the ICRC and Carrico had done with his corrections colleague in the run-up to the opening of X-Ray—namely, to insist on getting the people they needed into place. And there was yet another person General Lehnert would request to round out his team.

Accepting the absence of policy directives from Washington, Lehnert supervised his detention team as he had his construction and administrative team of Buehn and Meier. This arrangement solidified the unity of effort and command. Now, with the ICRC on its way and Colonel Carrico in place, Lehnert thought about his options for establishing a workable command. With both Colonel Carrico and the ICRC, he had struck, in theory at least, a good balance between the professional detention mission and the rights of the captives. Lehnert would be able to rely on tight security, knowledgeable guard units, and adherence to the law, even if the latter was no longer strictly required.

But there were still problems, one of which was triggered by the presence of the ICRC representatives. They could be helpful in drawing attention to the law as it applied to prisoners' needs. But they were not compelled to be loyal to him. They represented an outside interest, however well intentioned. And their primary loyalty was not to the national security of the United States but to the rights of the al Qaeda and Taliban captives. On the other hand, when it came to Terry Carrico, whose interests, as an army colonel, would primarily be those of national security, he would likely have as little sensitivity to the issue of the detainees as prison officials across the United States were often reputed to have for their charges. Nor could Lehnert be sure that Colonel Carrico would be someone with whom he could discuss these issues in an off-the-record, exploratory way. What Lehnert needed was someone to help him put this matter in perspective, someone loyal to the military and the nation's security but sensitive to the fact that the individuals who were about to be caged at Guantanamo were human beings, just as the Cubans and the Haitians who had last inhabited X-Ray had been. Rolling this over in his mind, Lehnert came up with an answer. He would ask for the services of a Muslim chaplain, someone who understood Muslim culture and who reported to him, so that decisions could be taken on the basis of informed discussions. With the arrival of the prisoners imminent, and the growing sense of confusion and lack of preparation on the part of his superiors, Michael Lehnert contacted the Chaplain of the Marine Corps and submitted his request for another new member of his team. It remained to be seen whether the brass would acquiesce.

As the arrival of the incoming group of captives approached, the general entertained a modicum of hope that his JTF could accomplish this task with some sense of decency while still satisfying the brass in Washington. But if he and his team thought so, they were soon to be bitterly disappointed. Within days, Michael Lehnert and the JTF would have a sense of just how wrong they were to think that they might have mastered this mission. Nor, it turned out, had they pushed back successfully against Washington's determination to withhold the label "prisoners of war" from the terrorist suspects at Guantanamo. The EPW classification was off the table for a very specific reason: it would have entailed binding legal rules about how the captives could be treated while in American custody.

On January 4, the order to execute was finally issued by the Pentagon. On January 6, Lehnert had arrived from Camp Lejeune to take up his post at Guantanamo with several hundred more Marines in tow. To acknowledge Lehnert's arrival, Bob Buehn called another town meeting, this one to introduce General Lehnert and to enlist his help in assuaging the community's fears about depletion of resources, security risks to wives and children in case a detainee escaped, and the possibility of being sent home. Warming to this role, Lehnert first assured the group of several hundred that extra supply barges would be used to stock the Gitmo commissary.

As for the security issue, Lehnert conveyed total confidence that he had the potential risks completely under control. "We'll keep 'em secured. You can be sure of that," he told his listeners with palpable self-assurance. When it came to the continued presence on the base of the military families, Lehnert let his audience know that he was on their side. He reported a conversation that he had had with the supervising authority for the naval base, Admiral Robert J. Natter. Lehnert had explained the potential downside of sending the families off-base, one of the many lessons gleaned from Operation Sea Signal. "In my opinion," he told Natter, "it's a matter of morale. Send the families home and you create a class of military personnel from whom something has been taken away." As it turned out, the matter was never raised again by the chain of command.

But the most interesting thing about this meeting was neither that Lehnert had carved out time from his frantic schedule nor that the civilian audience continued to be afraid of the everyday nuisance of dwindling resources and the nightmare scenario of escaped terrorists on the loose. What stood out on the balmy late afternoon was a fashion item. Throughout the crowd, meeting outdoors at the open-air downtown Lyceum, were scattered T-shirts, all white, bearing the same ironic phrase: "The Least Worst Place." It was an attempt at using humor to master a situation that was unknown and somewhat scary. Even Lehnert took it in stride. Far from mocking Rumsfeld and the base's new mission, which was not a possibility for this unwavering patriotic group, the slogan inscribed on the T-shirts nevertheless conveyed succinctly, albeit without conscious intent, the unthinking nature of the Pentagon's ostensibly rational plan.

This underlying lack of thought betrayed a lack of preparation even at the linguistic level, a circumstance that was nicely captured by the very words "least worst place." For in addition to the fact that there still was no agreed upon nomenclature for the captives about to arrive—they were "the Taliban," "the bad guys," "the terrorists"—and still no verbal or written confirmation that this was to be a penal mission, there was also a more glaring and unusual absence. There was no name for the mission itself. Military operations, both campaigns and humanitarian efforts, invariably have names: Operation Neptune (Normandy, 1944), Operation Urgent Fury (Grenada, 1983), Operation

Just Cause (Panama, 1989), Operation Desert Storm (Persian Gulf, 1990), even Operation Sea Signal. But the Guantanamo mission had no name, other than the one Donald Rumsfeld had given it: "The Least Worst Place."

Even after the order to execute was issued, JTF 160 remained nameless, uninstructed as to its mission, uncertain about the applicable law, and awaiting a group of prisoners to whom no familiar classifications could be applied. The fallback policy of Bush's Washington—to have no detectable policy—was nevertheless about to begin. And into the void—which the lawyers in D.C. created, which the lawyers at Gitmo and SOUTHCOM tried with little success to work around, and which Michael Lehnert inherited in its full emptiness—had stepped the men and women of the naval base. They christened the operation with its first name, indeed with the only name it would ever have: The Least Worst Place.

5

The Bad Guys First

I don't even know their names.
—Donald Rumsfeld

Standing beneath a sun-bleached sky, Michael Lehnert scanned the horizon stretching behind the remote airfield on the leeward side of Guantanamo Bay. It was exactly four months since American Airlines flights 11 and 175 struck the Twin Towers and AA 77 had hit the Pentagon and United Flight 93 had crashed into the field near the town of Shanksville, Pennsylvania. Inspecting the landing site from a rise 100 yards away, Lehnert tried to get an overall picture of his JTF's readiness for their first consignment of detainees, a group of 20 whom Lehnert described before they arrived as "the bad guys first."

What Lehnert saw comforted him. On the surface, at least, all seemed to be under control. The recently sleepy base waited expectantly. At attention, rifles clasped to their sides, Marines and soldiers readied themselves on the landing field, while sailors guarded the river's mouth and armored vehicles lined the roadways. Humvees bristling with machine guns and grenade launchers squatted on the tarmac, and a helicopter hovered over the waiting convoy of gun jeeps and a yellow school bus that had been refitted to transfer the arriving detainees via ferry to Camp X-Ray. Snipers and riot squads stood in position.[1]

On the plane from Afghanistan, security had been tight. The Chairman of the Joint Chiefs, Air Force General Richard Myers, had warned that any lapses in security might allow the detainees, endowed with satanic determination, to "gnaw hydraulic lines in the back of a C-17 to bring it down."[2] Accordingly, the guards during the flight, an Air Force special guard unit called the Ravens, wore body armor in addition to carrying stun guns and even pistols, which they were trained to use inside the fuselage.

Colonel Terry Carrico thought they had the security on the ground covered "from A to Z." Colonel William Meier felt confident in the endless drills to cover transport from the landing field to Camp X-Ray on the other side of the bay. "We were all very excited to be part of history-making," one soldier told me. "We were all pretty stoked or pumped that the United States military had captured individuals that were part of the disaster of 9/11."[3]

For his own satisfaction, Lehnert reviewed the extensive preparations that had been made in anticipation of this moment. Escape was impossible. There was a chance that someone among the troops would be injured. Preventing injuries upon arrival was a daunting task, as he explained to the press, because the prisoners "represent the worst elements of al Qaeda and the Taliban" and could attack their guards personally in unforeseen ways.[4] Lehnert had no reason to doubt this characterization at the time. JTF 160 had rehearsed over and over again the procedures for receiving the detainees, from the landing of the plane to locking up the prisoners in the cells. The idea, according to Colonel Carrico, was total control from the beginning. "We shut down every road. We had total control of the route."[5]

The captives would be arriving, as everyone did, on the leeward side of the bay. When the plane was down and the engines off, troops would circle the C-141, "their backs to it and their eyes on everything around it,"[6] apparently to make sure that a fearsome enemy from the other side of the world would not ambush the landing site in order to liberate the worst of the worst. The formal transfer of the prisoners from Air Force custody to Lehnert's command would take place as they stood on the tarmac. The prisoners would be taken to the bus with two guards accompanying each detainee, one to have a hold of the prisoner, another to serve as the "chaser" in case something unexpected occurred. They would be loaded onto a bus, driven onto a boat, ferried to the other side of the bay, and then bused nonstop up, around, and through the base itself via Sherman Road, then down the hill in the direction of the Cuban fence line. Outside the caravan of prisoners, armed Coast Guard boats would guard the passageway to the Guantanamo River and machine gun boats would patrol the rest of the bay and the river. To avoid any misunderstandings or last-minute glitches, Cuban authorities had been thoroughly briefed about the arrival plans.[7] And Raúl Castro would eventually reciprocate by announcing to the international press that any escapees from the detention facility would be sent back to U.S. custody.[8]

Of particular concern were the points of transfer, from the plane to the bus and from the bus to X-Ray itself. More realistic than fear of a rescue attempt was the worry that the detainees might be able to see where they were. The security of the base might be compromised if the prisoners could somehow locate themselves and thus have knowledge of the terrain. To limit the detainees' ability to see, the seats of the bus had been removed so that the only place to sit was on the floor. As an extra precaution, the windows along the sides had been covered with cardboard.

As he scanned the waiting troops, Michael Lehnert told himself that all the planning had paid off. Yet for all the machines, weaponry, and manpower in place, and for all the plans that had been well laid and all the procedures that had been practiced until they became automatic, "game-day butterflies" filled the air. Everyone was on tenterhooks, wondering what it would mean to have in custody "the worst of the worst." Despite the comfort he took in what he could see, Lehnert was experienced enough to be wary. He knew that there was only so much that could be controlled.

In fact, he had already had several reminders of how the best-laid plans can be disrupted by the unexpected. Even before the plane's arrival, Marine General James Mattis had e-mailed Lehnert from Afghanistan to inform him that gunfire had erupted at the point of takeoff in Bagram. There were no U.S. casualties and no damage to the plane. Nevertheless, it was an ominous sign, a stern reminder to Lehnert of something he knew full well.

Yet another indication that things might not go as planned had occurred in the lead-up to the date of arrival. The Pentagon had suddenly granted the press access to the base.

When it came to the press, SOUTHCOM had provided more policy guidance than in other areas. But it was still woefully inadequate. The general guidelines from the Combatant Command had provided standard directives outlining the "public affairs posture for this operation." The naval base, according to the memo, would be "serv[ing] as a temporary holding facility for Al Qaida, Taliban, or other terrorist personnel that come under U.S. control as a result of the ongoing global war on terrorism." Lehnert and the JTF he commanded, it continued, would preside over a detainee population "expected to incrementally increase to as many as 2,000 maximum security detainees." The Combatant Command promised that "holding conditions in the detention camps will be humane and consistent with the Geneva Conventions."[9]

The memo also provided guidelines "for what can and cannot be divulged... both to media, and to family members and friends outside Guantanamo Bay." It was boilerplate except for the decision to allow embeds, which simply replicated the policy in Afghanistan for permitting reporters to ride along with U.S. forces.

Tacked onto the public affairs office's memo was a sheet on "Media Q and A Guidance." Here, the chain of command's attitude toward the press regarding

Guantanamo was apparent. It considered eleven hypothetical questions—ones that could only be answered flatly "No" or essentially without comment. Such straightforward refusals to provide information were obligatory in response to all press inquiries about the route to Guantanamo, the specifics of the detainees on the flight, the date of the first arrival, and the names of the detainees. In answering other questions, as well, specific answers were discouraged. On the other hand, where they could, spokespersons were encouraged to emphasize the danger that the detainees posed. So, for example, the memo reminded those responsible for briefing the press that "The SECDEF said that there have been three or four incidents where these folks have demonstrated their determination to kill themselves, kill others, and/or escape."

Beyond these vague guidelines for selective transparency, Lehnert and his public affairs officer, Steve Cox, working with Lieutenant Colonel William Costello from SOUTHCOM, were left to fend for themselves. As Cox put it, he was "surprised at the lack of guidance through SOUTHCOM,"[10] and somewhat dismayed by the responsibility placed on him to improvise policy.

Chosen at the last moment (and largely because he was available), and arriving one day before the detainees were scheduled to arrive, Cox turned out to have excellent credentials for the job. He had served at Gitmo in 1992–93 during the Haitian migrant crisis, a challenging media stint at best. He also had field public affairs experience, having served during the Gulf War and elsewhere. Significantly for the history of Guantanamo's first hundred days, he was accustomed not only to controversy but to operating within the framework of the Geneva Conventions.

Cox took his lead from Lehnert, who thought that the stonewalling and evasiveness recommended by SOUTHCOM would lead to more trouble than it was worth. As he explained it to Cox, "If we had any hope in the world of getting public opinion on our side, they would have to see it for themselves." Cox was aware of Lehnert's scant experience when it came to press relations, and knew that he would have his hands full teaching the gregarious and straight-shooting General how to present himself to the media. But he agreed with Lehnert that transparency and access, within sensible limits, should characterize their relationship with the press. Before the detainees arrived, in other words, and before the reality of who the captives actually were had dawned on anyone in the chain of command, a tentative consensus was taking shape that openness rather than opacity should characterize the military's relation to the press. That journalists themselves would come to be seen as hostile intruders by Guantanamo authorities was the last thing that Lehnert and Cox could have imagined at the time.

The critical decision to allow press access to the base on the day of arrival was made neither by Lehnert and Cox nor by SOUTHCOM but by the Pentagon. In the days following Rumsfeld's official announcement about the opening of Guantanamo, the press corps applied relentless pressure, clamoring for permission to visit the detention facility.[11] According to the Pentagon's spokeswoman Torie Clarke, "They wanted every detail of every aspect—transport, clothing, interrogations, toilet facilities."[12]

Pelted with incessant demands for transparency, the Pentagon relented and decided to grant the media carefully choreographed access to Guantanamo prior to the arrival of the prisoners. Members of the press were invited to visit the base. They could take a whirlwind tour of the facilities, and they were expected to return home the day they came. This substitution of showmanship for transparency began what would be one of the more persistent, and fraudulent, characteristics of the Guantanamo operation. Insisting on their openness, the authorities demanded—and JTF 160 usually complied with—a policy that involved scripting every moment of the press's access.

Despite their attempt to extend the policy of total control to include the press, the Pentagon planners were blindsided by their own failure to predict how the people they were trying to control, in this case the journalists, were likely to bridle at the imposed constraints. For example, the media was given the date of January 10 for their first visit. From CNN reporter Bob Franken's perspective, the military had "grudgingly decided that they would show us the facility they were gonna use." Before their visit, the reporters did not know that the 11th would be the day the detainees finally arrived. Until the last minute, in fact, the timing was uncertain, as the date kept changing.[13]

Once the media representatives were on the ground, however, the buzz was out. It was confirmed. The first planeload of the allegedly worst of the worst would indeed be arriving the very next day. Within 24 short hours, some of America's deadliest terrorist enemies would arrive in chains. How could conscientious American journalists, following the biggest story of their lifetimes, simply pick up and leave? How, Carol Rosenberg of the *Miami Herald* wondered, could she pass up the chance to report on one of the few stories of a lifetime that would have no pictures, no video, but only the words of reporters to rely on for the moment and for the historical record?

It was a hard pill for the press corps to swallow—flying home on the eve of what promised to be a momentous chapter in U.S. history. To Franken it seemed like a dereliction of duty. More than unhappy, Franken was defiant. "I'm not going," he told the military's press officers, pure and simple. "I'm not going. . . . I am not getting on that plane," he said, referring to the plane waiting to take the reporters back to the States. Franken knew full well that they could pick him up bodily and throw him aboard. One chief petty officer, an imposing young man who towered over even Franken's 6'3" height, stood ready to take him on, to show how he would handle a weakling reporter.[14]

As the JTF would soon learn, however, word traveled seemingly at the speed of light from the island base back to the commanding heights in Washington. Soon enough, Franken was contacted by his CNN bureau chief, Katherine Kross, who, in turn, had already received an earful from Pentagon spokesperson Torie Clarke about Franken's intransigent refusal to abide by his previous agreement to come home on the 10th. "What the hell are you doing?" Franken remembers her asking. "My job, Katherine," he responded, informing her of his resolve to stay. Franken explains his theory of his job this way: "If a tree falls in the woods and it's not on camera, does it really fall? And the answer is, 'Of course not.'" The events of the next day were headline news, much too important for journalists simply to abandon their observation posts.

Torie Clarke later insisted that her "instinct" wasn't that different from the one Cox ascribed to General Lehnert and to himself. As Clarke tells it, she wanted "to open the place up. Let the cameras into GITMO so everyone—from our foreign critics to human rights organizations to everyday Americans who were legitimately concerned about what was happening there—could see what was happening. We had nothing to hide."[15]

Even a Pentagon with something to hide, admittedly, could foresee the negative consequences of physically ejecting American reporters on the day the detainees arrived. Such a highly visible press blackout was bound to excite unwanted journalistic curiosity and intensify the amount of criticism that Washington would confront. Moreover, the war on terror was to some extent a propaganda war, and the press, if skillfully managed, could be a useful vehicle for conveying to the world images and impressions that would benefit the American side. So the decision was made to allow a few members of the press, drawn by lots—one for each group: print, broadcast, and so on—to remain. Franken speculates that Lehnert's intervention, among other factors, had been crucial to the final decision. "I'm inclined to think that he [Lehnert] said, as far as he was concerned, that he would be okay" with the reporters staying to observe the arrival of the detainees. Lots were drawn, and Franken was chosen to represent television news.[16]

The next day, the remaining pool of reporters gathered on the hill beside the landing strip. Watching also was another cadre of press observers who had totally escaped the attention of JTF 160, SOUTHCOM, and the Pentagon. This second group of journalists was perched on a watchtower on a Cuban military base with clear sight lines to Guantanamo Bay. Castro had granted them the right to take pictures, which they continued to do in the future, most often from the vantage point of the ironically named Dollar Bar where they would regularly congregate.

The Pentagon's decision to allow American media access to the airfield on January 11 and the foreign media's capacity to observe events from Cuban posts drove home to Lehnert and the chain of command that, even prior to the arrival of the prisoners, the public, largely via the press, would be an integral part of the goings-on at Guantanamo.

Even without the burden of outside pressures, he faced a flood of problems that led Timothy Nichols to compare General Lehnert's job to holding back the dike. With the outside world looking in, it would take strategic stopgaps as well as wise overall policies to keep the barriers to disruption in place.

If asked to enumerate the cascading problems of his new mission, Lehnert might have begun with the problems not of the detainees but of the troops on the ground. One piece of the story that he would have to manage consisted of the passions of the men and women who populated the JTF. In truth, the troops were on the verge of an emotional eruption. They had worked around the clock since their arrival days before. What's more, layered over their exhaustion was a sense of the awesome magnitude of the campaign they were about to conduct. At least one soldier had a personal tie to 9/11—Randy Tulepan's father had narrowly escaped from the World Trade Center. The charged atmosphere was sensed by all and made apparent in the outbursts of patriotic hatred against the Taliban and in simmering disagreements between the Marines and the soldiers they were trying to train.

Lehnert had already registered another, perhaps even more worrisome, problem. In the few days since Terry Carrico had arrived, it had become clear that the two men saw their joint mission very differently. Carrico had firm ideas, despite his lack of direct prison experience, about how prisons ought to be run. As he explained to General Lehnert, the minute prisoners thought that they had any independence or personal control over events, they would begin to perceive the guard staff as weak, and then be emboldened to take disruptive, even dangerous, action. Once they arrived, Carrico said, the prisoners had to be under direct control at every moment—a job that he intended to give in part to the Immediate Reaction Force, a squad of

men trained to use brute force to physically overwhelm and subdue unco-
operative prisoners.[17]

Lehnert, for his part, made it clear to Carrico that he wanted to err on the
side of humane treatment. Carrico seemed at first to assent; he also agreed
with Lehnert that the Geneva Conventions should govern the guards' behavior.
Lehnert felt some confidence in Carrico's commitment to exercise restraint
as well as firmness. But he worried that this tenuous agreement could easily
unravel when his pumped-up and exhausted troops encountered dangerous
and potentially violent detainees.

Lehnert faced yet another challenge: persuading the various services to
work smoothly with one another. When first assigned to the JTF, many of the
individual troops were skeptical of serving on a mix-and-match joint mission.
It was the first joint mission for many, including Terry Carrico, and few rel-
ished the prospect of working with the other branches. Many were skeptical of
the viability of such operations. Some of them—notably Carrico's army units
and the Lejeune guards—were already deeply at odds with one another. Given
the heightened emotional environment that was sure to define X-Ray, Lehnert
knew that leadership in the matter of interservice affairs would be essential to
his ability to keep control over the nature of the detention effort.

Essentially, the Marines' job was to train the Army soldiers in the detention
effort. The Marines took their trademark gung-ho approach to this task, consulting the detailed manuals that they had lugged down to the base, creating
strict protocols where there had been none, and devising drills for the Army
troops to perform and perfect through endless repetition.

The Army troops chafed under this regime. To the Army troops, the Marine
Corps sometimes appeared less like a fellow branch of the military and
more like an exotic cult with its own bizarre codes and customs. "It was very
apparent...that there was this macho type" of Marine at Guantanamo. "We
always say, 'hey, diddle, diddle, up the middle.' Marines will never go left or
right...and they are proud of that." The Marines responded with "compla-
cency kills."[18] In sum, the divide was one in which the Marine guards insisted
that they were the ultimate professionals, and that their way needed to be followed by Army units that were lazier, less obsessive about drilling, and generally less up to the serious task at hand. For its part, the Army sought to make
the mission their own, as it would be theirs alone when Lehnert and his units
left, at a still undetermined point in time.

Lehnert kept his doubts at bay and trusted in the discipline, the training,
and the chain of command as his bulwark against underlying problems.

Whatever jitters infused the waiting troops and their general about the danger the detainees posed, whatever challenges had been countered and dealt with, he knew they'd done the best they could. Now, he was about to find out just how effective their best actually was—or could be, given what the next few hours would tell him about the detainees.

The plane from Kandahar was expected to land circa 1500 hours. Having dispatched one of his men to Afghanistan in anticipation of the arrivals, Lehnert knew just when the plane had departed. This first flight was a direct one, as there was still some worry about landing on foreign soil and thus violating laws of transporting prisoners. Braced for anything, the naval base community itself stood breathless. Touchdown came nearly an hour ahead of the estimated time of arrival.

As expected, when the plane landed and the rear hatchway of the C-141 opened, the first to appear in the opening was the head of the Ravens, who reported in with the waiting security force. The manifest was turned over and custody was formally transferred to the Marines, who would keep custody until they reached X-Ray.

Before the detainees emerged from the plane, troops aboard the plane lugged out a room-size metal container. Press observers gasped, thinking, in the fearful atmosphere of the day, that perhaps it was a type of cell—that perhaps the likes of Hannibal Lecter were on board, unable to be unrestrained and unboxed even for a moment. As it turned out, it was only an in-flight latrine.[19]

When the detainees finally did appear, they looked like anything but the "worst of the worst" that President Bush's press secretary Ari Fleischer had proclaimed them to be. Disheveled and frail, wobbly from their long trip, stinking of urine and wearing blackened goggles, earmuffs, orange socks, and knitted caps,[20] they looked like aliens perhaps but not like purveyors of danger and destruction. The spectacle shocked the guards on the ground. "We didn't know they would be like that—hooded and goggled—they didn't tell us they were coming in, you know, sensory deprivation."[21] Nor did they know that some of the detainees would be so weak they had to be carried off the plane between two guards—"105-pound guys," as one onlooker put it, "and the Marines just lifting [them] like . . . a bag of groceries."[22]

The Marines lifted the detainees' earmuffs as they entered the bus, "You are now the property of the U.S. Marine Corps," the Marines shouted in English.[23]

Once all 20 had been led off the plane and loaded onto the bus, the transfer order to the JTF custody was signed and Michael Lehnert was officially in charge of the detainees. The bus wound its way toward the ferry dock 300 meters away. As Shafiq Rasul remembers about the second flight, on which he arrived three days later, "[W]e sat cross-legged on the floor...and were thrown about because of the movement of the bus."[24] The bus climbed from the boat up past the road where Debi Buehn and her son Will, just home from school, waited. As soon as they had seen the ferry pull onto the beachhead by the salinization plant, they had jumped in the car to witness the passengers who would be riding by their road. Climbing toward Debi Buehn's vantage point, in the direction of the McDonald's, the post office, and the elementary school, the bus made it to the top of the hill where Debi and her son waited. She pulled Will closer to her side as the bus approached. When she glimpsed the silhouette of a soldier standing on the bus, the nose of his rifle pointed down at the detainees, she felt secure and somehow vindicated.

As First Lady of the naval base she contained her emotions under the professional demeanor of a member of the U.S. military. All that armor, the vehicles, the guns, the combat gear in full display, and then the yellow school bus designed to transport innocent American children now being used to convey the opposite of American innocents—namely, terrorists. Her observation of the incongruity apparent in the use of a school bus for the alleged terrorists was not unlike General Lehnert's own sense that the use of the military to handle a penal mission was disturbingly out of place.

Within days, the buses would be painted a grayish white, but the process of getting ready, the call to action, had been too rapid; there had been as little time for paint as for newly crafted policy. But as a writer, Debi knew that the image of the school bus was the one by which she would remember the day, the capsule shot that best explained the situation they were all now in—the unraveling of American icons in the wake of 9/11 and the usurping of institutions dedicated to American honor and decency.

From the moment the school bus pulled up at the gate to Camp X-Ray, the simmering conflicts inside Lehnert's command intensified. At Camp X-Ray, where the excitement was barely contained, Carrico's units stood waiting, as did the medical corps. The only relief was that the press had been left behind, escorted off to the communications room to file their stories.

The banning of the press from X-Ray at this pivotal moment was a lucky choice for the U.S. military, because it meant that no one would know that the first scuffle after the plane landed was not between the detainees and their guards or even among the prisoners. It was among the captors.

Just as the bus was entering Camp X-Ray, the Marine contingent, present primarily to observe their Army trainees, noticed that they were being pushed by the Army guards. They found themselves being moved along the dirt toward Bravo Block, a cell block that had been prepared for the first arrivals.[25]

The Marines, uncertain of what was happening, did not push back until they were inside the rows of the cell block. By then it was too late. They heard the loud, unmistakable click of the cell block gate locking behind them. Marine guards had become the first prisoners at Guantanamo Bay's Camp X-Ray. Humiliated and furious, the Marines could now only watch the proceedings. They stretched out on the parched ground and prepared to wait until their jailers let them out. The message was clear; the Army could perform their duties without the supervision of the Marines. They didn't need babysitters.

In subsequent days, the festering tension between the rival services would require Terry Carrico and Michael Lehnert to make some major decisions.

While this drama unfolded backstage, on the main stage events followed the script. After the bus entered the sally port and was cleared, the prisoners were offloaded one by one and escorted to an enclosure, where, still in their coats, goggles, and earmuffs, they were forced to kneel and wait under the still-hot late afternoon sun. While JTF 160 troops snapped photos, the prisoners were processed. Soldiers cut off their clothes and escorted them—two guards per detainee—to the showers and from there, covered only by a towel, to medical personnel for an exam. They were weighed and fingerprinted, swabbed for DNA, clipped for hair samples, and given a plastic bracelet embossed with their identification information. After a body search—an X-ray photograph of a prisoner in Afghanistan who had been discovered with a grenade in his rectum had been circulated—they were finally allowed to dress. The orange jumpsuits were much too large and had a gap that exposed the body from the waist to the top of the legs when the wearer bent over. Their goggles were taken off for the X-rays, and then put back on. All told, the detainees essentially spent over 40 hours blindfolded.

Still, as day turned to night, no prisoner had yet been taken to his cell. Aware of his responsibilities for the health of the detainees, if not out of compassion, Lehnert bridled at the "Army regs" that the guard units insisted upon following. The Army, he said, would ask the detainees, "What's your social security number?... suddenly these forms appeared... the ones that they learned a long time ago in some school in the Army." For Lehnert, it was bureaucracy for the sake of bureaucracy—and counterproductive at that. But the Army wasn't budging. Claiming that they had to follow the rules, they successfully stood their ground. It was all part of the philosophy that Carrico embodied: you stick to the rules, because if you don't, you risk unleashing chaos in your camp.

The military term for the posture taken toward the detainees was "positive control." Both Terry Carrico and Al Shimkus, the two men responsible for overseeing hands-on behavior with the detainees, agreed that such a policy was at the heart of any successful oversight of the detainees. Captain Shimkus stressed the way in which the rigid control that Carrico found essential guarded the "detainees' security." Carrico extended the benefits of "positive control" to the guard troops as well. "We wanted to ensure that we had that for the protection of the detainee and the protection of our people," he explained.[26]

The line between this "positive control" and coercive, even abusive, behavior was hard to determine, however, particularly at the outset. Several instances of abuse and rough handling were reported, on that first day as during subsequent arrivals—not only by the detainees but by military observers as well. At the point of disembarkation, small signs of anger on the part of the guards erupted, according to the Marine guards watching from their locked-in area as well as the detainees themselves.

The detainees who arrived on the early flights recalled being not only pushed, but punched and kicked. And according to the detainees, the medical part of the in-processing was an experience whose harshness and humiliation was hard to forget. Shafiq Rasul, one of the British detainees, recalls that after his shower, "I was walked naked to another table where a cavity search was conducted. This was both painful and humiliating." Not only had he not had access to any toilets, but "Having been subjected to the same search before we left Kandahar and having been kept shackled throughout the time we were transported, there can have been no purpose to this search other than to further humiliate or punish us."[27] According to one of the Marine guards, "[O]ne guy started bleeding over his goggles" because he was roughed up by his guards as he got off the bus, while one guard yelled at him, 'Remember 9/11.' "[28] Yet another detainee in the holding area caused enough of a disturbance for the guards finally to realize that he had a wound on his head that needed immediate attention.

Shimkus explained that a certain degree of roughness was an inescapable part of maintaining security. "It may have been perceived as rough. But I don't think it was any more rough than maintaining positive control."[29] Shimkus, Carrico, and the guards insist that they were handling the detainees professionally, without anger or emotion of any sort. As one guard explained, he had dealt with hardened criminals before and knew "how not to allow myself to think about what they might have done, but just to treat them according to the rules."[30]

The process may have taken too long and skirted the outer limits of acceptable treatment, but by around 11 P.M., nearly nine hours after the plane touched down, it was finished, and the last of the detainees was walked to his cell. No one had tried to escape. And if there were injuries, they were inconsequential. Their cells, referred to by various of the escorts as "dog kennels," "cages," and "cells," were 6 feet wide by 8 feet long, each sharing a wire mesh wall. Each block of cages consisted of four or five in a row, arranged in double rows. Dirt paths had been cleared between the blocks. The goggles and earmuffs had been removed from the prisoners. So, too, the shackles. In the cell was a bucket for bathroom use in between trips to the porta-john, as well as "2 towels, 1 blanket, 1 sheet, 1 small toothbrush, shampoo, soap, flip-flops and an insulation mat."[31] One of the towels was for washing, the other to be used as a prayer mat. The cell door was latched, and though the halogen floodlights stayed on, the detainees lay down and, for the first time in two days, slept.

By the time the sun came up on January 12, General Lehnert had learned a great deal that he hadn't known before about his mission. Most of all, he began to assess which of the problems he had anticipated were still important, which were cause for immediate worry, and which new ones to add to his list of concerns. The good news was that his instincts about handling the press, nurtured by Steve Cox, seemed to have paid off. The initial accounts were descriptive rather than condemnatory, fair rather than polemical. The articles mentioned the readiness of the U.S. forces at Guantanamo to maintain security at the facility, quoting Carrico's confident assertions about positive control. On the sensitive human rights issues, the press acknowledged the fact that Amnesty International protested the conditions of the detainees on the flight and that Human Rights Watch pointed out that, although the United States had determined that al Qaeda and the Taliban were not subject to the Geneva Conventions, international law called for the humane treatment of these prisoners. The press passed along the government's assurances that the Red Cross would be allowed into Guantanamo Bay and promises by Carrico and others about the Koran and a halal diet for the prisoners. Neither Cox nor Lehnert could have hoped for better.

But, beyond the press, Lehnert sensed that there were some problems that were not so easily handled. And the most challenging of these was JTF 160's ignorance about who the detainees were. The press may have been there for reasons of transparency, but the operation was not really transparent even to Lehnert and the JTF. On innumerable counts, Lehnert and his men were just plain ignorant, or rather unschooled. The names of the detainees were a mystery, as were their countries of origin, their ages, the languages they spoke, and what they had done to warrant transfer to Guantanamo. Later, Nichols and others would write e-mails to colleagues in Afghanistan, where he had recently served, to see what he could find out about individual detainees, but even then, little was known. And the troops he was responsible for had demonstrated on this first day of arrival a discomfort with not knowing who they had in their custody and therefore what precisely they were up against.

The detainees had arrived with numbers rather than names. Referred to as ISN numbers (Individual Service Numbers), they allowed the Americans to distinguish one detainee from another. The detainees often lied about their names and had been captured or traded with little or nothing by way of identification. Commonly used in prisons, where the names of prisoners are known, ISNs help strip captives of their humanity. But at Guantanamo, the detaining authorities really did not know the prisoners' names, and therefore had little choice.

Language was the core of the problem when it came to the lack of knowledge and information about individual detainees. During the first arrivals, the impossibility of communicating with the detainees highlighted the ignorance of the JTF with painful clarity. The Arabic cue cards were not particularly helpful because, to the apparent surprise of those who provided them, many of the early detainees spoke not Arabic but a variety of other languages, notably Pashto and Urdu. One of the principal aims of the Afghan campaign in the fall of 2001, besides denying sanctuary to the terrorists, was to capture and detain the 800 or so Arab fighters gathered around Osama bin Laden and Ayman al-Zawahiri. Bringing these Arab fighters to Guantanamo had presumably been what the initiators of the detainee operation had in mind during the earliest stages of planning. But the Arabs, including the leaders of al Qaeda, had escaped in mid-December from Tora Bora into the tribal areas of Pakistan, much to the embarrassment of the Pentagon and unbeknownst to most Americans.

If the Arab fighters had not escaped from Tora Bora, the Arabic cue cards would presumably have proved more useful. The same can be said for the

Arabic translators who had been sent to Guantanamo to help mediate the guards' communication with the detainees. The smaller than expected number of fluent Arabic speakers was disorienting to the Americans. The dominance of Urdu and Pashto added to the captors' sense of confusion. By pure happenstance, one of the Marine guards spoke some Urdu, having served 18 months in Pakistan. His translation skills were to come in handy at times. But many of the detainees spoke Pashto and only a smattering of Arabic.

Nothing seemed to flummox the American guards more, however, than the English-speaking detainees, at least at the beginning. Highlighting the ignorance of JTF 160, the fact that some of the detainees spoke English was a cause of great consternation among the troops. They were confused by this unanticipated circumstance, and soon began to think that maybe all of the detainees knew English and were keeping it to themselves as a ploy. To make things even more threatening to the guards, as if to say that the detainees had secret knowledge, beginning with the fact that they knew English, those who spoke English fluently did so not with Middle Eastern and South Asian accents but with British and Australian accents.

The American troops had been instructed to assert "total control." But the language barrier was potentially inflammatory. Thwarted by their inability to be understood and communicate, the likelihood of violence as a response to frustration increased. If the detainee couldn't follow verbal orders, then physical force would have to substitute. If the Arabic word for "kneel" conveyed nothing, then kicking or shoving the detainee behind the knees would make the point.

But language wasn't the only pretext for abusive behavior. The reported mistreatment of the English-speaking detainees suggests that culture was as big a divide as language. According to Shafiq Rasul, his use of English led directly to abuse at the hands of the guards. As he tells it, after six or seven hours of squatting in the heat during the in-processing, Rasul asked for some water. "The soldiers realized I was English and a man from the ERF team came and started kicking me in the back and calling me a traitor. . . . I wasn't allowed to move, if I did I would be kicked."[32] The military corroborates the story that they were shocked at the presence of English-speaking detainees—and that they saw this as a sign of guilt, both because it underlined the deceitfulness of those in their custody and because speaking English seemed to add a layer of nefariousness to the profile of the unknown captives.

Perhaps to avoid the unwanted attention meted out to Rasul, or perhaps to play games with their jailors, many of the other native speakers of English were determined not to let the Americans know that they, in fact, spoke the language. The Australian David Hicks, who arrived on the first flight, was one of these. So was Asif Iqbal, from the United Kingdom. The fingerprints of another early arrival came back from FBI analysis showing that the prisoner in question had been a student at the University of Nebraska. Up to that point, the man managed to keep completely secret his familiarity with English.

Where there was an information void, the members of the JTF filled in the blanks with their own invented stories. Routine administrative and medical record-keeping seems to have fulfilled a psychologically reassuring function, serving to calm the anxieties of ignorance. Captain Shimkus acknowledged this inadvertently when he contrasted Guantanamo Bay with the Afghan battlefields. In Afghanistan, he explained, omissions from the record are understandable. In Guantanamo, by contrast, "in a more controlled environment...you have to maintain sophisticated medical records."[33] With or without accurate data, a record was created and filed. The lengthier the forms about the detainees that they filled out, perhaps, the less ignorant the captors felt themselves to be, as if the mere recording of speculative and unreliable personal data meant that the detainees were being brought under control.

The tendency to fill in the blanks with whatever was on hand helps explain the wild rumor that took hold among dozens in the JTF that most of the detainees were maliciously concealing their capacity to speak English. It followed that all of the captives were, as Rumsfeld had explained, guilty of deceit and therefore guilty of terrorism. Lehnert saw clearly what he was up against— rumor in the place of knowledge, anger as the result of frustration.

The central issue about which there was such vast and discomforting ignorance was the issue of ethnic identity. If the detainees spoke Urdu and Pashto, then they couldn't be the Arab fighters, comrades of the 9/11 perpetrators, and allies of Osama bin Laden whom JTF 160 had expected. So who were they and why were they here?

Carrico's philosophy of detention interpreted any attempt to understand the detainees within their own cultural context as a kind of appeasement in the face of a lethal and unforgiving enemy. To try to see something from the detainee's point of view was to compromise the mission of penal detention.

The day of arrival delivered other powerful lessons. The culture of the detainees presented one element that would henceforth define the day-to-day decisions made about Gitmo. But the second cultural issue that had manifested itself—the clash of sensibilities about the proper manner of penal detention—threatened to color the future as well, for this philosophical divide reinforced the Marine Corps–Army split. Even in those first hours, Lehnert let it be known that because the detainees came from a culture that was relatively unknown to the American troops, it was important to think about possible cultural differences before taking action on behalf of or against the detainees. Their names were a case in point. Lehnert's notion was that the use of multiple names was "part of their culture," and therefore a reality to be understood rather than retaliated against in anger. For Carrico, this attitude was absurd and potentially dangerous. Interest in the identity of the detainees was tantamount to capitulation to the enemy. For Carrico, talking to the detainees was full of pitfalls. He let Lehnert know from the day of arrival that any such catering to the detainees would result in undermining the leverage of the detaining authority.

By the time that the last detainee was placed in his cell, Lehnert was even more convinced than he had been during the days of preparation and theorizing that the detainees were foreign in ways that his troops could hardly appreciate—dressed in their spacemen-like accoutrements as they exited the plane, the detainees' first appearance reinforced the sense that grew over the course of the day that they were wholly alien beings.

In the next days, the detainees gradually came to be distinguished as individuals by their captors. Although the detainees' real names remained unknown, they began to sport nicknames chosen by the U.S. troops.

The assignment of names happened within the first two weeks, as detainees awoke from their travel-induced haze. As Marine Master Gunnery Sergeant Marc Coudriet remembers it, "When they first came, they were complying...due to lack of sleep [and] fatigue from traveling...then, you know, they started having little attitudes."[34] From these attitudes and related behaviors came the nicknames. Each day, individual detainees earned nicknames from their keepers. Some were easily labeled—The Professor, the General, Crazy Horse, Al Qaeda Claus, and The Tipton Three from England, also labeled "the Beatles." Half-Dead Bob arrived, as did others, with that name already assigned in Afghanistan. He was the "expectant" who Shimkus worried might die. As he began to heal, the guards and others would refer to him as Quarter-Dead Bob and Eighth-Dead Bob.

Also noteworthy in the early days was Wild Bill. Wild Bill's antics in the camp startled the detainees as well as the guards. As one guard said, "it had to have hurt," referring to the seemingly continuous masturbating that the detainee indulged in. His pants more often off than on, his noises irritating anyone within earshot, he disturbed everyone. " 'He would eat his own feces, dump fresh water from his canteen and urinate in it and drink it,' a senior interrogator said."[35] The question in everyone's mind was whether he was crazy or putting this all on. According to Tim Nichols, it had been detected in Afghanistan that Wild Bill had "some type of impairment," but without adequate resources to assess things, they "sent him to me."[36] Warrant Officer Scott Bolman, curious himself, picked up the phone and called a buddy of his in Afghanistan and put the question: What do you make of this guy? The answer: He's crazy. He was then, and he is now. Wild Bill raised the level of discomfort throughout the camp. Eventually, he was moved to a cell far away from the rest of the detainees, and eventually from Guantanamo itself.[37]

The most notable among the Camp X-Ray detainees was "the Australian," David Hicks, number 002, who had arrived on the very first day. Hicks was a wayward boy from the outback who had traveled the world in search of adventure and meaning. While in Japan training horses, he had become interested in studying religions, and found himself particularly attracted to Islam. When he returned to Australia, he converted to Islam and embarked for Pakistan in 2000 for further study. Once there, he found his way to Afghanistan and the training camps of al Qaeda. Hicks knew just what his rights were, coming from a democratic society where the rule of law was familiar and submission to questionable authority something to protest against.[38]

Hicks was a challenge from day one. His English, though accented, made everything he said intelligible. And what he said corroborated the troops' worst fears. Reportedly telling the guards that he would kill them before he left, he gained everyone's attention. Rumors circulated among the staff that Hicks had superhuman strength. Acknowledging his rise to notoriety, Florida congresswoman Ileana Ros-Lehtinen, who saw Hicks when she was part of the congressional delegation that visited X-Ray two weeks after the opening of the camp, boasted, "We just all gave him the evil eye."[39]

It wasn't just what he said that aroused attention. It was also what he did. According to Major Coudriet, Hicks was the first to begin to defy the ban on communication among the prisoners. He developed a system of signals, involving whistles. He figured out a way, according to Coudriet, of using his food to make maps of the camp. Together, the whistles and the maps meant they were "planning an escape."[40] Others remember him counting out the guards' steps as they went from one place to another and keeping track of the time in dirt on the floor of his cell, also considered ways of mastering the geography of X-Ray. As Staff Sergeant Robert Farabee remembered, Hicks would move his mat to tell the time and count the steps of the guards to calculate distance. And he could sit in a given position for hours, all of which greatly impressed the guards.[41]

Early on, the detainees and the guards began to absorb their impressions of one another and, in the days to come, they would begin to act upon those impressions. They would be helped in these exchanges and observations by the arrival, days after the first planeload of detainees had come to Guantanamo, of the International Committee of the Red Cross. Lehnert intended to do everything in his power to have the ICRC diminish his own and his troops' ignorance about the detainees—even if such information came packaged inside a respect for cultural differences. Better understanding of the detainees, he believed, was bound to strengthen his position, helping him resist Carrico's determination to turn what he thought should be a detention facility into a penal colony. As it turned out, the arrival of the ICRC would be only the first salvo in an internal battle at Guantanamo that pitted the intense desire for information against the reality of elusive identities and scant evidence.

6

The Petting Zoo

You'd bring in folks, and they'd walk around. We'd show them the interrogation booths.
We'd show them the medical facility. We'd show them where the reaction force is.
They'd walk right past the detainees.

—Lt. Col. Timothy Nichols

Across the globe, from allies and critics alike, the photograph had ignited a blaze of protest. "Torture," accused the caption in Britain's *Daily Mail*. "Strongarm Tactics," cried the *Mirror*. "Fudg[ing] or blur[ring] the edges," scolded Mary Robinson, UN human rights chief and former president of Ireland. "Outsourcing…moral obligation," the Toronto *Globe and Mail* headlined, quoting a Canadian MP. French foreign minister Hubert Védrine and British prime minister Tony Blair sought assurances from their American counterparts that the United States was, after all, intending to follow international law. "Inside Camp Terror," read the caption from Sydney's *Daily Telegraph*.[1]

The U.S. press took scant notice of the photograph. The *New York Times* buried it on page 14 of the Sunday edition. The accompanying story bore the lackluster general headline it used for the war on terror, "A Nation Challenged." The *Washington Post*, too, downplayed the image, publishing a story about the British outcry but failing to mention any domestic criticism. But despite the muted American press response, the photograph did provoke a torrent of criticism from human rights advocates inside the United States as well as abroad.[2]

The Guantanamo photo was indeed memorable. And it soon began to play a decisive role in the war of images that accompanied the war on terror. There were the detainees, in a full-color snapshot—the prisoners from Afghanistan captured on film on January 11, the very day they arrived. The image that would come to define Guantanamo forever in the eyes of the world displayed the detainees, kneeling in the day's heat, goggled and earmuffed, bound and shackled at the wrists, dressed in fluorescent orange jumpsuits and caps and turquoise face masks, facing away from one another and bending in submission toward a concertina wire fence. They were awaiting in-processing huddled in the holding pen prior to their medical exams, their showers, and their assignment to cells.

The image appeared in newspapers worldwide in blatant disregard of international law. Articles 13 and 14 of the Geneva Conventions make it imperative to safeguard the dignity of such prisoners and therefore to keep their identities undisclosed. Accordingly, their faces should have been off-limits. The same prohibition applied to any images of the detainees shackled, or even just in custody, from which the prisoner might be identifiable. Citing the Geneva Conventions, the DOD's public affairs office for Guantanamo had strictly forbidden photography at Guantanamo.

Yet the photograph did appear, bringing to public consciousness serious questions about the legitimacy of the Guantanamo operation: Was it a place that would abide by human rights law, as Lehnert had reassured the press and counseled his team of officers? Were the prisoners being treated in accordance with what prisoner-of-war status demanded, even if they were not officially labeled enemy prisoners of war? Or was the United States violating its sworn treaty obligations, not to mention its own legal codes, as the photograph seemed to suggest?

Both Lehnert and Rumsfeld, in their different ways, realized immediately how much damage the photograph could cause. For Lehnert, the damage would be personal as well as professional. Not only would he be branded henceforth as the "Lash of Gitmo," but his prior assertions about humane prisoner treatment at the camp suddenly seemed duplicitous. Donald Rumsfeld, for his part, became aware for the first time that Guantanamo's geographical remoteness and isolation did not mean that the Pentagon could control the way the detention facility was seen by the world. He also learned that his own office did not fully comprehend the supreme delicacy of the mission, or the potential pitfalls of even limited and managed press coverage.

Rumsfeld's immediate reaction to the appearance of the photo in the press was to hastily place a videoconference call to Lehnert and other officials at the camp. The Secretary wanted answers. How did this happen? Who was responsible for this travesty? Who took these photos? He had thought the media was under control. The SECDEF was looking for someone to call on the carpet, someone to slap down.[3] So the culprit his inquiries unearthed came as something of a shock. To his impatient inquiry—"Who is to blame?"—he received a disconcerting answer: "The Pentagon."

Indeed, the Pentagon itself had given the picture to the press. The photo had been one of many taken on the day of arrival by Navy combat cameras.

They were part of a pro forma documentation of military procedures, preserved on film as a matter of course for their archival and lessons-learned value. Navy Petty Officer Shane McCoy had taken the photos. McCoy was part of "an elite unit that took secret pictures not for the public but for the Pentagon brass."[4] As *Miami Herald* reporter Carol Rosenberg found out in her interview with him six years later, McCoy was the only military photographer allowed at X-Ray that day. The other combat photographers shot pictures earlier in the day at various points of arrival and in-processing.

After the photos arrived in Washington from Guantanamo, the Public Affairs Office at the Pentagon had decided on its own, without consulting the Office of the Secretary of Defense, that it would be an effective PR move to release this one picture in particular to the press, presumably because it showed how effectively the United States was handling the world's most dangerous prisoners. DOD spokeswoman Torie Clarke took responsibility for the decision to publish the photos. As she later would say, in an attempt to rationalize the decision, "The pressure from the media was unbearable... I felt that releasing select images could allay some of our critics."[5]

For both Lehnert on the ground in Cuba and Rumsfeld back in D.C., the appearance of the photograph crystallized much of the debate that would hound the two of them throughout the initial months of the Guantanamo mission. For his part, Lehnert began to take realistic stock of his limited ability to prevent the planned detention camp from turning into a notorious penal colony. Rumsfeld, on the other hand, plunged with gusto into an attempt to shape the public narrative that defined Guantanamo. To do so, he did what he liked most to do: he called a press conference.

As it turned out, the incriminating photo could not be covered up with eloquent words. It would define the remainder of Lehnert's days at the camp. As events leading up to and following the photo's publication made clear, moreover, JTF 160 and the Office of the Secretary of Defense were on a collision course. Competing ideas about detention and the war on terror would henceforth test the relative strength of the uniformed military and the civilian leadership at the Pentagon. Bureaucratic infighting and competing agendas, if not competing sensibilities, set the stage for what happened next.

In the week between the arrival of the first planeload of detainees and the publication of the indelible photo, Camp X-Ray sprang to life. Over a hundred new detainees arrived, some of them severely wounded and sick. The JTF did not know most of their names or countries of origin, but they obviously represented an ever-broadening array of nationalities. Multilingual, weak, and frail, in their increasing numbers they compounded the questions that lay festering and unanswered. The detainees' eccentricities, the logistical problems of the camp, and the personalities of both prisoners and guards began to have a defining impact on the detention program during these early weeks. Much as they had been doing before the arrival of the prisoners, Michael Lehnert and his team continued to apply untested resolutions to novel circumstances, improvising command decisions about nearly every aspect of detainee life, including medical policies, legal considerations, press relations, and religious observances, trying their best to ensure that the detainees' "physical, mental and spiritual needs were met."[6]

While they were struggling with their novel responsibilities, Carrico, Lehnert, Meier, Buehn, and Shimkus were also under the constant and skeptical scrutiny of visitors, not all of whom were journalists. Barring visiting photographers from taking pictures of the detainees and their conditions was one thing; avoiding the prying eyes of the outside world was another.

Passengers landed at the air base nearly every day hoping to catch a glimpse of America playing tough in the war on terror. The endless stream of incoming flights included Navy "rotator" planes brimming with military personnel, jets out of D.C. bearing congresspersons and other governmental VIPs, small commercial nine-seaters crammed with journalists and intelligence agents from the United States and abroad, and private charters laden with contractors. Members of the task force called these official visitors "looky-looks," or "looky-loos": visitors, civilian and military, who took up valuable time and resources without adding to the operation, voyeurs rather than contributors.

The nearly daily comings and goings not only gave shape to the camp's routine but also influenced decisively the overall character of the mission. These touring busybodies and drive-by experts turned Guantanamo essentially into a national-security tourism hotspot—to see it was to be able to say one had seen it, even if the day-trippers left without a clear sense of what exactly they had seen. Was it humane? What kind of enemy was the United States up against? What did a terrorist actually look like? How adept was the United States in handling the worst of the worst?

Shepherding them around became a time-consuming occupation, not to say preoccupation, of the staff. The JTF officers quickly scripted a routine for the visitors, one that included the allegedly more sensitive aspects of the operation. Whatever they wanted to see, "We'd show 'em," Tim Nichols, Lehnert's intelligence officer, recalled. First and foremost, the visitors got to see the detainees in their open-air cells, with Shimkus, Lehnert, Carrico, and various other staffers available to provide a running commentary. They were also allowed to observe the daunting Immediate Reaction Force, ready to nip dangerous outbursts or rebellions in the bud. All these peeping Toms irked Nichols. X-Ray had become, in his words, a "petting zoo."[7] There for all to see were the cages, mute prisoners, open urination and defecation, cement floors, and exotic accoutrements, isomats (foam pads), prayer beads, and truncated toothbrushes, proof of the unfamiliar and less than human nature of the inmates.

The first group of visitors clarified for Lehnert the questions that would help him manage his operation. The trip, arranged by Jim Haynes, general counsel for the Department of Defense, was a site visit by the War Council, accompanied by some of its fringe players. Arriving on January 15 on a UC-35, the group included Alberto Gonzales; David Addington; Will Taft; Jim Haynes; Air Force General Counsel Mary Walker; John Yoo; Deputy Attorney General Larry Thompson; DOD's deputy general counsel for legal counsel, Whit Cobb; DOD's deputy general counsel for international affairs, Charles Allen; Eliana Davidson, a lawyer in Haynes's office; Manuel Supervielle, and others. In other words, the lawyers who were struggling to discover—or invent—a legal rationale for indefinite extrajudicial detention, unregulated by American or international law, had come down to see, however briefly, the flesh and blood reality that their ongoing work affected.

The problem was that there had still been no definitive agreement on detainee policy. In fact, in the five days leading up to the plane flight, the disagreements had grown rather than diminished.

When Haynes's group boarded the plane for Guantanamo—as when the detainees had arrived several days earlier—there was still no resolution to the legal dispute between Taft's staff and the lawyers working to satisfy DOD's War Council. The president and his advisors had not yet made up their minds. But those who opposed dispensing with the Geneva Conventions—notably Taft's legal team—knew that the political momentum was already strongly against them. And they knew just how far their opponents would go to get what they wanted.

Taft had already been given some indication of the direction the ultimate resolution would take. On January 14, John Yoo had sent back an answer to Taft's response to Yoo's own January 9 memo.[8] Yoo's answer attempted to make the case that, however it appeared on the surface, there were many fundamental agreements between the lawyers at State and those at the Office of Legal Counsel. Yoo had tried to insist that given the conditions of detention at Guantanamo, there was shared recognition that the treatment of prisoners was humane and lawful. But the fact was no one on Taft's team knew what those conditions were. Moreover, Yoo, "behaving like an aggressive advocate" and "hell-bent on security immunity for the leadership," according to Taft's lead lawyer for drafting the response, tried his best to parse the document so that he could conclude that in essence there was agreement between the two groups, even though there clearly was not.[9]

Lehnert, still left without guidance on the ground, understood that the January 15 group of visiting lawyers contained people adamantly opposed to the presence of the ICRC at Gitmo. These were the same lawyers who insisted that the detainees were not prisoners of war, and thus that the United States did not have to treat them in accordance with the Geneva Conventions. And they had unintentionally brought along an ally for Lehnert as well. It was Manuel Supervielle, the Cuban-American JAG colonel from SOUTHCOM who, without consulting his superiors, had invited the ICRC, in line with Common Article 3, to come to Guantanamo in the first place. Supervielle had been summoned to the Pentagon, and had been shuttled immediately not to the Office of the Secretary of Defense but straight to Andrews Air Force Base. Prior to the flight, therefore, there had been no time for a discussion with the Washington lawyers of his call to the ICRC.

No sooner was the plane airborne and stabilized than Jim Haynes, seated in the front of the plane, shouted back to Supervielle and asked him to please explain why in God's name he had invited the ICRC to Guantanamo. "It seemed like the legal thing to do," Supervielle remembers answering. "We're supposed to follow the Geneva Conventions except where it would impede operational security. So, I didn't think operational security was compromised by the presence of the ICRC." Supervielle then hastily added in his defense, "And the generals at SOUTHCOM and the acting head of SOUTHCOM all agreed with me." From there, Supervielle launched into a speech detailing the rationale he had used originally, all the while stealing looks out the window to see when Cuba's island landscape might come into view.[10]

For the remaining 30 minutes of the flight, the Bush administration's leading lights in crafting policies for the war on terror lambasted Supervielle about his apparent soft spot for the Geneva Conventions. They let him know that, as John Yoo had written to him days earlier with characteristic dismissiveness, "This is not your area." Prisoners captured in the war on terror, Yoo and the others had argued, were nothing like any of the enemies that the United States had previously known. Anyone steeped in the laws and practices that predated 9/11, as a result, was operating in an obsolete framework. To meet the new, unprecedented threat, the old rules had to be thrown out. Still, the possibility that executive-branch officials might use Cuba to do an end run around the American Constitution wasn't something that readily occurred to Supervielle, even as he fended off his questioners.

By the time the plane landed, Supervielle understood in no uncertain terms that this group of advisers thought that inviting the ICRC presence was a grave mistake. The Red Cross would be treading on U.S. territory and poking its finger into a highly sensitive mission that was really none of the organization's business.

"Well, is there a way to back out of it now?" someone finally asked Supervielle.

"I don't think so," he responded.

"Can they be sent to D.C. first?" someone asked. "Or maybe to Miami, to SOUTHCOM?"

Supervielle shrugged his shoulders. "As far as I know, they're in the air already, coming from places like Lebanon and Somalia—and they're converging in Jacksonville. Besides," he added, "it wouldn't be my call to turn them away. I wouldn't have that authority. I'm just a punk colonel."

At this point, Whit Cobb, according to Supervielle, sighed and extracted a piece of paper from his briefcase, a single sheet listing those points on which he and the others thought that the Geneva Conventions could apply at Guantanamo. It was a notably succinct list. It included permission for some religious practices, some degree of medical attention, and authorization for a religiously appropriate diet.

Many members of the Washington contingent on the plane knew just how fierce a battle lay behind that single sheet, copies of which Cobb distributed to the plane's passengers. For the two days prior to the trip, the lawyers in Haynes's department and their allies at OLC had browbeaten the lawyers on Secretary of State Powell's team, led by Taft, in an effort to secure a bottom-line agreement on the policy that would be in place when the detainees arrived. The squabbling lawyers barely made it to the finish line in time, and left many details to work out.

By the time of this flight down to Guantanamo, however, the main contours of America's new detainee policy were in place. And its basic elements were in no way to Taft's liking.

Donald Rumsfeld and Dick Cheney were deftly outmaneuvering Colin Powell. It was somewhat inevitable that the Pentagon's lawyer, Jim Haynes, and the vice president's lawyer, David Addington, with their determination to minimize the legal constraints on matters related to the detainees, would get the better of Will Taft and the Department of State lawyers, who were reluctant to bend the rules on detainee treatment, even though no one could be sure of this at the time. The inequality of the bureaucratic fight had become apparent in the first two weeks of January, just prior to the trip to Guantanamo.

Looking at Cobb's list, Supervielle registered its extraordinarily limited recognition of the rights that were to be extended to the prisoners at Guantanamo. Its resemblance to the Geneva Conventions was superficial, and its purpose was more to withhold rights than to extend them to the prisoners. By way of reply, he drafted his own document—the bubble chart that he and his team at SOUTHCOM had stayed up all night preparing even while, unbeknownst to them, the lawyers in Taft's office were doing much the same. Supervielle's lawyers—one from each of the services—had divided up the 143 sections of the Geneva Convention III articles and had made recommendations about which ones the United States would definitely not be able to follow in the context of Guantanamo and which ones, by contrast, it might be possible and therefore advisable to follow. This became what Supervielle came to call the bubble chart.

Rather than the meager, slapdash list Cobb had distributed, Supervielle's was a meticulously prepared point-by-point legal document. At one moment during the trip to Guantanamo, as if fending off the verbal assault by his fellow passengers, he held up the fruits of his team's efforts—his bubble chart—for his attackers to see. Supervielle explained, "Here is another approach to consider. We've gone through the Geneva Conventions—Article III—and color-coded the rules with red, yellow, and green." The red category—a full "No, we can't allow this"—included those items in the Conventions that could not possibly be followed at Guantanamo, either for security reasons or for logistical ones, such as paying the prisoners for their labor, housing them barracks-style with many men to a room, or allowing them access to a canteen or musical instruments or the right to congregate. The yellow category included those articles that were borderline, whose applicability depended on the specific context. Green represented those articles that could be easily followed without any substantial harm to the operational mandate or the security of the prisoners or staff.

Supervielle explained to his fellow passengers that his chart was meant as a guide for the commander on the ground, in this case General Lehnert.

Supervielle emphasized that case-by-case interpretations should be left to the general's discretion and that, above all, "fluidity" was called for. Even though the JTF officers and their superiors at SOUTHCOM had been consulted in preparing the chart, things could and would change over time and perhaps even from detainee to detainee.

As the plane prepared to land, Supervielle turned his mind from the interagency sparring to other, more personal things. This was the first time he would be returning to the land of his birth, and it meant something to him. He suspected that he would be the only member of his family to ever see Cuba again.[11] On landing, Supervielle realized that he would be able to do for himself a favor that he had asked Lehnert to do—bring back a handful or two of sand for his father and grandfather. He passed his bubble chart along to Lehnert, and he then toured the rest of the base along with his fellow passengers.

As a team player, the thought also crossed his mind that, despite the sparks flying, he wasn't seriously at odds with his fellow passengers; he was just giving the best counsel he could. But whether or not he wanted to acknowledge it or even understood it fully, Colonel Manuel Supervielle had undertaken the two most pronounced and effective steps in pushing back against the developing American policy of violating the Geneva Conventions, first in calling in the ICRC and now in preparing a detailed guide for adhering to the spirit of the Conventions, leaving room for "fluidity" but erring on the side of following the Conventions' rules.

Lehnert began his initial presentation to the D.C. group with an ill-fated attempt at humor. The first slide he showed them, of the island of Guantanamo, came with Lehnert's commentary: "Welcome to the Least Worst Place in the Caribbean." Supervielle remembers chuckling to himself, thinking the joke funny, but noticing that no one else in the room seemed to appreciate the humor. Unfortunately, Lehnert's attempt to lighten up the atmosphere was not his only initiative destined to fall dismally flat.[12]

Supervielle's difference of opinion from the majority of those in the D.C. group did not go unnoticed, either by Lehnert or by Haynes. After an overnight stay, the visitors boarded the school bus for the return ferry ride to the airfield. Haynes turned to Supervielle, catching the JAG off guard for the second time on the trip. "You're gonna stay down here, right?" he said, issuing a command in the form of a question. "You'll make sure things are working down here, right?"

There was little doubt as to what Jim Haynes had in mind with this order. Within a day of the War Council's departure, the ICRC, which Supervielle had invited down, had landed. "You invited the troublemakers," Haynes seemed to be saying. "You can stay here to deal with them."

But for Lehnert the presence of Supervielle was a blessing. It meant that he now had on his team a military lawyer who shared his commitment to treating the detainees essentially as prisoners of war. And, once the ICRC landed, Lehnert's unexceptional plan to manage Guantanamo by the book, in accord with the Geneva Conventions, would be one step closer to realization.

"Fluidity," Supervielle's stab at reconciling the Geneva Conventions with the unprecedented nature of the Guantanamo project, became the mantra of necessity rather than choice during these first days of Gitmo. For a week or so, Lehnert and his team continued as they had before the detainees arrived. They made up policy on the fly as problem after problem arose. But the flexibility was not without rhyme or reason. It was flexibility, after all, not arbitrariness. Dominating their decisions were two directives—caring for the well-being of the detainees and keeping the troops out of harm's way.

Lehnert and his officers quickly discovered that the Pentagon's initial expectations about the detainees' needs fell short of the reality. Food was a primary concern. Committed to serving halal food, the JTF had originally settled for vegetarian MREs (meals ready to eat). But as Al Shimkus pointed out, the detainees' digestive systems were already severely compromised by the destructive regime in Bagram. Due to the changes in climate and ingredients, they had a very difficult time adjusting to their new diet. Under Lehnert's direction, Shimkus set up frequent weighing of the detainees—a custom that has lasted until today—in order to monitor weight loss and gain. By the end of week one, however, the JTF already knew that it would need more than scales to see to their captives' nutritional needs.[13]

When it came to medical realities, the problems were even more overwhelming. Shimkus had been told to expect infectious diseases and battlefield wounds. He therefore screened the detainees for tuberculosis and set up an ICU inside the naval base hospital. Early on, he had also had the foresight to set up an isolation unit with special ventilation. And, as he had little choice, he readied beds in the naval hospital for other cases. Still, for all of his preparation and ingenuity, as the first flights of detainees showed, the problems were of a much greater breadth than anyone had anticipated. "Virtually every one that came to us had some kind of health issue," one medical administrator told me.[14] They indeed had battlefield injuries, but by now the wounds were infected, requiring major treatment interventions. Some prisoners had diseases that no one could recognize or that seemed chronic, but the detainees offered little to no information about their conditions. Others were old—90 in one case, late 80s in another—and at least one detainee arrived at death's door, "expectant," in the words of the medical staff. Everyone recognized that the death of a detainee, at the onset of the detention project, would have been devastating to the image of X-Ray. Determined to perform well as a medical professional, even if it meant going beyond the normal limits of his medical rank, Al Shimkus was not about to be derailed by the evident difficulties. He saw the problem: "We had no idea about what prison medicine was," he recalled. And while he may have assembled the best equipment available, what he really needed was the expertise to diagnose and treat these unknown diseases. At a minimum, he needed at least a first-rate ophthalmologist, a dermatologist, and a tropical disease expert. He could also have used a cardiologist and a gerontologist. Shimkus was given carte blanche to call in whomever he needed.[15] Our directive, Shimkus's chief deputy explained, was "to take good care of these people." They were told: "Your job is to keep them alive. If you need something to do that, you need to let us know."[16]

Shimkus also needed facilities well beyond the few beds in the naval hospital and the medical hut at X-Ray. And judging from the condition of some of the inmates, he was going to need a crash course in the burial customs of Muslims.[17]

That kind of expertise was particularly lacking. No one seemed to know the answers to basic questions about Islam. One detainee had arrived with a Koran, but others soon began to request their own copies. And apparently the detainees needed to know which way was east in order to face toward Mecca while praying. Questions arose over prayer beads as well: What were they for? Who needed them? What were the rules and expectations surrounding the call to prayer?

The religious issues, the JTF began to discover, were not separable from the rest of the detainees' lives. When the otherwise docile prisoners reacted strongly to being undressed and touched, the Americans were at first surprised. They soon learned that Islam regulated how the body was to be handled for both daily care and medical purposes. The "clash of civilizations" was nowhere exhibited more vividly, in fact, than in the pained recoiling of the prisoners over the presence and involvement of female attendants. Nakedness was an issue as well, for the detainees seemed unaccustomed and unwilling to be seen naked in front of others. So was cleanliness, which is central to Muslim ritual and observances. Muslims are required to wash before prayer, which occurs five times daily, so they required frequent access to washing facilities such as showers. The JTF soon began to realize the multiplicity of problems connected with cleanliness and other culturally tinged customs, but they didn't quite know enough to pinpoint the specifics, or even the religious theory behind the problems they faced on a daily basis.

The detaining authority's lack of knowledge about the religious culture of those being detained soon became a major obstacle to the smooth management of the facility. Acknowledging the growing sense that ignorance dominated life inside X-Ray, Lehnert talked each day with Galen Jackman at SOUTHCOM, emphasizing the need for a kind of expertise that was culturally sensitive as well as practically adept. Sympathetic to Lehnert's demands, Jackman went to work to push his requests up the chain of command.[18] But even as he waited for his superiors to make arrangements, Lehnert was counting on relief to arrive sooner—in the form of some visitors he had asked for and the first of whom, so he had heard, were on their way.

Help landed at Guantanamo, ironically, the day before the publication of the infamous photograph. On the evening of January 17, the International Committee of the Red Cross arrived.[19] The coincidence of defensive action at the Pentagon and pragmatic activity at Guantanamo, the one intended to paint a misleading veneer on things and the other intended to try and fix them, would be replicated throughout the days of Lehnert's command at Guantanamo. It was the perfect symbol of the fact that the Pentagon's agenda and Lehnert's agenda were moving forward on parallel tracks, if not on ones that might someday collide.

From the moment the plane bearing the representatives from the ICRC landed, Lehnert and the task force let them know that they were welcome and were expected to be an integral part of the detention facility. To make sure that the relationship got off on the right foot, Bob and Debi Buehn—following an idea hatched by General Lehnert and Manuel Supervielle—hosted a welcome party for the international group on the evening of their arrival.[20] They wanted to socialize with the newcomers before the hard work of negotiating priorities began. There, on the newly refurbished Cuban tile floor, surrounded by the mahogany woodwork of the Buehn home, the just-arrived Red Cross officials mingled with Carrico, Shimkus, Buehn, Lehnert, and others.

The ICRC's four-man delegation, headed by Urs Boegli, brought not only the clout of the ICRC but much needed expertise as well. Boegli, at fifty, was the ICRC's chief Washington delegate, responsible for all of North America.[21]

By his side were Paul Bonard, deputy head of the ICRC Protection Division in Geneva; Christian Mehl, a linguist; and Raed Aburabi, a doctor. As constituted, the group could help with better communication with the detainees and with the medical details, the human rights issues, and the legal challenges that confronted JTF 160.

Boegli, who gave up a lucrative career in international business to become a relief worker, had worked for the ICRC in Angola, Sudan, Lebanon, Thailand, and Cambodia and knew how to put the end result—humane treatment—above grandstanding or shaming. The ICRC's neutrality, he believed, meant that its job was not to expose or denounce but to make things better. Taking the easy road of exposing violations of human rights to the press could prove futile, even self-defeating, for the ICRC's purposes. "[I]f we stick to the facts and do not shrink from admitting that the world is a complex place," he told a London crowd in 1998, "if we recognize the value of taking the trouble to listen to those who truly know a situation, if we exercise caution, if we spontaneously distrust the shocking figures that pop up so often in our line of work, then we will at least be taking steps towards greater credibility. And credibility is vital."[22] In other words, his primary aim was to improve situations, not to shame individuals or organizations.

Lehnert was especially relieved to finally have some knowledgeable individuals on the base who could help address the gaps in knowledge left by the policy vacuum in which JTF 160 was being forced to operate. Boegli's and Lehnert's immediate respect for one another was mutual and heartfelt. As Boegli told the New York Times, the JTF had essentially greeted them with, "Good to have you busybodies here."[23]

With Supervielle there for legal guidance and the ICRC in place, Lehnert could begin to make decisions about the care and custody of the detainees with legal and humanitarian counsel by his side. And starting the next day, the new actors began to help implement policies designed to address the needs of the detainees.

The first thing the ICRC wanted to do was to interview each detainee. Setting up an open-air table within sight of the cages, the representatives began their questioning. If the ICRC representatives had had their way, the detainees being interviewed would not have been shackled at all. But the JTF command structure was not about to allow anything that would expose the ICRC men to serious harm. A compromise was reached. Each detainee was seated in a chair facing a table at which the interviewers sat, asking their questions and taking notes. This afforded the shackled detainees a modicum of dignity. The

JTF acquiesced to the ICRC's demand for privacy during their interviews, settling for placing the guards a "sprint's distance away" but out of earshot, as the ICRC asked the detainees questions that no one had yet posed. Who were they? Where were they from? What had happened to them prior to arriving at Guantanamo? What were the conditions of the plane ride? How had they been treated so far in their few days at X-Ray? Had they been beaten? Harmed? Were they able to pray? Did they want to send cards or letters home to let their families know where they were? And, above all, what did they need in order to follow their religion and to feed and clean themselves as their religion required?

After they absorbed what they had heard, the ICRC men started to make suggestions to Carrico, Shimkus, and others, often conferring first with Supervielle. Some of the requests should have been evident to anyone, without the need for interviews. For example, the ceaseless exposure to the elements was almost unbearable. In the late afternoon, the scalding sun streamed through the west side of the cages, making the detainees swelter. The guards protested at first that closing off the cages would make it impossible for them to keep their eyes on the detainees at all times. So a compromise was struck: the guards agreed to place plastic sheets over one side of the cages during the afternoon hours.

Another early consideration regarded sleeping. As the first detainees settled into their daily routines, the construction of new cells at X-Ray continued around the clock, bringing with it the endless noise of machinery and tools. To guide the work, halogen lights rimmed the perimeter of the camp 24 hours a day. Between the lights and the noise of construction, it was nearly impossible to sleep, especially once the initial exhaustion of the manacled plane ride had passed. The task force agreed to the ICRC suggestion that the detainees henceforth be allowed to use earplugs and eye masks.[24]

Equally important was the ICRC's counseling in religious matters. Almost immediately upon their arrival, the ICRC ordered Korans for everyone to supplement the single, shared Koran on hand when X-Ray had opened. They instructed the JTF about the five-times-daily call to prayer, crucial to devout Muslims. They explained as well about the halal diet and that the preparation of the food—for example, how an animal was killed—was as important as the food itself.

More sensitive religious discussions involved the Muslim attitude toward their body and bodily functions. So, for example, the ICRC team informed Carrico that posting guards in the showers violated the Islamic prohibition against men being seen naked. Together, the ICRC and the task force wrestled with this dilemma. Showers without guards were out of the question. And then someone on the task force remembered a cache of thousands of pairs of underpants that had been left over in a Guantanamo storage depot from the Sea Signal days. The solution suddenly became obvious. The detainees would wear the underwear when showering. Out of such ad hoc concessions and improvisations, Guantanamo detainee policy took shape and grew.[25]

Other issues concerned bodily excretions. Toilet considerations outweighed all others at X-Ray. Given a bucket to urinate in, the detainees often used it for defecation as well. One of the very first things that the detainees learned was to hold up for the guards to see one finger for urinating and two for defecation. Transporting the detainees to the porta-johns was time-consuming, requiring two guards per detainee, and was simply impossible at a moment's notice. Then, there was the matter of toilet paper: how and when to dispense it to the detainees for their own use, an issue of cultural sensitivity. Many of the detainees, as the task force would later find out, were accustomed to washing their genitals immediately after going to the toilet. Furthermore, if a detainee had a wet dream or masturbated, he was not allowed to pray before cleansing himself. But access to showers, as to the toilets, was infrequent. Discussions about some of these matters began at the time of the ICRC, but solutions would be found only at a later date.[26]

The ICRC tried to introduce some comfort items as well. They asked that the detainees be allowed to smoke, for example, but were turned down on the grounds that inside X-Ray no one, not even the guards, could smoke. They were more successful when they sought to remedy the absence of salt and other customary ingredients in the detainees' diet.

The ICRC's greatest contribution was probably to the medical program run by Captain Shimkus. Especially at the outset, having the ICRC present was a much appreciated gift to Shimkus. The ICRC counseled him about matters of consent, about prohibitions on nudity, and about the use of females to deliver care. They also taught him about some of the diseases with which he had been previously unfamiliar. He was also able to discuss with them the detainees' apparent intolerance for the diet being provided. Many of them suffered from gastrointestinal symptoms when exposed to this new diet, and the ICRC group was able to explain to Shimkus what was going on.[27]

They offered other diagnostic help as well. The doctor who came with the ICRC knew the symptoms of leishmaniasis, the skin disease that Shimkus had discovered on several of the detainees, one form of which can penetrate the skin and destroy internal organs. He also helped identify which injuries were old and which were fresh. In one case—a detainee with an eye injury—the ICRC determined that the injury was not recent, as the prisoner claimed, but at least eight years old.[28] After the ICRC doctor coaxed the detainee into admitting the truth—he believed that he would be denied treatment unless he claimed that he'd suffered an injury in the war in Afghanistan—Shimkus arranged for surgery to remove the eye and restore eyesight to the other glaucoma-plagued eye. Shimkus considered this one of the great achievements of his time at the JTF.[29]

The JTF officers did not always yield to the ICRC's requests or advice. Colonel Carrico did not agree to stop assigning women as shower escorts, which was vehemently protested by the prisoners, but did work out a way to have burlap cover the lower half of the shower before the underwear solution was found. And Captain Shimkus would simply not agree to replace female medical providers with male counterparts or to work around their presence as Carrico had been willing to do in the case of the showers. Women constituted roughly 40 percent of his staff. As the detainees had protested on their own, and as the ICRC was to reiterate, it was forbidden under Islamic law for men to be touched or seen naked by women who were not their wives. But Shimkus and Carrico refused to budge on this issue. Their mission, he explained, was the well-being of the detainees, and their well-being depended on getting the best care possible. As it happened, some of the most highly skilled of his medical attendants were women.[30]

By virtue of educating the officers and the troops, the ICRC began to fill in the gaps in knowledge and awareness that had plagued the mission since the arrival of the detainees. The humanitarian representatives recognized the power of knowledge to calm an otherwise tense situation. To the surprise and gratitude of the officers of the JTF, the ICRC shared much of what they learned with the task force. For example, they passed on the names of detainees, which they were told in order to send letters home. The ICRC was also the first to learn the countries of origin of many of the detainees—either in their interviews or when they asked where to send the letters written to relatives. The humanitarian group automatically conveyed this crucial information to the task force Indeed, they shared any confidential information that they thought might constructively aid the task force in handling the detainees more humanely. They did this not simply to gain the trust of the Americans but to enable the task force to better minister to the detainees' well-being, both as patients and as inmates.

Far from "interfering" with a highly sensitive American mission, as the War Council had worried, the humanitarian group was making the detention operation work more smoothly. The JTF had finally broken through the detainees' wall of silence. They were finally getting reliable information about the individuals they had in their custody. And they ferreted out this information not by cruel and degrading treatment but, on the contrary, by following Common Article 3 of the Geneva Conventions.

Within days of working side by side, the rapport between the ICRC and JTF 160 leadership was solid, even despite the infamous photo of the kneeling prisoners and all the outrage it had provoked. The JTF quickly came to understand that the ICRC reps were there not to take unilateral action but simply to advise them. As Lehnert summed it up, "They tried as much as possible to be honest brokers, and to be neutral."[31] Carrico and Shimkus, the two officers whose staffs had the most direct interaction with the detainees, agreed that the presence of the ICRC substantially increased their own ability to function as professionals. The ICRC, for its part, learned that Lehnert's expressed desire to listen was genuine, that he was not only open to their way of thinking but that he would work diligently with his men, notably Carrico and Shimkus, the two whose staffs had the most interaction with the detainees, to help implement agreed-upon policies. Before the week's end, Boegli reported how pleased he was to Tom Gerth at the State Department. "You have the right man for the job," he wrote, referring to Lehnert.[32]

But there were still some discrepancies between the anticipated needs of the detainees and the more realistic demands that the ICRC was able to articulate to the camp leadership. Lehnert was counting on the arrival of another contingent to provide some practical solutions.

Patrick Alford and a staff of 145 medical specialists arrived at the same time as the ICRC. Alford's attentiveness to detail was a boon. His proximate task was to set up a new hospital, Fleet Hospital 20, and to do so quickly. He and Shimkus immediately set to work.

Alford quickly recognized what his commanding officer Al Shimkus already knew only too well, that the ignorance about prison medicine was a gap they would have to bridge by their own intuition and street smarts. Fleet Hospital 20, in fact, taxed the imaginations of both. And while at one point they were able to bring in a specialist in prison medicine from Leavenworth, it was not until months later that Shimkus was able to send staff from Guantanamo to observe the medical facilities at a U.S. prison.

Illustrating the wisdom of military training, Alford and these men had been part of a larger group of approximately 250 individuals from Camp Lejeune who had been sent to Camp Pendleton in California during October 2001. They were there to train in setting up an expeditionary medical unit. Originally, they had been told they would be sent to Ramstein Air Base in Germany, a way station for American troops in Afghanistan. But on the eve of the Gitmo detainees' arrival at Gitmo, they were told that their destination would be Cuba.

Alford's team spent five days unpacking, staging, and erecting the prefab hospital—a series of air-conditioned tents with floors and walls—and stocking it with everything from beds and shelves to X-ray machines and laboratory equipment. They had completed the setup by January 26, proving General Lehnert's claim that "Navy medicine," the skeleton on which the JTF medical effort was built, was "indeed expeditionary."[33]

Expeditionary or not, there was another element to Fleet Hospital 20, one that spoke to a second part of the JTF operation, and that was the other half of the care and custody mission. Care focused on food preparation and delivery, on medical attention, physical as well as psychological, and on allowing for religious practices. Custody, on the other hand, focused on the methods and means of containment for the prisoners. Custody, in other words, pertained not just to the kept but also to their keepers.

Guantanamo Bay, Cuba (photo by Manuel Supervielle)

Colonel Manuel Supervielle on his first trip back to Cuba, January 15, 2002 (photo courtesy of Manuel Supervielle)

Interrogation-style booths under construction at Camp X-Ray (photo courtesy of Robert Buehn)

Medical SEA huts under construction (photo courtesy of Robert Buehn)

Cells at Camp X-Ray (photo courtesy of Robert Buehn)

Toilet (photo courtesy of Robert Buehn)

William H. Taft IV (left) and Colonel Manuel Supervielle (photo courtesy of
Manuel Supervielle)

Brigadier General
Michael Lehnert
receiving instruction on
driving a small vessel
across Guantanamo
Bay (photo courtesy of
Timothy Nichols)

Major Timothy Nichols (right) and Lieutenant Abuhena Saifulislam, JTF 160 Chaplain
(photo courtesy of Timothy Nichols)

Chaplain Saifulislam (photo courtesy of Timothy Nichols)

Captain Robert Buehn at his home in Jacksonville, Florida (photo by Karen Greenberg)

Captain Albert Shimkus in front of the USNS *Comfort* (photo by Karen Greenberg)

7

The Caribbean Hilton

I think it's too good for the bastards.

—Congressman John Mica (R-FL)

As head of the Joint Detention Operations Group, or JDOG, Terry Carrico was the point person on penal policy. Consistent with the lack of expertise at the ready for the Guantanamo detention effort, he was a military policeman (MP), not a corrections specialist. Still, as we have seen, he was adamant about the need for firm authority in his prison, Camp X-Ray. To his mind, his goal was to exert control in a manner that left absolutely no room for the detainees to think that they had any freedom of activity at all. This was not about cruelty or abuse. This was about maintaining order and calm in the camp. To Carrico's mind, unyielding authority was essential to maintaining order and to preventing an outbreak of protests or violence. Tasked, as was Shimkus, with making sure no one was harmed or killed, Carrico wanted to do what it took to maintain order.

Had Carrico had a more professional setup, he might have softened his policy stance. But in three areas he was lacking the right people for guarding the detainees. First, he had at the outset no prison specialists from the American Correctional Association or the Bureau of Prisons on hand with whom to consult. If he had, he might have been persuaded that some form of deference to prisoners' sensibilities could enhance the power of prison authorities. Otherwise, this perspective holds, morale can deteriorate quickly into despair and random acts of rage and violence. Secondly, he did not have troops with a background in the kind of prison they were overseeing. They simply weren't trained to respect the Geneva Conventions. For this, he would have needed not just regular MPs but those experienced with, or at least instructed about, wartime captives.[1] And third, he was operating with reservists rather than regular duty soldiers. He had MP units, it was true. But they weren't internationally trained. They were not even fully trained, as regular Army MPs would have been, in military incarceration. Just as the JTF had no say about which captives in Afghanistan were selected to be sent to Guantanamo, so also they had no say about who was detailed to the camp as guards.

Following his more or less untutored instincts in this void of policy and expertise, Carrico patched together a number of policies. Central to his approach to the prison environment was a gag rule, a general prohibition against talking. There was to be no communication between the guards and the troops. Nor was there to be any among the detainees. Both bans spoke to the matter of security. Communication among the detainees would enable them to plot and conspire against their captors, to mount an uprising, to attack a guard, or even to plan an escape. Communication with the guards could lead them to sympathize with their charges, many of whom were their own age. Such fraternizing, Carrico thought, would necessarily corrode the authority structure of the camp.

To Carrico's mind, sending a message to detainees was only one goal. He was also determined to prevent his troops from coming to harm. Indeed, Lehnert and his entire staff had acknowledged from the beginning that this was a two-sided effort involving both care and custody of the detainees and keeping the troops out of harm's way. For Carrico, this meant impressing each detainee with a show of indomitable force at all possible points. Thus, though shackled and bound, no detainee was allowed to move with less than two guards in atten-dance. If it meant fewer showers and fewer bathroom runs, so be it. Carrico also arranged for the Immediate Reaction Force to be available at all times. They strutted, dressed in full riot gear, including helmets and face shields, protective vests, shin guards and batons, transparent Plexiglas shields, and nonlethal ammunition (bean bags, wooden plugs, tear gas), able to intimidate from outside the cages at even the slightest hint of dissension or deviation from the rules. When necessary, they would enter the cages, a group of five dressed in riot gear. Four would seize a limb each, and one would grab the detainee's head. They would then press the rowdy or unlucky prisoner face-down to the cement floor to achieve total incapacitation, preventing any movement at all. Over time, the detainees learned to assume the prone position, arms behind their backs, so as to reduce the roughness of the IRF team.

Nor was the danger to the troops something to be taken lightly. The reserv-ist MPs themselves, as opposed to enlisted troops, were certainly fixated on the threat to their well-being. They may have been less formally and consis-tently trained than enlisted men and women might have been, and therefore not as psychologically inured to the threats of the detainees, but they were liv-ing under duress that warranted sympathy and flexibility. Carrico understood the grounds for this fear, as well as the downside of belittling the fear and thereby crippling the mission.

The detainees, for their part, learned early and perhaps too well to fan those anxieties. As they awoke from the stupor induced by their long plane rides and their traumatic captures and incarcerations in Afghanistan and elsewhere, many of the detainees began to express their seething anger and hatred toward the Americans. They spat at the guards. They pissed all over them at times. They threw their feces at them through the wire mesh sides of the cages or when the doors were opened. The guards naturally feared contagion from tuberculosis or malaria through saliva. They cringed at the thought of diseases borne by human feces. Some detainees repeatedly threatened to injure the soldiers physically if given the chance. Worst of all, they threatened to harm the families of the guards as well.

And the soldiers reacted. They worried about being attacked in the cages if they needed to enter. They imagined that the detainees might sharpen items in their cells and use them as weapons, as had happened in New York City in the case of Mamdouh Mahmud Salim, a defendant in the embassy bombings trial, who stabbed a guard in the eye with a sharpened comb. They feared that their captives might manage to attack them on the way to and from the medical facility, the ICRC trailer, or the bathroom facilities. And, above all, they were frightened by the threats of harm to those they loved.

To counteract the growing fear, the JTF leadership did what they could, nowhere more so than in the medical area, where the hazards of interaction with the detainees were numerous. Inside the medical rooms, the troops were trained to defend themselves. The medical providers learned how to handle sharp instruments in ways that would make it hard for their patients to snatch them from their hands. They learned not to talk in the room with the patients, so as not to inadvertently transmit information about themselves or about Camp X-Ray.

Shimkus organized classes on health and hygiene and transmittable diseases to calm worries about contagion. He reminded the troops that surgical masks were given to the detainees on the planes and worn until they were screened for communicable diseases during in-processing. Following their instincts, Shimkus and Alford learned to space the beds so that the detainees could not possibly touch one another, and faced the beds to the wall rather than the center of the room, to limit the ability of the detainees to see one another. They left enough room between beds so that a detainee from one bed couldn't jump from behind any clinicians attending to a detainee in another bed. In sum, as Alford put it, "We treated them as high-security, high-risk, potentially threatening individuals." And, at all times, guards and military police were present.[2]

But the troops were not so easily reassured. Their anxieties were exacerbated by their own uncomfortable living conditions. As a gesture toward the Geneva Conventions requirement that detaining troops and the detainees share similar circumstances, the soldier and Marine guard detail slept in tents. While the Seabees assigned to construction and troops involved with support for the operation slept in housing units, the guards lived in a tent city originally called Camp Freedom where conditions were barely tolerable. The only toilet facilities were porta-johns and although there was running water available outside for washing and for showers, there was no hot water.

Some of the early "looky-look" congressional delegations expressed horror at the conditions in which the troops were living. Congresspeople told Lehnert and Carrico that it was unacceptable for American servicemen to be treated this way. But even without the pressure of the congressional delegations, Lehnert and Carrico were attentive to the situation. To combat the resentment of the troops, they devised a rotation system in which the guard troops spent three to four days inside the wire, sleeping in the tents, followed by two to three days in houses that had been reserved for them elsewhere on the base. Debi Buehn and the other wives from the naval community offered to chip in as well. Debi started an "Adopt a Serviceperson" or, more colloquially, "Adopt a Soldier" program designed to bring the servicemen and women into resident homes for meals and for general outreach, including the provision of comfort items and the like.[3]

But these well-meaning gestures of concern proved insufficient to contain the anger of the troops. Rather than dampening resentment on the part of service personnel, they legitimized it. Theirs was a thankless task on more levels than just the living conditions. For example, the soldiers watched the culturally sensitive attentiveness to the religious needs of the detainees with at best mixed feelings and at worst uncomprehending resentment. Providing comfort, however minimal, to those associated with 9/11 was like a slap in the face. As Donald Rumsfeld repeated often, "our job is to be humane but not to make them too comfortable."[4] But the guards didn't only resent the fact that they had to cater to the detainees. They also chafed at being less well attended to by the JTF than the worst of the worst. The contrast between their own treatment and that of the detainees was galling. Sergeant Michael Marshall tried to explain the feeling many weeks later. "The Red Cross," Marshall summarized, "steps in [and suddenly] they are pushing for more things for the prisoners than they are for the service members that are here. It gets under our skin a little bit."[5] So here was the ordinary soldier's, as opposed to the War Council's, argument against the ICRC. Indulgently humanitarian treatment of the captives was a slap in the face to the captors. It upended the crucial distinction between the victors and the vanquished.

For the guards, sleeping in tents was only a small part of a much larger context of humiliation and deprecation. Positioned inside the wire, the troops were demoralized on several fronts. Unlike the infantry outside the wire, or the Marines who supervised them, the Army guards were not allowed to bear arms. The job of prison attendant, as opposed to active soldier, was unglamorous at best. And they were further demeaned by what was required of them—namely, the doling out of food three times a day, transporting the detainees to the showers and to the porta-johns, and keeping a vigilant eye trained on individuals who were basically contained and therefore required little intervention.

Above all, their role as bucket bearers for the detainees rankled them. In the absence of sufficiently frequent porta-john runs, their job was to carry the slop to a disposal site. Even though Al Shimkus pointed out that this was a potential health hazard, there really was no practical alternative, given the amount of time it took to transport each soldier securely to and from the porta-johns. But the bucket bearers were not focused on the health hazard. They were morally as well as physically disgusted by their task, namely, carrying the waste of individuals who, in their minds, had murderously attacked the United States of America.

In this simmering hostility between the detainees and the troops, symbols loomed large. For example, the soldiers were seriously upset by restrictions on displaying the American flag and playing the national anthem, imposed in deference to the sensibilities of the detainees. Sergeant Marshall saw correctly that the ICRC could get the detainees to cooperate, to some extent, by accommodating their allegiances—specifically, by doing everything in their power to make devotion to Allah possible. But this meant reducing the opportunities for the American soldiers to exhibit their own patriotism and points of honor. "They can play their call to prayer five times a day, but we have to fight to hear the anthem during colors . . . and we have to fight just to get a flag out here. Just little things like that," Sergeant Marshall explained.[6]

The flag was the chief symbol around which the umbrage of the soldiers and Marines coalesced. Referring to a flag on the hill overlooking X-Ray, Marshall said, "The first day we had it, we played colors, the national anthem, into the loudspeakers down at the compound. I guess that raised a fuss with the prisoners. They complained to the Red Cross and then it stopped. We went about a week, a week and a half without any music, anything with the colors, and then our companies would fight . . . it got so that they did play the anthem . . . at night when the flag came down. Did the prisoners stand up for that? I'm sure they can hear it. The first day when they played it down at the compound, I guess they covered their ears."

Food was also a focal point of competition between the detainees and the troops. At one point in the spring of 2002, Debi Buehn recounts, lamb was flown in for the detainees who were celebrating the Muslim holiday of Eid al-Adha. But a hunger strike was in process. So the detainees refused the lamb. The families on the naval base asked if they could have it instead. To their astonishment, their request was denied, presumably in order to prevent allegations of giving the food of the detained to their jailers.[7]

Tensions between the detainees and the service members, which arose naturally during the first days of Guantanamo, would endure for the life of the detention facility. As late as 2006, during my visit to the camp, apprehension about weaponized feces typified the disgust and irritation with which the guards viewed the detainees. Camp Five was a maximum security facility originally modeled on a medium security prison in Indiana. The upper floors outside the cells were originally made of an open wire mesh that allowed light into the spaces below. The mesh eventually had to be lined with a solid material to prevent excrement from falling through on the heads of those walking beneath. Food envy was also alive and well. Troops stationed at the base in 2006 complained to me that the detainees were fed fresh strawberries while U.S. personnel had to settle for canned fruits.

The resentment festering in the minds of their predecessors, the first JTF troops, led to other kinds of outburst as well. In addition to feeling humiliated by their tasks, the guards were humiliated by their peers. The tension that had been brewing between the Army and Marine troops prior to the arrival of the detainees, and that had bubbled over when the Army locked up the Marines for that short period of time, continued to grow. The Marines flexed their muscles, and the Army retaliated by asserting their ownership of the mission.

One night, for instance, Marine guards manning the towers at the perimeter of X-Ray spotted a guard sleeping on duty. They woke and berated him, chewing him out in true Marine style. The soldier replied, with time-honored disrespect, by flipping the Marines off, using universal sign language to say "Fuck you." The Marines were furious. Several days later, two Marines drove a jeep into X-Ray at the end opposite the sally port. Their objective was to demonstrate, once again, the scandalous laxity of the Army guards. How can you consider yourself on top of things, they asked, when we can drive a car into

X-Ray not only without passing a guard but without catching anyone's notice? It was a mean-spirited stunt, even if its goal was to expose an unacceptable lack of professionalism on the part of the Army troops.[8]

For Carrico, whose mission relied completely on maintaining the morale of his men, this was an unacceptable state of affairs. Lehnert had wanted his men there to train "because most of the soldiers had just studied it in school. They had never run brigs before," but training and humiliating were two different things. In response, Carrico removed the Marines from X-Ray and had them put on transports from the airfield to X-Ray. Moreover, he hardened his resolve to find ways to improve the situation of the men and women under his command, considering ways, for example, to rotate them out of Guantanamo after a certain number of days.

Worried about the stability of his operation in the light of these tensions, he decided to take a new request to Lehnert. Until this point, Carrico had yielded to Lehnert's imposition of an order with which he did not agree. One close member of Lehnert's team told me: "[M]y perception is that, if left to his own devices, Carrico would have been tougher at X-Ray than we actually were." To soften the implications of this revelation, my informant then added, reassuringly: "Not that Carrico was offering to go way off the page or do anything crazy."[9] As Lehnert remembers it, Colonel Carrico didn't get into many discussions. "He just said, 'Yes, sir.'" But now, as January drew to a close, he had something to ask. Direct and to the point, Carrico was not known for complaining or protesting. So when he asked for something, he knew that Lehnert would be especially attentive.[10]

General Lehnert heard the request with more than a twinge of foreboding. Years later, he recalled Terry Carrico presenting the case to him, "The guards don't want the detainees to know who they are. We don't want them to be able to identify the soldiers. You know, to harm them later. To go after their families."[11] To preserve their anonymity, the Army guards, with Carrico's support, were seeking permission to cover the names on their uniforms— to duct-tape out their identities or, if they had the new kind of Velcro name patches, to tear them from their left shirtfronts, leaving blank plastic and cotton strips instead of names. Their request, Lehnert knew, did not come out of the blue. It was a logical culmination of the strained relations that developed during the first few weeks of X-Ray as the detainees and the guards got to know one another and began to stake out their reciprocal roles in the Guantanamo drama.

But Carrico was not simply seeking a gesture of recognition for the predicament of his guards. He was also initiating a campaign of pushback against the policy that Lehnert had devised and was now implementing with the help of the ICRC. Perhaps Carrico had forgotten that it was originally Lehnert himself who had requested his presence. In any case, Carrico was hell-bent on stopping what he saw as a slide toward excessive leniency before it was too late. In his mind, the detention project was going seriously off course. Rather than isolating the detainees and teaching them who was in control, the Lehnert–ICRC partnership was conveying the opposite message. These overindulgent custodians were signaling that communication between both the detaining authorities and the detainees and among the detainees themselves was not only possible but welcome.

Even today, Lehnert does not hesitate to defend his point of view: "I think the uncertainty and the lack of knowledge of where they were...was going to create a sense of despair. Or a sense of rebellion. I wasn't trying to make nice with them. But I felt that there are certain things that human beings in a cell have a right to know."[12] He had witnessed firsthand the explosive potential of feelings of despair when he ran the detention effort at Sea Signal. He knew, therefore, that he could not allow hopelessness to develop in this detention operation but instead needed to get out in front of it, stave it off. The experienced ICRC group reinforced Lehnert's commitment to active engagement with the detainees, because this was the very basis of their ability to represent the detainees' interests to the JTF leadership. In fact, when he expresses appreciation of the ICRC, it is almost always on the grounds that the humanitarian agency "erred on the side of communication" whenever there was a chance that communication would "benefit both the detainees and those...incarcerating the detainees."[13]

For Lehnert, it was a question of management. The best way to have a camp he could control, Lehnert believed, was to create an environment, physical and psychological, in which the prisoners were treated as humans, not chattel, which, practically speaking, meant three things above all: bathrooms, walls, and communication.

To Carrico, whether Lehnert was trying to "make nice" with the detainees or not, the general's overall approach revealed seriously misguided thinking. Allowing the wishes of the detainees to change camp policy was eventually going to cause significant unrest. Giving the detainees even a modicum of power was a prescription for disaster, in his view. Carrico tried his best to explain this to Lehnert. "General Lehnert was there running a refugee camp.... And I had to sit down many times and look him in the eyes and say, 'Sir, this is not a refugee camp.'" In the kind of refugee camp that Lehnert used to run, Carrico went on to explain, you could use lenient policies more readily. In a penal detention camp, it was more difficult. More stringent methods were required.[14]

Lehnert did not try to paper over his difference of opinion with Carrico, referring to it as "crosstalk." He simply let decisions rather than words speak for his point of view. The significance of the nametag request, however, did not go unnoticed by the general. He knew just how well it highlighted the philosophical differences between the two men. Lehnert, therefore, didn't want to answer without giving the question a great deal of thought. As he processed the request, he considered the present, the recent past, and the tenor of things in Washington. First, he was aware of the emotional stress that the guards were under, just as he was aware of the thankless nature of their task. Second, there was the fact that the detainees themselves, up to this point, still had no names. Why, then, one might reasonably ask, should the guards? Reciprocity required that the troops sleep in tents rather than houses. So why shouldn't reciprocity also be used to lighten the psychological burden on the detaining guards? Third, he recognized that 9/11 had increased the appeal of anonymity throughout the armed forces in general. Shortly after 9/11, he recalls, the military, across all forces, told its officers to scrub their online bios, both on military databases and where necessary on more public sites where they might appear. They wanted the names of spouses and children deleted in the interests of safety. That way, jihadi terrorists would not be able to track down the families of American service personnel. And when the War Council visited Guantanamo following the arrival of the detainees, even Manuel Supervielle automatically covered up his name before entering the blocks at X-Ray. In assenting to this particular request of Carrico's, therefore, General Lehnert could comfortably defer to the trend embraced by both the military's higher authorities and a general consensus about the dangers that the detainees posed.

Yet Lehnert knew, by instinct and by his comprehensive reading of history, that anonymity among guard forces was not without potential dangers, that it could allow for an absence of accountability. Without a name, a soldier can do anything he wants, unafraid that his misdeeds will come back to haunt him. Anonymity might shield the guards from future retaliation by their wards, but it would also protect them, to some extent, from disciplinary measures imposed by the chain of command.

Philosophical differences aside, Lehnert freely acknowledged how much he needed Terry Carrico. He had not forgotten why he had asked for Carrico's services in the first place. He needed some form of corrections expertise. And while Carrico didn't have exactly that, he was enough of a professional to get up to speed quickly and to be able to assess the recommendations of his corrections specialists and sense how to apply them in a judicious and fair way. Lehnert knew enough to be grateful for Carrico, despite their clashing conceptions of how to run a detention facility. He knew, too, that his entire operation was dependent not just upon Carrico but also upon Carrico's men and women. Lehnert had little doubt that Carrico's deference to the anxiety of the troops contained a measure of wisdom. If the guards didn't have steady nerves, the entire detention process could spin out of control. The decision, then, pitted his determination to treat the detainees correctly against his concern for the psychological state of the troops who were implementing his policies.

Lehnert came up with a compromise. He agreed to cede to Carrico's request, but only partially. He informed Carrico, "Okay. You can do this. But I don't want to order it. You can give the troops a choice. If they want to cover or remove their names, they can. But they don't have to." The policy would cover the medical facilities as well as X-Ray. Perhaps Lehnert guessed that some soldiers and Marines would take it as an insult to be told to hide from danger. And, in fact, the Marines refused to disguise their identities, true to their cult of courage in the face of any conceivable threat.

Splitting the difference in this fashion made good sense in the post-9/11 psychological context, which necessitated a certain acceptance of fears, however irrational, that plagued many Americans. And it reflected Lehnert's understanding of the political reality at Guantanamo. He could keep control of his camp, he was sure, by balancing humanitarian concerns and detention rigor in a just and moral way. He made the no-names decision, certain that he could maintain control and knowing that Carrico respected the chain of command and would without question do as he was ordered. From Lehnert's perspective, a small concession to the custody side of the mission could end up strengthening his hand by lessening the divide with Carrico. And, to boot, it could also bolster his efforts to make humane treatment the norm.

But the decision highlighted certain tendencies of Lehnert's that could, in more tense and complicated circumstances, be exploited. According to his subordinates, he commands quietly, reluctant to exercise power as a weapon and disdainful of officiousness, on occasion willing to remain in the background rather than push his stature forward. He expects compliance from his subordinates without having to order it, and reserves the direct exercise of power for serious decisions of high moment.

Asked about this decision to agree to the no-names policy, Lehnert confessed years later that he considered it to be an error of judgment on his part. "If I had it to do all over again, I would have insisted that they at least wear numbers if not names."[15]

But if there was an error in Lehnert's reasoning, it wasn't about the no-names policy, it was the notion that he could maintain a commonsensical policy—and one that complied with the Geneva Conventions—in the face of Donald Rumsfeld and his plans. Lehnert could handle Carrico, who, as a professional, followed orders and respected decency and the law. Lehnert could easily counter Carrico's insistence that punishment and rigidity were more effective deterrents to prisoner misbehavior than leniency and too much flexibility. But Carrico was a potential enabler in a much larger discussion, one that was still playing itself out in Washington. Lehnert felt the reverberations of indecision and infighting at the highest levels of government on a daily basis. And, as January drew to an end, he began to detect just how difficult it was going to be to maintain control of his camp.

The first signs of what Rumsfeld had in store for Lehnert's vision of Guantanamo came during the press conference that he'd called days after the release of what Steve Cox understatedly termed the "damaging photograph." It was several days after the arrival of the ICRC and of Pat Alford. Acknowledging the serious nature of the questions raised by the photo, Rumsfeld informed the journalists in attendance that he was willing "to stay here and answer as many detainee questions as need to be answered," adding "it's time to tamp down some of this hyperbole that we're finding."[16]

In the details of his answers, Rumsfeld showed a familiarity with the tensions at Guantanamo that was both insightful and comprehensive. Comfortable with himself and his audience, feisty and charming, Rumsfeld praised the troops for "handling a tough assignment in a very professional and truly outstanding way....The allegations...that the men and women in the U.S. armed forces are somehow not properly treating the detainees under their charge are just plain false....And let there be no doubt, the treatment of the detainees in Guantanamo Bay is proper, it's humane, it's appropriate, and it is fully consistent with international conventions. No detainee has been harmed, no detainee has been mistreated in any way."[17]

Rather than calling the photographed scene an aberration, Rumsfeld made light of the allegations of abuse, choosing not to apologize but to justify and legitimize the treatment displayed in the photograph.

Rumsfeld went on to emphasize the need for tight security due to the level of threat that the prisoners embodied. Like Carrico, but with the power to put his ideas into action, he was intent upon justifying any measures that the United States sought to impose. He pointed to the severe danger that the prisoners posed and the heinous crimes they had committed. "These men are extremely dangerous. Lest we forget, in Mazar-e Sharif, the al Qaeda prisoners broke loose in a bloody uprising. They killed one American, they killed a number of Afghan troops, and some prisoners were carrying grenades under their clothing."

Rumsfeld paid the requisite homage to human rights issues. But his theatrical gestures of disbelief at allegations of abuse did not seem wholly sincere. "Oh my goodness!" he exclaimed early in the press conference. "Now look, is he [John Walker Lindh] being treated like the other detainees, shackled, hooded, and what have you? Oh! Well, let me say about that. . . . When people are moved, they are restrained. . . . It is because in transit . . . is the place where bad things happen. That's what happened in Pakistan when the Pakistani soldiers were killed . . . in the uprising in the bus."[18]

Invoking the dangers posed by the captured "terrorists," Rumsfeld refused to back away from the prerogative of the U.S. government to use harsh methods to ensure the safety of the troops and the nation. "And will any single prisoner be treated humanely? You bet. When they are being moved from place to place, will they be restrained in a way so that they are less likely to be able to kill an American soldier? You bet. Is in inhumane to do that? No. Would it be stupid to do anything else? Yes." His tone indicated an annoyance with the questions about human rights and the conditions of the detainees. Asked about the heat in the open-air cells, he took a cavalier attitude: "There are a lot of people in Cuba with no air-conditioning. I know that will come as a surprise!" For emphasis, he added, "I was in Washington before there was air-conditioning and the windows used to open. It's amazing."[19] If the press corps persisted in considering the treatment evident in the photograph as inhumane, then they were just plain "stupid."

Tiring of the repeated questions, Rumsfeld finally invoked a fairy tale about repetition and rumors, making an analogy to the press. "[I]t's perfectly possible for anyone to stand up and say, 'Henny Penny, the sky's falling, isn't this terrible what's happening?' and . . . have someone else say, 'Gee, I view with the alarm the possibility that the sky's falling!' And then it gets repeated. And then some breathless commentator repeats it again. . . . Now, does that make it so? No." To Rumsfeld's mind, not only weren't the detainees mistreated, they were positively being pampered. They had "warm showers, toiletries, water, clean clothes, blankets," Rumsfeld said, and "regular, culturally appropriate meals, prayer mats, and the right to practice their religion; modern medical attention far beyond anything they could have expected or received in Afghanistan; exercise; . . . writing materials, and visits by the ICRC (International Committee of the Red Cross)." Rumsfeld summed up his point: "Just for the sake of the listening world," he said, addressing critics everywhere, "Guantanamo Bay's climate is different than Afghanistan. To be in an eight-by-eight cell in beautiful, sunny Guantanamo Bay, Cuba, is not inhumane treatment. And it has a roof." Contradicting the message of the photograph as a display of cruel and inhumane treatment, the Secretary was adamant. "I am telling you what I believe in every inch of my body to be the truth . . . [I] haven't found a single scrap of any kind of information that suggests that anyone has been treated anything other than humanely." Basing his confident assertions on the winning strategy of Lehnert to utilize the ICRC, Rumsfeld embraced as a public relations ploy what the War Council had fiercely and successfully opposed.

In essence, Rumsfeld handled the press conference as he might have handled one of his wrestling matches. This was bureaucratic political wrestling, full of the shadow jive for which he had once earned a reputation. He had taken the strengths of the opposition and turned them to his own advantage. He used a press conference to turn the ICRC and Lehnert's oversensitivity to the detainees into a building block for his own narrative about Guantanamo as a perfectly humane front line in the country's struggle to contain the looming danger.

But Rumsfeld was a fighter who had learned that dominance was not victory. He had won many battles only to end up losing the wars. The most dispiriting example happened when he had sought the vice presidential slot in Ford's failed campaign for the presidency in 1976. Rumsfeld had succeeded in knocking out his two opponents, Nelson Rockefeller and George H.W. Bush, only to lose the nomination to Bob Dole. Now, decades later, he was determined not to claim premature victory. Rather than rest on the laurels of his successful press conference, where his media audience laughed and traded jokes with him, he planned a second public relations maneuver to solidify the ground he had gained. Perhaps as a result of the prodding he had received from one reporter, who had noted that all of Rumsfeld's information about Guantanamo was secondhand because he had not been there himself,[20] he decided to follow up the photo op with a trip down to sunny Guantanamo the following Sunday.

On January 27, the day of Rumsfeld's visit, Bob Buehn, Al Shimkus, and Michael Lehnert gathered at the usual meeting spot for their Sunday morning run. Nearly three weeks into their lives with the detainees, there was almost too much to talk about—the growth of the detainee population to 158, the arrival of the ICRC, the publication of the Navy photograph, and the constant tension between the guards and the detainees, among other topics. Enervated but still engaged, they had a few hours to step aside for a moment from the world they had built. Together, they were silent, reflecting on the pace and contours of their run toward Windmill Beach instead of the chaos that had engulfed their tiny piece of Caribbean coastline. As a cat-size iguana ran across the road, the trio recalled, almost in chorus, the press conference that the Secretary of Defense had given earlier that week. "If someone looked down from Mars on the United States for the last three days," Rumsfeld had said at the press conference, "they would conclude that America is what's wrong with the world." Rumsfeld was determined to set his audience straight: "America is not what's wrong with the world." It was only a matter of time, the Secretary continued, until the American people and "the people of the world" would see that the Guantanamo Bay detention facility was humane, reasonable, and necessary. He attributed his confidence, in part, to the fact that the commanders down there were "talented and responsible people."[21]

Rumsfeld's visit, Lehnert hoped, might offer a chance to clarify matters. The primary question in his mind was about whether or not the Secretary understood just how long it would take to extricate the country from this awkward situation by trying and/or releasing the prisoners.

Since the decision to use X-Ray, there had been talk of building a more permanent detention facility at Radio Range, where the migrants had lived during Sea Signal. As an engineer, Lehnert knew just how to do this. He was ready at the first go-ahead to open up the 40-foot containers that would create a new detention site. The new location would be called Camp Delta. It would consist of individual cells inside buildings with roofs and sides. There would be plumbing in each cell and a physical recreation area outdoors. He knew just what such a facility would entail in terms of equipment, materials, and men. He had some of the fundamentals with which to get started. And he knew that until that happened, Camp X-Ray, a series of cages fit for animals, was all that the world would ever know of Guantanamo and all that the detainees would ever experience.

Already, the Fleet Hospital occupied a piece of ground at Radio Range. And there was no doubt that a new camp would be built. But Lehnert's question was not about physical realities, it was about policy. How quickly, he wanted to know, did Rumsfeld think he could undo the situation that had been created at Guantanamo? Did he think of this as a long-term mission in which the trial or return of the prisoners could take a substantial amount of time?

Bringing members of Congress along for the trip, Rumsfeld made the case for an increase in appropriations and construction at the detention facility. His fellow travelers included four senators: Dianne Feinstein (D-CA), Kay Bailey Hutchinson (R-TX), Ted Stevens (R-AK), and Daniel Inouye (D-HI). Each senator held a position that would be pivotal in deciding upon future funding and building at Guantanamo. Inouye was the chairman of the Senate Appropriations Subcommittee on Defense. Stevens was ranking member of the Senate Appropriations Committee and served on the Subcommittee on Defense. Feinstein was the chairman and Hutchinson the ranking member of the Subcommittee on Military Construction and Veterans Affairs. "We need to know how much it's going to cost," Hutchinson said.[22] Also present were General Myers, head of the Joint Chiefs of Staff, and Major General Gary Speer, acting head of SOUTHCOM.

Beyond the symbolic show of support for Guantanamo's future, Rumsfeld had very few details to offer. Loquacious and effusive, Rumsfeld made a politician's tour of the base, shaking hands with everyone he could, listening, and observing. He even spoke with the young sailor who had taken the notorious photograph. As the sailor later recounted to Carol Rosenberg, "I told him, 'Hey I'm sorry my photos caused all these problems.' . . . He told me not to worry about it, I was doing my job."[23] Rumsfeld observed X-Ray and its inmates. But he made it clear that he was essentially there for the photo op, the extension of the press conference from earlier that week. Rumsfeld viewed the cells in which the detainees were sitting or standing and made a general tour of the facilities, including the medical facilities.

At one point, Lehnert was able to corner Rumsfeld out of earshot from the others. He knew just what he wanted to discuss. At his press conference, the Secretary had said, "It is certainly not the first choice of the Department of Defense to be in the business of detaining people for long periods of time." He also denied plans to raise the number of detained to "as many as a thousand," despite internal memos that mentioned the possibility of 2,000 prisoners.[24]

Knowing it was not his place to offer policy advice, Lehnert asked, "Mr. Secretary, what are your plans for the future? I'm just wondering—are you thinking of this as a long-term operation?" Rumsfeld was clear in his response. "This is a temporary effort. Only temporary. Short-term." The Secretary was adamant with the general.[25]

For Lehnert, this answer was at best problematic. It meant that the civilian leadership had yet to assess, in a realistic fashion, the implications of the detention effort they had undertaken. He informed Rumsfeld as politely as he could that he disagreed, that he thought this might not be such a short-term effort. Lehnert's reasoning, which he did not mention to the Secretary, came directly from his Sea Signal days. It had taken months to find ways to send Cubans to third-party countries. The diplomatic quagmire, Lehnert had learned, was time-consuming and labyrinthine. And in this instance, where the world was watching, where human rights abuses would have an incendiary impact in the countries of origin, and where the detainees were associated with terrorism, the consequences of lengthy detention seemed magnified. Lehnert was certain of it: they were in this for the long haul. Rumsfeld listened but said nothing.

However disheartened Lehnert may have been by his private exchange with the Secretary of Defense, the trip to Guantanamo was considered a success both for JTF 160, which had displayed an impressive attention to the care and custody of the detainees, and for Donald Rumsfeld, who had accomplished more than met the eye by his trip.

As it turned out, the fallout from the photograph was only one part of Rumsfeld's motive for flying down. In the time between the publication of the photograph on the 19th and 20th and Rumsfeld's visit to Guantanamo eight days later, the halls of the executive had been further enmeshed in the dispute over the classification of the detainees. For Rumsfeld, there was political capital to be gained by a well-staged visit to the detention facility.

Although Lehnert had been told even as he arrived at Guantanamo that the detainees should be treated in a manner "consistent with the principles of the Geneva Conventions" but "not bound by them," and although the War Council's trip on January 12 had demonstrated an attempt by administration and SOUTHCOM lawyers to grapple with that directive, the policy received a public face on the day that the photo was released. As the DOD stood behind the necessity of keeping prisoners exposed to the heat in outfits ensuring sensory deprivation, the new attitude to the Geneva Conventions as irrelevant to the current context was apparent.

The course of events in Washington followed suit by codifying the policy. To his great disappointment, Will Taft, the State Department's lawyer, learned upon his return to D.C. from Guantanamo that the president had endorsed the Office of Legal Counsel's interpretation; that the Department of State's efforts to stem the course of John Yoo and the others who supported the January 9 memo had been futile.[26]

Then, on January 19, Rumsfeld informed the Joint Chiefs in writing of what General Lehnert had been told as he moved down to Gitmo: that "The United States has determined that Al Qaeda and Taliban individuals . . . are not entitled to prisoner of war status," that they were to be treated "in a manner consistent with the principles of the Geneva Conventions of 1949" only "to the extent appropriate and consistent with military necessity."[27]

On January 22, the same day that Rumsfeld held his press conference responding to the inglorious photograph, OLC sent a memo—this time not a draft—to Alberto Gonzales and Jim Haynes, which solidified the War Council's position and dismissed the opposing views of Taft and his lawyers as outlined in their January 11 memo. According to the January 22 memo, al Qaeda was a nonstate actor and the Taliban represented only a failed state. On these grounds, both could be exempted from the protections of the Geneva Conventions. Echoing Yoo's earlier assertions, the memo contended that there was no category under international law that could be properly applied to the detainees. In Yoo's words, "Common Article 3's text provides substantial reason to think that it refers specifically to a condition of civil war, or a large-scale armed conflict between a state and an armed movement within its own territory."[28] The January 22 memo further argued that "neither the federal War Crimes Act nor the Geneva Conventions would apply to the detention conditions in Guantanamo Bay, Cuba, or to trial by military commission of al Qaeda or Taliban prisoners" and that customary international law "has no binding legal effect on either the President or the military. . . . "

Taft's team thought otherwise. Reviewing the negotiating history, they were convinced, as mentioned earlier, that the term "non-international" referred to any armed conflicts other than those occurring between nations, including those involving the Taliban and al Qaeda. There was, therefore, no need for a new body of law when considering either the Taliban or al Qaeda. There was, contrary to the assertions of John Yoo and others at the Office of Legal Counsel, no new legal paradigm needed for prisoners in the war on terror. Having been out of the country for the bulk of the memo dispute, Secretary of State Colin Powell protested directly to the president upon his return, but to no avail. A military man who played by the rules, Powell seemed to be out of his league when up against those for whom the rules were merely an obstacle to be overcome. The president, upon hearing Powell's dissent, threw him a bone by agreeing to let him address the National Security Council the following Monday. But over the course of the weekend, the cards were taken out of Powell's patient hands by Addington and Rumsfeld.

On Saturday, January 26, the *Washington Times* published a memo dated January 25 signed by Gonzales and addressed to President Bush.[29] The leaked memo, which Powell was certain came from Addington's office, laid out, in four short pages, the pros and cons of not applying the Geneva Conventions to the detainees. It acknowledged but discounted the views of Powell's legal team, noting for the record that "the Legal Adviser to the Secretary to State has expressed a different view." The document further addressed the implicit threat that bypassing the Geneva Conventions could make the lawyers vulnerable under the War Crimes Act. The memo labeled the reasoning displayed by Taft's department as "unpersuasive." "OLC's interpretation of this legal issue," Gonzales wrote, "is definitive."[30]

As the battle lines grew more formal, the magnitude of stepping outside the law, its constitutional and ethical implications, began to set in. As one lawyer on Taft's team said, "I began to wonder whether they remembered that they'd taken an oath . . . everything here violated Article 2 of the Constitution."[31] What the War Council needed was to legitimize the basis of their new paradigm; namely, a renewed emphasis on the danger they faced and their professed willingness to follow the Geneva Conventions whenever they could despite the fact that they weren't legally obliged to do so.

The next day, Rumsfeld boarded the plane bound for Guantanamo. On the plane ride down, Rumsfeld took the opportunity to put his own spin on the brewing debate with the Powell/Taft group. As the press listened, the Secretary defended the notion that the detainees were not prisoners of war. Referring obliquely to the *Washington Times*'s allegation that Powell disagreed with this stance, Rumsfeld denied any dissent on the part of the secretary of state. Grabbing at the chance to defend the new policy, Rumsfeld warned against "blur[ring] the distinction between lawful combatants and unlawful combatants." Any approach that overlooked this distinction was "fundamentally flawed."[32]

The Secretary's trip had two aims. It targeted, first, the critics of the detainees' living conditions, and secondly, those in the Department of State who believed that the detainees should be classified and treated as prisoners of war. It provided a visible forum for powerful senators to express their support for Rumsfeld's determination to strip the detainees of POW status. "I'm doing what we need to do to make sure that we detain as many people as possible until we get a handle on the tentacles of these networks," said Senator Hutchinson. Senator Inouye, asked whether he was "in favor of reviewing the status of each of these detainees," said "I think the position that the Secretary has taken is the correct one." Senator Stevens described Rumsfeld's position as "absolutely correct."[33]

Powell's presentation to the National Security Council on the following Monday was thus undermined before it was made. He could address the NSC, but the leaked policy, and the implicit rebuke to Powell, had defanged the secretary of state's protest.[34] And Rumsfeld could now hold Guantanamo up, backed by Senate leaders, as an exemplar of human rights treatment for clearly dangerous enemies. As Senator Diane Feinstein announced, she was completely convinced that "They're going to go out and kill again, and just as they say, they're going to kill innocent civilians."[35] For this reason—and because they could now rest assured that the detainees had food, medical treatment, and religious amenities, comforts that Florida Republican congressman John Mica called "too good for the bastards"—the congressional delegation gave Rumsfeld its full support.[36]

Rumsfeld's visit, and the machinations that led up to it, may have put an end to effective opposition by Powell, Taft, and the others who viewed the Geneva Conventions as a source of practical wisdom in managing military detainees.

Yet, ironically, the decision to jettison legally binding standards for humane treatment made Congress more amenable to funding for a more viable detention operation, something Lehnert himself desired. Rumsfeld had found a way to use Guantanamo as proof of the grave dangers facing the United States and thus as ammunition in the administration's campaign to bend and skirt the law. But he had also shown Lehnert, however inadvertently, that humane treatment at Guantanamo could allay doubts and embarrass critics and was therefore in and of itself a powerful propaganda tool. As Lehnert understood it, despite the Secretary's public protestations to the contrary, the visuals of X-Ray were one reason that X-Ray would have to be abandoned.[37] The men were living like animals in cages, and the photograph, despite the government's defensive assertions otherwise, meant that better conditions would have to follow soon.

In the brief span of Guantanamo's first few weeks, Lehnert had learned much. He had learned that Rumsfeld's and Carrico's agendas, though different in intent from one another, overlapped when it came to the actual policies of the camp. He recognized that there were forces mounting against him, practical, political, and philosophical. Lehnert had also discovered, thanks largely to the publication of the photograph, precisely where the central lines of division lay over the future of Guantanamo. Rumsfeld's imperious annoyance with human rights protests merely reinforced the more practical concerns of Carrico about managing unruly detainees.

Much as the photograph disclosed a philosophical tension, it also illuminated much about Michael Lehnert. While the picture had shocked the world, it had also put a dent in Lehnert's conviction that he could administer a command that adhered to a strict moral code even in a context that diverged from ordinary legal and ethical norms. For Lehnert, the photograph was incontestable proof that X-Ray could not be sustained. So, too, it meant that he himself couldn't hide from the fact that as long as X-Ray existed, he bore some of the responsibility for its appearance. The photograph was like a mirror, and it reflected back not the picture of humane treatment but a portrait of mistreatment. "They looked like dog kennels," he acknowledged, an image that showed how the two pieces of his mission, care and custody, were in direct conflict with one another and raised doubt as to whether he was administering a humane policy. True to his growing awareness of the untenable nature of his task, Lehnert found himself most surprised not by Rumsfeld's denial of the long-term nature of the detention mission but by the fact that the legal rights of the detainees were never raised as an issue during the visit to Gitmo.

Lehnert was right to be surprised by this. The emphasis on satisfying some of the demands for creature comforts required by the Geneva Conventions had allowed the legal rights of the detainees—in particular their access to habeas and federal courts and to military commissions—to go without attention or discussion. Inadvertently, Lehnert's approach had given Rumsfeld just the back door he needed to escape the criticism that the Geneva Conventions were being ignored. They were, but not in the areas that were then being given most attention. Lehnert had put humane, internationally acceptable policies into place. The result was that those policies were being used, contrary to his intent, to obscure the absence of legal conditions and treatment.

For now, the one comfort Lehnert could draw from Rumsfeld's words to the press was that the Secretary had at least been compelled to publicly maintain the appearance that human rights were being upheld. Rumsfeld might have invoked danger in order to justify goggles, shackles, and exposure to the Caribbean sun, but at the same time he had been forced to insist that he and his department respected the human rights of the detainees, even if he did so flippantly. This gave Lehnert's attempt to maintain humanitarian and legal standards at Guantanamo a foothold that boded well for his agenda. He had learned to identify his allies and to be generous to those who might otherwise be antagonized by his beliefs about how best to manage detention.

As he pondered the lessons of January and the challenges that lay ahead, he thought about his own strategy going forward. For even as he watched Rumsfeld twist the humanitarian efforts toward his own end, even as he sensed that Rumsfeld had a plan he wasn't sharing, even as he confronted the prospects of a long-term prison colony that he would have to direct for a little while longer, and even as he acceded—knowing better—to the pressures of the "no names" policy, he carried with him the knowledge that his best weapon was yet to be deployed. For at the very time that Rumsfeld had been giving his press conference in D.C., Lehnert was expecting the arrival of another ally who was landing on the leeward side of the island. Lehnert was placing his hopes for a future Guantanamo—one that would uphold his professionalism and satisfy his conscience—on the shoulders of this newest member of his team.

8

The General and the Chaplain

Well, at a certain point, you've got to start trusting somebody. Particularly when
they're wearing the uniform of a U.S. soldier."
—Maj. Gen. Michael Lehnert

On January 23, Navy chaplain Lieutenant Abuhena Saifulislam flew into the air
base at Guantanamo Bay on a sleek C-21 military transport plane. "I'm here
for the JTF," he explained to a soldier at the hangar. "I'm the new chaplain."

The tenor of the chaplain's arrival, haphazard and accidental like so much
else in the early days of Guantanamo, was familiar to the lieutenant. Even his
name had come about due to happenstance. Prior to joining the U.S. Navy, the
Bangladesh-born naturalized American citizen had gone by the name of Saif
ul-Islam (meaning "Sword of Islam"). But the military authorities kept writing
his name as one word on official documents. He tried to correct them several
times, and then finally gave up and just decided it was easiest to change his
name. Henceforth, he officially adopted the version used by the Navy. Now, he
was known as Saifulislam, Saif for short.[1]

His whole career prior to Guantanamo, in fact, had displayed this kind of ad
hoc reliance on chance and acquiescence to what fate held in store for him.

Saif had originally come to the United States in 1989 to obtain an MBA in
finance, which he successfully completed at what was then known as New
Hampshire College (now Southern New Hampshire University). In 1992, with
his degree in hand, he was working part-time as a floor clerk at Williams-
Sonoma in New York City, frustrated over the stagnant job market, when a
coworker suggested to Saif that he might consider joining the military. And,
as it was possible for a noncitizen—as he was at the time—to enlist in the U.S.
military, Saif made a phone call to a recruiter for the Navy—Saif's favorite service thanks to the World War II movies he'd seen.

Saif joined up as an enlisted man, and with his finance background, was
assigned in 1994 to the payroll department at the Pentagon itself, a rather
lackluster position. By coincidence, that year the first Muslim naval chaplain
(and the second in the armed forces overall) arrived at the Pentagon. U.S. Navy

Lieutenant Junior Grade Monje Malak Abd al-Muta' Ali Noel, Jr., conducted regular Friday services, the Muslim equivalent to Sunday Mass, there. Chaplain Noel had more in common with Saif than just his religion. Lieutenant Noel had, like Saif, attended New Hampshire College and, also like Saif, received an MBA. Comfortable with the new chaplain on both personal and religious grounds, Saif became a loyal attendee at Chaplain Noel's services. And after a time, Saifulislam decided that he had found a "more noble" career for himself— that of a military chaplain, a profession which then included only a handful of chaplains who could minister to the 4,000 Muslims in the armed services.

The road to the chaplaincy hinged upon becoming an officer, and to do that, he first had to become a citizen[2] (as officers need to be able to get security clearances) and then pass a review board for admission to the officer corps.

To overcome these hurdles, Saif, though unpretentious and seemingly naive in demeanor, behaved with the wisdom and wile of a schooled strategist. Once he became a citizen, he called in an old promise from a retired admiral who agreed to help put together Saif's review board. That done, Saif got the impression that the review board showed a reluctance to grant him entry to the officer corps. At that point Saif mentioned that he planned to be a chaplain and that he was already helping to organize prayers at the Pentagon. Suddenly, doors began to open for him. His commission went through without a hitch.[3]

Thinking about those days, Saif frequently acknowledges the unexpected support of those who had positions of authority over him. Whether it was the Pentagon chaplain or his mentors at officers' school, "they seemed to like me," Saif will characteristically say with a low chuckle. From there, Saif completed a degree at the Graduate School of Islamic & Social Sciences in Ashburn, Virginia—a new program that had been approved by the DOD.

The new chaplain came on active duty in August 1999, and was assigned to Marine Corps Base Camp Pendleton in California starting Sept 1. Through his association with the military, he had demonstrated his willingness to trade egoistic concerns for the rewards of being in the U.S. armed forces. After 9/11, Saif was assigned a tour of duty in Egypt and then in Amman, Jordan. When he returned from Jordan, he learned that his services were requested at Guantanamo.

After initially being alerted to the possibility of a Guantanamo posting, Saif was then given mixed signals about whether or not it would actually happen. On the one hand, he was receiving periodic phone calls directly from Guantanamo: "When are you coming?" "Can you come now?" On the other hand, he could detect little movement at the bureaucratic level. As Saif explained to his impatient callers from Cuba, "It's not up to me. I can't just board a plane without orders." The higher chain of command was apparently dragging its feet on the appointment.

In the context of the other deployments to Guantanamo, which had left but hours for packing and farewells, the lackadaisical approach in this case seemed more like an intentional delaying tactic than incompetence. Saif waited through the New Year and nearly until the end of January without receiving any further word.

Then, suddenly, on the evening of January 21, while he sat watching TV at home at Camp Pendleton, his eyes fixed on the scroll bar at the bottom of the screen. The words streaming across the screen said that a navy chaplain was on his way to Guantanamo. Confused, Saif called the chaplain's office: "I hear that somebody's heading out and I'm still at home." His deployment order had finally come down. Television reporters had been told, but no one had bothered to tell Saif himself. Within hours, he was packed and at the airport, ready for an overnight flight, a stopover in Miami for a briefing at SOUTHCOM, and then another flight to Puerto Rico. He arrived at Guantanamo on Thursday afternoon, January 23.

Coincidentally, a whole shipment of Korans had arrived on that very day, per the request placed earlier by the ICRC. This signal that the detainees might now be able to practice their religion was a welcome twin to the arrival of the chaplain.[4]

Now, standing on the airfield, unexpected, Saif made his own phone calls to the navy base to see if someone could come and meet him. The soldier on the tarmac stared back at this travel-weary, unshaven, dark-skinned man in civilian clothes. The JTF command staff were expecting a Muslim chaplain, but not until a commercial flight arrived later in the day. The soldier's bewilderment was the imam's initiation into the confusion that reigned at his new post.

Even as Saif was dispatched to Cuba, the disarray of the Pentagon's effort at Guantanamo suggested the need for an improved understanding of just who these detainees were—a lack of understanding that Lehnert was hoping Saifulislam could help reverse. Two days earlier, the *Miami Herald* had reported that an imam had emerged among the detainees themselves.[5] Reporter Carol Rosenberg based this story on the reports of several guards who had informed her that a one-legged, heavy-set man seemed to be leading the call to prayer. The detainees were allegedly deferential to this authority figure. Normally, as the JTF command staff and guards understood it, the soldiers in Afghanistan are "thin . . . they're not well fed . . . and a lot of times they're not well groomed.

But the generals and the higher officers, they're normally fat or fatter because they're fed well. They live well."[6]

The Pentagon was caught off guard by the *Miami Herald* report. As Rosenberg heard it repeated back to her, the reaction was "if the guards knew this, why didn't we?"[7] Apparently, rumors of the self-proclaimed and community-acknowledged leader had not made their way into any of the intelligence reports that shot up the chain of command. The news raised an even more disturbing question than the quality of intelligence at Guantanamo: Were the detainees now organizing themselves?

The alleged emergence of an imam was not the only sign of cohesion among the detainees. Guards were trading stories: The detainees were whistling and tapping pebbles to communicate with one another. They were scheming to map out the camp. They had spit on one guard and tried to bite another. The men in boxes, it seemed, were becoming restless and maybe even dangerous. The military's own imam could not only satisfy the detainees' need for a religious leader, the thinking went, but could possibly be able to stem some of the discontent and anger brewing inside the wire.

Setting his eyes on the new chaplain for the first time, Lehnert observed the easy way he carried himself and the unbothered, peaceful look in his dark eyes. Saif conveyed a sense of being both dutiful and contented. Small, soft-spoken, and laid-back, the chaplain was anything but a threatening presence, suggesting that use of his skills and their ability to heal the rift between the detained and JTF 160 might not be such a pipe dream after all.

The general and the chaplain got down to business. Innumerable decisions had to be made during the next few days and weeks. But for starters, Lehnert had several questions on his mind to which he needed answers right away.

The assumption behind this first conversation was that Saif would be interacting with the detainees, a proposal that spoke directly to the simmering differences of opinion between General Lehnert and Colonel Carrico.

If Saif were to engage the prisoners directly, his presence would poke at two of the issues that dominated life at X-Ray. First, he would be a living, breathing example that Lehnert was determined to end the ban on talking. As it happened, Lehnert had finally put an end to the no-talking policy the day before Saif arrived. Lehnert explained his decision in the following way: "When you make dumb rules that are easy to break, you aren't empowering the guards, you are empowering the detainees." He had come to see the no-talking rule as positively ludicrous in the context of X-Ray. As he explained:

I reversed the ban because it was an unenforceable rule. The cells were open. Two detainees lying on their mats with their heads 18 inches apart could appear to be sleeping but actually whispering to one another. A guard 8 feet away wouldn't be able to tell it was happening. I repeatedly told the guard force that you don't make rules that you cannot enforce. My logic was simple . . . [8]

Logic aside, Lehnert had made a tactical move against Carrico's by-the-book inflexibility. In the course of his January 23 conversation with Saif, the tension apparent in the camp, as seen through Lehnert's eyes, manifested itself. Saif was there to keep the detention center humane and to enforce to the best of his abilities the Geneva Conventions and, as a means to that end, to thwart Carrico's control over the detention regime.

Saif was therefore at Gitmo from the outset as a pawn in a power struggle over the definition of the camp. But even before he began to hear what the detainees had to say, his very presence spoke to yet another pronounced tension in the camp, that between the detainees and the guards. A Navy chaplain was already in place for the naval base, but Saif was expected to serve the detainees rather than the troops. In fact, at this point in time, there were no Muslim servicemen or women at X-Ray.[9] As in the case of Captain Shimkus and the medical services, expecting Saif to minister to the prisoners would mean altering the nature of his role in the military in that medical personnel and religious leaders ordinarily tend to U.S. troops. Thus, Saif's chaplaincy was one more instance of the detainees receiving special treatment.

Saif grasped both these political implications of his presence almost immediately. And before the meeting was over, he had come up with several suggestions for next steps. First was the question of whether or not he would wear a uniform at X-Ray. Saif was already somewhat embarrassed by the fact that he had been given no time to change and felt a bit disrespectful in the presence of the general. The two men deliberated over the issue, sharing the concern that if Saif wore a uniform, it would put more distance than desirable between the detainees and the imam. On the other hand, they reasoned, wearing military garb would enhance the sense of transparency that Lehnert had tried to emphasize since the detainees had arrived. Saif made the call. He was American military, so why not make that fact clear? Why begin by trying to hide anything? And Lehnert readily agreed. He would wear his uniform, wanting above all to make the detainees trust him, and certain that candor was the best first step in that direction.

A second question concerned language. How was he to speak to the detainees, given the wide array of languages they represented? Did he want a translator, and if so, what would his requirements be? Saif's mother tongue was Bengali. He spoke Urdu and Hindi besides, but only rudimentary Arabic. He had been fluent in English since his boyhood years in Bangladesh, where he attended a school run by Catholics. His preference, again, was for less rather than more distance from the detainees. His languages would have to do. Besides, Saif explained, displaying his understanding of how the languages of the region worked, the detainees could translate for one another, for example, through Urdu. Saif therefore was not dependent upon the services of a translator when it came to dealing with the detainees.

Readily absorbing Lehnert's sensibilities—the desire to have someone he trusted in contact with the detainees—and the urgency felt by Lehnert for this contact to occur as soon as possible, Saif made a suggestion as the meeting neared its end. "Why don't I call them to prayer tomorrow morning?" This simple proposal was aimed directly at the heart of the problem. In that way, he would speak to the detainees on their own terms, those of religion; in the language of prayer, Arabic; and as a group, letting them learn as a group who he was and why he was there. The symbolic gesture could only be a step in the right direction, and a strong signal that the end of the no-talking regime was but a first step in the direction of improving conditions at the camp. Lehnert agreed enthusiastically, grateful for the indication that the new chaplain was indeed going to help solve the political-philosophical divide that had already come to characterize the JTF 160 operation.[10]

Five times throughout the day, Muslims are called to prayer by the muezzin, who leads believers in a recitation in praise of Allah. Usually, the call is sent out from the top of a minaret, the muezzin's voice descending over all those who are ready to pray.

The next morning, just before dawn, Carrico picked up the new chaplain at the Bachelor Officer Quarters where the JTF command staff resided. Lehnert was already waiting at X-Ray.

Absent a minaret, a more rudimentary system would have to suffice. At 5:17, sunrise, on that Thursday morning, 12 days after the first detainees arrived, Saif sat on the ground cross-legged, wearing his camouflage, and projecting his quiet voice into the handheld bullhorn. There had been no formal call to prayer since their arrival 13 days earlier. "God is great, God is great... Mohammed is his messenger, come to prayer,"[11] the imam called, and was heard not just by the detainees but also by the base residents who were housed in the neighboring Villamar complex.

Shafiq Rasul, detainee #86, remembers being startled when the call to prayer filled the air. Even as Saif offered the reassuring news that once the detainees had completed their ablutions, they would all pray together,[12] the sudden piety only added to the general atmosphere of uncertainty in which he and his fellow detainees had been living for nearly two weeks.

Sitting beneath a sign pointing to Mecca, Saif chanted as the prisoners knelt on towels and prayed together.[13] Saif remembers that, however startled or confused the detainees were, "I offered the prayer and everybody joined me from their own cell." At the end of the service, Saif explained his presence: "I am the new chaplain. I am here for you. My name is Saifulislam."

Afterward, Saif and the general walked through the blocks. Introducing himself to each of them, Saif's first message to them was simple: "I will be around to talk to you later. I just want to introduce myself now."

The midmorning walk of the chaplain and the general through X-Ray was a transformative moment for the camp. Whether or not the detainees would accept the ministering of an American military chaplain, whether or not they would pray with him or even talk to him, remained to be seen. But Lehnert was trying to send a message: that the U.S. military was trying to find a way to accommodate the detainees. The question of whether their detention was legal was out of Lehnert's reach. In the meantime, he offered what he could— the chaplain and his call to prayer. It was a gesture in compensation for the lack of legal clarity about the status and future of the detainees, a symbolic act that could communicate the good intentions of the on-the-ground detaining authorities. Or so Lehnert hoped.

By the time Saif arrived, the guards and others were well on their way to replacing ignorance with stories based on observation, however overlaid with conjecture and even rumor. Given the language gap and the ban against talking, there was no way to measure or evaluate these stories. That changed with the presence of Saif. The chaplain spoke some of their languages, he belonged to their religion, he knew the lands they came from, and he was apparently not out to hurt anyone.

Spending the better part of his days inside the cell blocks, he would walk up and down the rows of cages and ask if anyone wanted to speak with him. He could ask questions, he could listen to complaints. He could stay all day and all night if they wanted. Saif's presence, though, was only a beginning. Whether Saif could gain the confidence of the detainees was a wholly different matter.

Saif was optimistic about his prospects for gaining insights into the detainees. At the outset, he felt welcome, "like a doctor who treats a wound, regardless of how the wound occurred. 'I look into their soul to see what they want from me, and how I can help them spiritually.' "[14]

But the challenges turned out to be much more complicated than Saif's early optimism had anticipated. Opinions differ about how the detainees viewed Saif as time went on. Among the guards, there was the sense that the detainees mocked the voice of an American Muslim. As one recalled, the rapport between the detainees and the chaplain was limited, if present at all. "When [Saif] came in and did the call to prayer, the detainees turned the other way. It was embarrassing."[15] Many of the detainees verify this account, insisting that they resisted such an obvious attempt at cooptation. "We were just standing there watching him," Shafiq Rasul reminisced about Saifulislam's first call to prayer. "And all the [detainees] go, 'What the hell is this guy doing?' "[16]

Saif took the resistance in stride. He knew that they talked behind his back, that some cursed him out as a hypocrite, as Satan. Yet he persisted in his daily walks through the camp's cell blocks, attempting to talk to them. Not surprisingly, he developed special ties with the Bangladeshis in the camp, who, as he remembers it, always stood up for him. And, he recalls, the detainees from Afghanistan were less hostile than others as well.

Of greater note, perhaps, is how infrequently the detainees have commented upon Saif. In the handful of memoirs and interviews that have come out, very few have seen fit to mention him at all. But there is some evidence that he had an impact on them. Saif saw to it that some of the detainees' complaints were addressed. At his request, their customary foods and prayer beads were provided. He also reinforced the case that the ICRC was making about issues of modesty such as the use of females as shower escorts. He explained the frustrations over not being able to worship "shoulder-to-shoulder, ankle-to-ankle." He convinced the detainees to take medicines that would help heal their wounds. He ordered the traditional white knit skullcaps and copies of the Koran in Urdu, Arabic, and large type.[17]

The detainees trusted Saif at least enough to complain to him about the most personal matters of their prison lives. When they found themselves awaking in the morning after having had a "wet dream" the night before, or when they masturbated prior to rising, they turned to Saif. Under Muslim law, they were forbidden to pray after ejaculation until they showered. Saif would call the guards and try to arrange this. So, too, they confided to Saif about the need to wash themselves after going to the toilet as was customary for them. Saif arranged for an additional bucket to be put inside their cells.

Detainees confided in Saif about impending pregnancies back home, about rough handling by the guards, about a kinsman located elsewhere in the camp. Furthermore, the detainees broached the larger policy questions with the chaplain. What was going to happen to them? What were the plans? Was this temporary, as the primitive cages suggested, or long-term?

Whether or not they treated him as an imam to be trusted with religious concerns, the detainees clearly benefited from Saif's presence at the camp. On the other hand, he also participated wholeheartedly in the propaganda campaign aimed at the press. And yet, neither reflected the primary reason he had been asked to Guantanamo. As Saif himself tells it, he was there for one reason and one reason only: "I was there for the General," he said, ready to keep an eye on things all around and to give the general access to the kind of knowledge that others on the task force simply did not have.

From the moment he arrived at the camp, Saif became Michael Lehnert's window into the world of the detainees. Before Saif's arrival, Lehnert had done his best to educate himself, watching from afar, listening to what the guards were telling him, even requesting his own copy of the Koran so that he could read it for himself. Now, with Saif by his side, he could have more trustworthy insights into the gripes, medical needs, and overall dissatisfactions on the minds of the detainees, or even just their general unhappiness.[18] The small group around Lehnert saw Saif as essential to the general and deferred to the highly unusual relationship. Overall, they explained it to themselves as "a good check" on the guards as well as the detainees, and therefore as wise from a management point of view, however unprecedented. In addition, the detainees and the ICRC both learned to approach Saif as a short-cut to Lehnert—and thus a quicker way of eliciting a response, a way that bypassed the usual chain of command.

Once Saif arrived, he and the general became an inseparable pair at X-Ray. As frequently as was possible for General Lehnert—basically every day he was on base—the two walked through the cell blocks together, stopping to ask questions and listen to those detainees who wanted to talk, and generally observing daily life there. The detainees shared their medical complaints, their dietary needs, and their wishes to be moved near friends. Some protested that their detention was unfair or a mistake, and that they were friendly toward the United States. According to his own account, Lehnert mostly listened, trying his best not to make promises about their futures, over which he knew he had no control.[19]

With Saif by his side, Lehnert felt empowered to ask questions and to get answers. And every morning and afternoon, the two would meet so that Saif could brief the general on what he'd seen and learned.[20]

Without apologies, the general made Saif his closest ally—"a younger brother" to some, a "son" in the eyes of others. "His relationship to the chaplain was different than it was with the rest of the staff," says Colonel Meier.[21] Lehnert gave Saif privileges that were unique to him, such as round-the-clock access to his refrigerator—where he kept foods that Saif particularly liked, among them chili peppers and apples—and let Saif know that his office was open to the chaplain at all times. Lehnert gave Saif the sense that he was included everywhere, in every meeting, at every level. "Lehnert would bring me, include me in what he was thinking. . . . I became a part of everything he did." And "he used to bring me chili peppers . . . from his home." Saif saw Lehnert's message as, "Whatever Saif needs, we'll do . . . " For Saif, the arrangement catapulted him to a position of importance unlike anything he had known before.

Lehnert's goal, with Saif as his eyes and ears on the detainees, was not so much to find out what their comfort issues were—this Saif could do without him—but to discover their state of mind. He wanted to know what concerned them, what their religious sensibilities were, what angered them, what confused them, and above all, he wanted them to know that he was listening. For Lehnert, it was the best he could do to forestall the kind of despair and hopelessness that he feared could set in, the kind of depression and anger he had seen among the Haitians when their hopes for a future in the United States were dashed. With the knowledge Saif could help provide, he hoped to pacify the prisoners as he had the migrants in the past.

Before Saif's arrival, Lehnert had been dependent on the ICRC for information about the detainees, not to mention subject to the limitations of Carrico's ban on communication, which he hadn't seen fit to reverse prior to Saif's presence. Now, with his own advisor, he could find out about the detainees for himself. And the learning would not be limited to the demands of the detainees. Inside the cell blocks, Saif became privy to more than just their requests for Korans and prayer beads, their need for showers and their desire for a sense of their futures. He learned a bit about who they were—where they came from, who their families were, and how they thought about the world.

Saif says that he kept some of the information he gleaned from the detainees to himself, deciding not to share it with Lehnert. In a fashion befitting a chaplain, he respected the privacy of the members of his congregation. But there were moments when the two shared impressions of the detainees, went over their files together, and tried to fill in the blanks about precisely who they had in their custody.

There was arguably a built-in conflict of interest in this relationship and its premises. As many of the detainees suspected, Saif was the sidekick of the general, and his allegiance was more to the general than to the detainees, though he tried his best to satisfy them both. Lehnert had initiated this gray-area chaplaincy, and in so doing had deftly acquired both a spy and someone who could truly help the detainees. But the fact remains that Lehnert's intentions were to keep peace in the camp, and to do so without being able to bring the rule of law—in the form of legal procedures or a more lenient detention supervisor than Carrico—into the camp.

"I went into the detention facility every single day that I was there. I would talk to the detainees, I would talk to the guards, I'd talk to the chaplain, I talked to everybody." Often, Lehnert recalls, these visits would occur at night. The demanding logistics of the day made after dark the easiest time for the general to visit; a time when he wasn't meeting with visiting VIPs or tending to construction or policy-related issues. "I would do it at all times. Sometimes it was 2 A.M. I would come in there, unannounced, and just drive in and say, 'Let me in. Let me talk. Let me see what's going on.' "[22]

Lehnert was concerned not just about the detainees and what they had to say but also about the behavior of the guards. The unexpected nature of the late visits appealed to Lehnert additionally as a measure of accountability. "They never knew when I was going to come. They never knew how long I was going to stay there. And I did that for a reason. Not because I didn't trust people, but people do well what the boss inspects." Unannounced visits would deter misbehavior—something he didn't like to talk about, but of which he was continually wary. This attentiveness to potential misconduct on the part of the guards was an important factor in the life of the camp. For, as the detainees later reported, random acts of abuse occurred frequently. Lehnert was trying his best to counter the occurrence of such acts, through policy, through his order to Carrico, through his own presence, and now through Saif.

Recognizing the significance of Saif to the general, the rest of the command staff deferred respectfully to the closeness of the relationship. Even Carrico kept quiet, despite the fact that Saif's presence was a rebuke, however subtle, to his way of doing things. Reflecting on Saif, Carrico—who wouldn't speak at length on the subject—acknowledged that "my code" was that "you don't talk to prisoners." Thus, his general impression of Saif's behavior was that Saif was "out of his lane." As Carrico explained with matter-of-fact regret, Saif didn't work for him. "I didn't control him."[23]

Control was one thing. Trust was another. Neither Carrico nor the troops fully trusted the chaplain.[24] Because he spoke the detainees' languages and secured comforts for them, he continually had to dodge suspicions about the possibility that he was an enemy infiltrator—as did all of the chaplains who came after him. Carrico's guards, watching Saif communicate with the detainees in languages they could not understand, chafed over their own ignorance and leapt to conclusions about the potential treachery of someone who was, like the detainees, of darker skin, from South Asia, and speaking the languages of the enemy.

Lehnert tried to nip the rumors over Saif's potential duplicity in the bud by offering to have an interpreter accompany Saif at X-Ray. According to Lehnert, the response from the guard force was, "Well, we don't know if we can trust the interpreters." In other words, anyone who spoke the languages of the detainees was suspect. Lehnert met with Carrico, Meier, and Nichols to discuss the issue. The conclusion was that the same xenophobia triggered by Saif would apply to the interpreters. Lehnert's reply, as he describes it was, "Well at a certain point, you've got to start trusting somebody. Particularly when they're wearing the uniform of a U.S. soldier." From that moment on, distrust of Saif was uttered, if at all, only privately. Lehnert maintains that Saif's role was basically to maintain a balance of perspectives between Carrico's sense of things and that of the ICRC; it was a means of legitimizing his command as neither too indulgent toward the prisoners nor too harsh. "For every person, like in the ICRC, that was saying, 'you need to be doing it this way,' there was somebody else" with a countervailing opinion, 'Oh, you know, by golly, we've got to show them the fist.' And what I was trying to do was balance those two very competing directions."[25]

Lehnert also maintains that his concern for the detainees was part of his overall concern that imprisonment not be the occasion for the abuse of power. In his early days as a captain, he had overseen the prison at Subic Bay and had earned himself the reputation, according to Father Tom Dansak, who was there with him at the time, of having no incidents of alleged prisoner mistreatment or of prisoner protest within the prison under his command. Lehnert has never really shown his full hand, either then or now. He has never spoken out on the guilt or innocence of the detainees. But the fact is that Carrico's sense of things was accurate. The introduction of Saif was not just about balance, it was about pushing back against Carrico's harsh rules and humanizing somewhat the life of the detainees who all of a sudden were given a voice, someone to talk to, and access to the commander of the JTF.

Lehnert bridles at the suggestion that he was a "softie," a "kinder, gentler, kind of fuzzy Marine general." He insists that he "didn't spend time wringing my hands saying, 'Oh, my God, these poor individuals endure vile [conditions]." Instead, he says, "I was absolutely convinced . . . that, as a nation, we claim to stand for something." He didn't want to preside over a shameful incarceration like the internment of Japanese-Americans during World War II. For him, preserving the dignity of the detainees was about honor—his own and the nation's. "From a standpoint of our stature in the world," he summed up, "the juice isn't worth the squeeze."

Though Lehnert insisted that the presence of Saif was "all about balance," he was also motivated by sympathy for the detainees. Had he been locked up without any sense of their futures, without access to lawyers, with no prospects of a trial and no word on what his destiny would be, he told me, "I would have felt the same way."

Lehnert's identification with the detainees was not just about himself. As the days passed, he began to realize that the people in his custody were more like the young men he commanded than like hardened criminals determined and able to bring down the world. He knew about lost adolescents in search of trouble. He understood the mind-set of those who boasted of evil aims and were incapable of doing much harm. Some were very likely bad guys, he thought, but for the most part they seemed to him like mixed-up boys with bad intentions—followers rather than leaders, and "knuckleheads" rather than trained jihadis. And, guilty or not, they were living in animal-like conditions, risking a beating by the Immediate Reaction Force if they dared disobey the command to stay mute.

Lehnert wasn't alone in seeing the detainees in this light. Notably, the detainee about whom the guards thought they knew the most was also the one with whom they felt some kind of personal identification. David Hicks, detainee #2—a white, English-speaking, working-class kid from Australia, with no college degree, in search of adventure and a sense of belonging—seemed to many of his guards to be very much like themselves. And his remarkable capacity for self-discipline particularly impressed many of them.[26] Even the other detainees noted the sense of identification between the guards and Hicks. As Rasul and a later arrival, Moazzem Begg, detainee #558, both agreed, the soldiers and Hicks were essentially cut from the same cloth.[27] At least one of

Lehnert's Marine guard force shared the perception, confessing, "He could have been one of us . . . I could have made him a Marine."[28]

The identification with Hicks had a double significance. It humanized the detainee population, but it also suggested a sign of danger to the guard force—and even to Lehnert. If David Hicks could be so easily recruited, then he was truly a danger. As a white male who spoke English, he could penetrate organizations easily as a spy or a terrorist who could successfully escape detection.

The identification with Hicks was one thing. But Lehnert's sense of the identification extended beyond this single prisoner. He identified not with Hicks alone but with the detained population in general. For him, the idea of a young man being deprived of justice and his rights—including possible punishment—was intolerable. This empathy for the Arabs and the tribal Afghans as well as for Hicks would in subsequent days prove pivotal to the general's fate at Guantanamo.

This sense of mirroring recognition reinforced the growing observation that had begun the minute the first detainees—wafer-thin, docile, and weak—appeared in the hatchway of the C-17 that brought them to Guantanamo. Day by day, the idea that they were America's most dangerous enemies—the worst of the worst—came up against the reality of the detainees themselves. And once the ban on talking was lifted, once the detainees could be heard by those who spoke their language, once there could be communication between the U.S. forces and the enemy, the sense of doubt about precisely who was in custody grew.

Prior to Saif's arrival, the alien character of the detainees had dominated the atmosphere at the camp. Their unknown languages, their indecipherable customs, and above all their foreign religion had allowed the troops to minimize the connection between themselves and the detainees.

Saif's presence bridged the gulf between the Muslim community and the troops. Although both the detainees and the guards considered him an infiltrator of sorts, they had no other choice but to rely on him as the main point of translation between the two groups of young men. Saif offered to answer any questions the guards might have about Muslim culture, attitudes, practices, and the like. Toward that end, Saif reached out to the troops, offering classes on Islam and letting the guards know he was available at all times to answer questions.

In essence, the addition of Saif satisfied numerous agendas. It placated critics of the inhumane aspects of Gitmo. It counteracted the dehumanizing policies of Carrico. It defied the Pentagon's apparent preference to keep the detainees as nameless, indecipherable, subhuman creatures to their keepers. Most of all, it brought knowledge of each party—the detainees and their keepers—to the other. The guards' ignorance about Islam was replaced by information about the need to treat the Koran as a sacred object, the need to worship shoulder to shoulder and hip to hip, the days of fasting in the Muslim calendar, and the Islamic codes about personal hygiene. And the detainees absorbed bits and pieces of information about their possible futures in the outside world.

Saif's insights into the universe of the detainees—however distant they may have been, they were the best the military had—gave General Lehnert power in the face of the increasingly worrisome policies coming out of Washington. Furthermore, it provided a focus for moral questions. Morality, after all, was something few wanted to be accused of violating. It was one thing to be protective of America's security and quite another to be seen as behaving outside the bounds of human decency. Saif's presence, and his close alliance with the commander of the camp, put moral concerns on the front burner at Guantanamo.

But it also highlighted one of the central ironies of the detention mission, the way in which Lehnert's determination to create a humane environment helped the Pentagon put an acceptable face on—and thus continue with—an otherwise unacceptable policy: the detention without charge of individuals in conditions that were barely civilized. Saif, inadvertently, abetted this Janus-faced agenda more than anyone else at the camp.

As soon as they could, the JTF command staff introduced the chaplain to the press. Following the first call to prayer, the chaplain was whisked away to face a media group consisting of more than 20 members. Saif had no experience with the press and, by his own account, "no clue"[29] about what to say, but it turned out that he was a natural when it came to interacting with the media. In the words of CNN's Bob Franken, he was "Mr. Television."[30] Saif loved the camera and the camera loved him back.

Lehnert's public affairs officer, Steve Cox, immediately saw the opportunities that were unleashed by Saif's comfort with the press. The very fact of a Muslim chaplain had been a "boon" to the detention effort: "[I]t lent more credibility to our claims of... doing the right thing, being in step with what the ICRC wanted and in step with the Geneva Convention and so on and so forth."[31] But the willingness of Saif to become a champion of the detention effort was an unexpected plus. As Cox pointed out, Saif "very easily could have come in there and said, 'You know what? I'm not really comfortable with this, and I really don't want to do it.' I still could have played up the idea that we had a Muslim chaplain there. But to have him be willing to participate was simply phenomenal.... I can't think of a time where he told me 'no.' ... And he participated as a full partner in every process, every step of the way."[32]

It was an obvious—and successful—tactic. "He was the front man," Franken says with his characteristic directness. "He was their token," trotted out to give the party line and doing so only too willingly,[33] to get the message out that Guantanamo Bay wasn't really such a bad place for prisoners after all. As Rumsfeld had said, it was virtually a Caribbean vacation.

A pivotal figure in the JTF's campaign to improve Guantanamo's image in the world, Saif thus helped peddle the story that the veritable "petting zoo" was actually a humane environment. The press would often repeat his press conferences and interviews verbatim as proof not only of his good intentions, but also of his beneficial influence at the camp. " 'I've been received very, very positively,' said Navy Lt. Abuhena Saif-ul-Islam in a telephone interview yesterday from U.S. Naval Station Guantanamo Bay in Cuba. 'In fact, they are very eager to see me every day and everybody wants to talk to me.' "[34] The press did not call these accounts into question. All around, no one seemed willing to view the chaplain or his role with a critical eye, least of all General Lehnert.

But while the gesture of inviting in a Muslim chaplain and the easygoing gentleness of Saif were a propaganda success, Saif also played an essential part in the Guantanamo that Michael Lehnert was determined to create, a Guantanamo in which public relations took a backseat to the successful management of a humane detention facility.

With Saif's help, Lehnert satisfied two contradictory concerns at once. He answered to his own code of morality, which for him was indistinguishable from the Marine Corps code of honor, and he gave his Pentagon bosses what they wanted—a veneer for an inchoate policy and a questionable legal agenda.

In general, Lehnert saw the press presence at Guantanamo as no better than a necessary nuisance, much like what he called the "media worm of the ouroboros," a reference he makes to the mythical snake that feeds on its own tail. So, it would follow, he shouldn't have been bothered by feeding them what they asked for, particularly as it helped him to achieve what he wanted. But Lehnert seems to have been discomfited early on by the conflict between Saif's dual roles as a minister of religion and as a propaganda tool for the Pentagon.

Even as he was using Saif to cover over the Pentagon's neglect of Guantanamo, Lehnert was indirectly raising objections that he could not make directly. An example was his relationship to one reporter, Carol Rosenberg at the *Miami Herald*.

Rosenberg had been among that first batch of journalists who arrived on January 9 and among those who benefited from Bob Franken's insistence that at least some of them be allowed to stay for the first arrival of detainees. Rosenberg's presence at Guantanamo, like that of Saif and the ICRC, exerted a pressure upon the JTF. Rosenberg, who has logged more days at Guantanamo than any other journalist, served a purpose for Lehnert, who came to rely upon her to ask the questions of conscience, including those about rumors circulating in Washington about military trials, interrogations, and detainee treatment. By giving her access, he made it possible for her to ask the questions that he could not, and thus to express his frustrations with the lack of policies from Washington—not to mention his determination to follow the Geneva Conventions.

As he told his staff, "If she's asking it, others will."

Using Rosenberg to prick the conscience of those outside the camp—those in Washington and the public in general—was evidence of the subtle, indirect ways in which Lehnert liked to work.[35] With the press, embodied by Rosenberg, helping Lehnert signal to the world the questions that needed to be asked, and with Saif bolstering legitimacy inside the camp, Lehnert had, by the beginning of February, found new and effective allies in his plan to assure decent care and custody for the detainees at Guantanamo.

Yet for all of his successful strategizing and maneuvering, even as he was making progress thanks to Saif's presence, the course of events was being yanked in a direction that his parrying and counterpunches could not resist. It was time, according to Lehnert's superiors in Washington, for the real purpose of Guantanamo to begin. It was time for serious interrogations to take place.

9

Missing Pieces

We want them to tell us everything they know.

—Paul Wolfowitz, Deputy Secretary of Defense

Donald Rumsfeld's signature glower suddenly materialized on SOUTHCOM'S video teleconferencing screen. It was the end of January. Nearly two weeks had passed since the first detainees had been consigned to JTF 160's custody at Guantanamo Bay, and the self-confident SECDEF was displeased. Bristling, the Secretary was pressing SOUTHCOM for some—any—sort of explanation. He wanted to know where the interrogations at Guantanamo Bay stood. What had JTF 160 done to get him the information he needed from the detainees? The SECDEF wanted to know: where was the intelligence he had anticipated? Where was the evidence? Didn't SOUTHCOM, overseeing JTF 160, understand the reason for this whole mission? Didn't they fathom the urgency of the matter?[1]

If January had belonged to JTF 160, February, it seemed, would be Donald Rumsfeld's month.

At SOUTHCOM, Rumsfeld's implicit criticism came as a surprise. JTF 160's first few weeks may have been hectic and confusing, but the detention mission was progressing along a consistent path, in line with a single governing idea: that of keeping captured enemies off the battlefield *and* complying with the Geneva Conventions (despite the relatively free hand sanctioned implicitly from above). Lehnert, with the aid and guidance of the International Committee for the Red Cross (ICRC), of Saif, and of the legal team, had all made it perfectly clear. For practical purposes, the prisoners were to be treated as enemy prisoners of war. Assigned a complex detention mission, but not given any detailed guidance about policy or future plans and knowing little of substance about the detainees, the task force had done a commendable job, at least according to the ICRC. The Red Cross representatives at Gitmo had praised the JTF's reactions to many situations that had emerged, including the helter-skelter arrival of assorted American personnel, the inherently disagreeable mission of locking individuals in cages, and the unforeseen glitches that were bound to occur when managing a population of alien and possibly dangerous detainees.

While the JTF had scrambled, with erratic guidance from SOUTHCOM, to put the first pieces of Gitmo into place, the command staff was increasingly aware that Washington was in disarray over detainee policy. As Lehnert puts it, with characteristic understatement, he had the sense that a "healthy debate" was going on in Washington.[2] Isolated from the center of decision making, Lehnert actually had little clue about the palace intrigue transpiring at the pinnacle of power. In fact, as he would discover soon enough, the "healthy" debate in D.C. was already virtually closed, though its controversial resolution was at this time known to only a few.

The War Council was using a variety of techniques, ranging from intimidation to secret agendas, to triumph over opposition and neutralize pushback from the State Department and the JAG corps.

Rumsfeld's video teleconference (VTC) was thus a watershed moment in the Guantanamo mission, anticipating the legal backing for the interrogation regime. Now, at least, there could be few doubts about the purpose of Guantanamo from the SECDEF's point of view. Its mission was to provide information for the Pentagon. Accordingly, following this phone call, SOUTHCOM and the country's entire national security apparatus began to reorient itself toward a new mission—that of interrogation.

In the wake of the VTC with SOUTHCOM, the developing strategies of the War Council began to coincide with Rumsfeld's push at Guantanamo for more and better information. Suddenly, the Guantanamo that Michael Lehnert had been struggling to create stood to encounter a whole new set of challenges.

From his national-security perspective, Secretary Rumsfeld's anger and frustration were arguably understandable. Theoretically, at least, the detainees assembled at Guantanamo might be withholding time-sensitive information about future attacks on the United States, in Afghanistan or elsewhere. Intelligence, after all, was the key to the war on terror. The plans in the minds of terrorists constituted information that could keep the United States safe. These captives had to be questioned as quickly and effectively as possible. "[P]robably there's a good chance that one or two or all of them know of the next [terrorist] event," General Richard Myers remarked at a press conference with Rumsfeld in early February.[3] Myers's comment also inadvertently admitted that interrogations of the Guantanamo detainees, rather than being focused inquiries based on individualized suspicions about the captives being questioned, were more open-ended than specific.[4]

The issue of interrogation masked a mixed message from the Pentagon. Standard interrogation policy posits two basic types of information: tactical and strategic. The time for tactical information—the kind relevant to upcoming battles and imminent security threats—had likely gone by for the detainees at Guantanamo. Prisoners generally reveal useful tactical intelligence only within a few hours or days of their initial capture. The more time passes, the more dated, fabricated, watered-down, and tactically worthless the information is likely to be. In the words of the Army Field Manual on prisoner interrogation used in 2002, prisoners are most vulnerable and likely to divulge what they know at the point of capture, which is "traumatic for most sources." Once that moment has passed, "much of an individual's susceptibility to interrogation is gone." Moreover, as an early manual spells out, when information is passed from short-term to long-term memory, a "conservative estimate" of 70% is "lost beyond recall."[5] Conveniently, these passages were removed when the Army issued an updated version of the interrogation manual in 1992 (still in effect in 2002), but the worry about "the rate at which people forget detailed information" remained a focus of interrogation tactics.[6]

The first detainees' ability to give tactical information had been compromised well before their arrival at Guantanamo. Many of them had not been interrogated at the end of November 2001, immediately upon capture by Northern Alliance forces in Afghanistan. Even worse, the first arrivals had been subjected to at least six excruciating weeks of additional traumas, culminating in their nightmarish 30-plus–hour airplane flight. Blindfolded, dehydrated, suffering from dysentery and deprived of toilets, freezing, shackled, and manhandled, unable to hear or communicate, they suddenly found themselves in an unidentified foreign land. The Army Field Manual on interrogation suggests that such a period would render tactical interrogation nearly useless.

Still, no one in Rumsfeld's entourage, not even the SECDEF himself, seems to have considered that the weeks that had passed since the detainees' initial capture ruled out the possibility of fruitful interrogations that might furnish actionable intelligence for the immediate future, either on battlefield tactics or on upcoming attacks on the United States.

Strategic interrogation took things one step further than tactical and operational interrogation. Tactical and operational interrogations were geared toward obtaining "time-sensitive, perishable information about foreign entities" relevant to an ongoing battlefield operation. Strategic interrogation, on the other hand, was "intelligence whose principal consumers are national-level civilian and military policymakers." This kind of information was "broader in scope, and more encyclopedic," focused on the "capabilities, plans and intentions" of the enemy, and included "biographic data, economic, sociological transportation, telecommunications, geography, political and scientific and technical intelligence."[7]

As for strategic information—about networks, chains of command within the al Qaeda structure, terrorist leaders and tactics—this, too, could falter, given the fact that, as Rumsfeld acknowledged, the names and the identities of the detainees were unknown. Yet no clear distinction was drawn publicly or down the chain of command to Guantanamo between the two interrogation goals.

Pentagon officials apparently thought that whether they wanted tactical or strategic information, extending the trauma that began at capture could loosen lips. They seemed to believe that the destabilizing effect of being thrust "into a foreign environment over which they have no control"—one of the conditions suggested in the Army Field Manual on interrogation—would prove effective on one level or another.[8]

Rumsfeld's fierce impatience seemed to stem not only from his fear that the mission was being botched with each passing day but also from the fact that he was accustomed to issuing orders and having them followed. And as the VTC made clear, he was convinced that he had given an unambiguous order for seriously vigorous interrogations to take place. Yet, somehow, the policies being implemented did not reflect the instructions he had issued. Now, on the VTC, the SOUTHCOM officers let the SECDEF know that there had been a serious misunderstanding. "The reason you're not getting information is that we're not doing interrogations," a staff officer confessed.[9]

In fact, interrogations were going on every day at Guantanamo, but not under the auspices of SOUTHCOM and JTF 160. Instead, they were being conducted, somewhat haphazardly, by a series of intelligence agency interrogators. Following in the footsteps of their colleagues in Afghanistan, the interrogators asked repeatedly about the whereabouts of Mullah Omar and Osama bin Laden. According to one of the staff officers participating in the teleconference, "Rumsfeld went through the roof" once he heard that the JTF was not part of the intelligence collecting mission.[10]

The discrepancy between SOUTHCOM's and OSD's understandings of the Guantanamo mission had numerous causes. Like the conflation of tactical and strategic information goals for interrogation, the Pentagon's initial public pronouncements about the rationale for Guantanamo had consisted of mixed messages. In press briefings, congressional hearings, and elsewhere, Rumsfeld, Wolfowitz, Myers, and others had focused on detention rather than on interrogation. That is, their stated goal was to take the bad guys out of circulation rather than to extract information from them. This stood in contrast to the justification for detention in Afghanistan, where DOD officials emphasized intelligence gathering. "We've been interrogating them, we're gathering intelligence information," Rumsfeld told the press in mid-December. "We've been trying to put pressure on people who are terrorists or people who are helping terrorists and to make it uncomfortable, unpleasant."[11] Similarly, at a press conference that same day, Wolfowitz clarified the purpose of the roundup. "[W]e've made it clear that where there's any reason to think that they're al Qaeda or senior Taliban people that we would like to get our hands on them to interrogate them." Wolfowitz illustrated the point with an example. "There are 15 [prisoners] that are moving from Sherberghan [sic] to Kandahar," he said. "My understanding . . . is that they were selected because we concluded . . . that these were people who might have important information or might be themselves senior people."[12]

But this stress on intelligence gathering, however ill-defined, as the most urgent task of the detaining authorities faded somewhat as DOD's focus shifted from Afghanistan to Guantanamo. As the *New York Times* noted, "Mr. Rumsfeld implied that there was nothing special about these prisoners in terms of their informational value. 'We just have to keep the flow going, and that's what's taking place.' "[13] An anticipated human-rights disaster in Afghanistan, due to overcrowding, insufficient supplies, and the onrushing Afghan winter, was integral to the decision to move the detainees out of the theater of battle. But the imperatives of intelligence gathering were never forgotten, even though the subject was momentarily passed over in silence.

But whatever confusing signals he had given out at first, at his hour-long press conference on January 22, 2002, at which he responded to the publication of the notorious photo, Rumsfeld communicated his intentions to use Guantanamo primarily as a means of obtaining critical information: "[T]he most important thing for us from our standpoint is gathering intelligence," he said, adding that "we feel not just entitled but an obligation to try to gather intelligence about future terrorist attacks and how the network functions. And that is what we're doing."[14]

Guantanamo would evidently be an interrogation center, not merely a holding facility, for perpetrators of the global war on terror.[15] To complicate—and obfuscate—the matter further, there was also the matter, still not yet specified, of military commissions and what kind of procedures would be set up to get evidence and testimony for building cases against the detainees.

SOUTHCOM may have resisted the OSD's plans to turn Guantanamo into an interrogation camp for another reason besides confusion. Galen Jackman believed that the "interrogation capability" required to carry out the mission Rumsfeld had in mind did not exist within the entire military. Just as it lacked recent experience with detaining prisoners of war, the American military was not well prepared for strategic information gathering via interrogations. There were simply not enough professionally trained military interrogators and analysts with the linguistic skills and cultural background knowledge to do the job. The military was equipped, as General Jackman explained, to do "tactical level interrogation. Capture somebody off the battlefield. Pull him back... as you're moving him to the rear... you're screening for intelligence." This was the Afghanistan scenario, one the military was used to. But when it came to strategic interrogation capability, "We had to develop interrogators," Jackman recalls.[16] We had to "start digging" historically and operationally to find out what the U.S. Army had done in World War II and who could be trained to help us now.

Historical digging would have shown that the U.S. military had conducted interrogations of prisoners throughout the 20th century. Moreover, during World War II the United States had engaged in a "strategic interrogation operation" aimed at Nazi prisoners of war on its own soil. Interrogating Nazi prisoners of war who were being held in Fort Hunt, just outside D.C., the MIS-Y program, as it was known, was a "carefully guarded secret."[17] The 3,451 POWs who came through the Fort Hunt interrogation process between August 1942 and the end of July 1945 provided strategic intelligence that proved significant for Allied victories in World War II.[18]

Needless to say, the U.S. military continues to train and rely on intelligence officers. Military staff structure has six categories, one of which is the J-2, specializing in intelligence and security. General Lehnert had brought Tim Nichols to Guantanamo to be his J-2 staff in charge of intelligence and security, none of which involved interrogations. In Nichols's own view, the GTMO J-2 job consisted of four tasks. First, he had to keep Lehnert "situationally aware": "We thought we might get detainees from other regions," he said, "that we would have to keep our eyes on the world." Second, he was to watch for any sign of a new migrant surge of Haitians or Cubans or others from the Caribbean theater and stay ready to respond. Third, he was to look out for "threat indications and warnings"; if, for instance, the United States had really captured the worst of the worst, then the detention facility might become a priority target for a sneak attack. Finally, Nichols listed the "amorphous task" of interrogation, which he saw as a matter of supporting interrogation operations rather than participating in them.[19]

Jackman was concerned about this discrepancy between the SECDEF's interrogation mission and the J-2s' training and experience. Overall, J-2s are trained for operational and logistical information gathering, and their means of gathering information come largely from observation and information analysis. By contrast, interrogation missions were largely the responsibility of the Pentagon's Defense Intelligence Agency (DIA) and of the units trained at Fort Huachuca, Arizona. Established in 1971 and located in the southern part of Arizona, Huachuca houses the U.S. Army Intelligence Center and School. Here the Army interrogators subsequently assigned to Guantanamo were trained on the basis of the Army Field Manual on interrogation, FM 32–54, updated in 1997, which specified the various aims, purposes, and techniques available to Army interrogators.[20]

Additionally, it was a well-known fact that the most comprehensive and searching interrogations had been carried out historically by the CIA, not the Pentagon. Sometimes employing extralegal techniques, the CIA had dominated the interrogation side of U.S. intelligence gathering in the latter decades of the 20th century. Even before 9/11, Donald Rumsfeld had been concerned about a general weakness in the military when it came to matters of intelligence and interrogation. In 1998, the Commission to Assess the Ballistic Missile Threat to the United States, which he chaired, concluded that "eroding" American intelligence capabilities was one of the chief obstacles to the ability to evaluate that threat.[21]

By the time he reassumed the office of secretary of defense, this time under George W. Bush, little had changed. On paper, Rumsfeld made intelligence an immediate priority. The September 2001 Quadrennial Defense Review had made much of the need for the Pentagon to build up the country's military intelligence. It was Rumsfeld's stated intent to create a more robust intelligence network within the military, partially in order to reduce the Pentagon's dependence on the CIA, where much of the nation's intelligence-gathering capacity lay and which was outside the purview of the Pentagon. But not even the initial steps toward that goal had yet been taken prior to September 11, 2001.

In addition to intelligence capabilities, one bureaucratic glitch threatened to hinder intelligence gathering prior to launch. According to one of

SOUTHCOM's lawyers, Rumsfeld had never signed the execute order for such a mission. A "be prepared" order had been drafted for an intelligence operation at Gitmo, but the mission had not been activated by the SECDEF's mandatory sign-off prior to the arrival of the detainees or at any time in their first couple of weeks there. In other words, Rumsfeld had told SOUTHCOM to fire its engines but had never given the command for takeoff. This time, the secretary of defense left no room for interpretation. He approved the execute order.

With or without an execute order, General Lehnert was in no way prepared for the mission of creating a serious interrogation operation at Guantanamo. As JTF 160 commander, he had understood that he had been given one mission and one mission only: that of detention, which he understood to mean overseeing the care and custody of the individuals who were sent from Afghanistan to the distant holding area.[22]

But in reality, the interrogation mission was always there, haphazard rather than well organized, but never absent. From the earliest days of X-Ray, the polo-shirt-wearing agents from DIA, CIA, FBI, the Secret Service, and elsewhere were carrying out interrogations even while policy makers and lawyers continued to debate interrogation policy.

And they did so with help from JTF 160. From the very first days of X-Ray, the task force devoted scarce time and resources to constructing interrogation huts on the perimeter of the camp, indicating that intelligence was already a priority. JTF 160 personnel transported detainees, one by one, to and from the huts, where agents questioned the physically shackled detainees one at a time.

The command team also looked after the interrogators, transporting, feeding, and lodging them as necessary. And because of a policy born of Lehnert's concern for humane treatment of the detainees and Carrico's worries about legal liability, JTF guards witnessed the interrogations, providing some protection for the detainees.

Still, aside from this peripheral support, the command staff didn't give much thought in the early weeks of Gitmo to interrogation as a systematic or even particularly pressing purpose of X-Ray. For those on the ground, the day-trippers were more of an oddity and a nuisance than a serious impediment to JTF 160's detention mission. For Lehnert, given the mission of care and custody, interrogation was something he personally seems not to have thought about, and if he did think about it in these early days, it was to conclude that it was something above his pay grade.

Thus, from the perspective of those in charge in Miami and at Guantanamo, the eventual role of Guantanamo as a center for intelligence gathering remained totally unclear for the first weeks of Gitmo's operating existence.

But interrogation was foremost among Rumsfeld's priorities—no matter the practical realities or the lack of expertise available to SOUTHCOM, and no matter how Lehnert might have pretended otherwise. At the end of the video teleconference, Rumsfeld ordered SOUTHCOM to begin immediately to conduct vigorous interrogations by the next morning. Within moments of the conference call's conclusion, Lieutenant Colonel Ronald "Buck" Buikema, stationed at SOUTHCOM, was dispatched to Guantanamo. His orders were to be in a cell with a detainee by 0900 the following day, even if it was only to ask the detainee his name. Of course, this type of questioning was already under way, and it was not what Rumsfeld was looking for. But the immediate, and perhaps the only, goal for Buikema was to be able to get word to the Secretary that SOUTHCOM and the JTF were into the interrogation business—even if that meant making merely cosmetic efforts as a prelude to setting up something more substantial, a more detailed and organized plan for mounting a systematic intelligence effort on the ground.

When Buikema arrived, he first had to acquaint himself with what Tim Nichols, the astute J-2 of JTF 160, had been doing. On January 17, for example, Tim Nichols flew to SOUTHCOM with his "counterintelligence guys to discuss exploitation so that the global war on terror could benefit from this." According to Nichols, at that moment "the focus switched from construction to intelligence. And that has been the focus ever since."[23] The difference was that intelligence was not yet a policy. So, for a time, intelligence at Guantanamo was there but not there—a shadowy activity ongoing but not yet named or categorized, or aimed at a clear strategic goal.

For Nichols, before Rumsfeld's VTC and Buikema's arrival on the base, intelligence was not specifically about interrogation. It was mostly about arm's-length information gathering. His tower guards kept careful track of the movements and personal interactions of the detainees, and his analysts tried to decipher the budding hierarchies and chart out the lines of communications among them. He was ever on the lookout for telling "signs and signals." The goal was to understand the environment: Who knew whom? Who were the leaders? Who was the henchman? Who delivered the *adhan*, or Muslim call to prayer? Knowing the answers could help him and his team discern the group dynamics and thus improve both detention policies and intelligence-gathering efforts.

Having taken possession of the files and pocket litter that arrived on the planes with the detainees, Nichols rummaged for additional information from prior investigations. He read through the files, debriefed the guards after every shift, studied the guards' reports, and discussed with Lehnert the identity of the detainees and what they could make of it all. Observing and analyzing, he had documented the patterns of sociability among the prisoners and made some headway, figuring out the hierarchy that seemed to have spontaneously emerged within the camp. When Lehnert lifted the ban against talking on January 22, Nichols's job as well as the psychological comfort of the detainees was eased.

Tim Nichols's observation and analysis work had provided some basic groundwork for intelligence gathering. Nichols's specialty—honed during exposure to Afghan and Arab culture during his service for CENTCOM in Afghanistan—was studying the detainees and their interactions for intelligence. For him, the way enemy forces communicated among themselves was a window into their larger organizational structure, at least in theater. With Nichols in charge, passive observations by guards in the towers and inside the wire could disclose rudimentary facts, such as relations of authority and deference, that if nothing else would help preserve discipline in the camps.

Nichols was concerned about the mandate to interrogate, largely because he and his staff lacked the preliminary background information necessary to carry out effective interrogations. Nichols's approach followed from the assumption that good interrogation comes from knowing as much as you can about the person in custody. Before going into an interrogation, an interrogator studies the person's history as well as his belongings, which can include anything from the food in his pocket to his computer hard drive. The point is to convince the person being questioned that his interrogator knows him, knows a great deal about him, and if he lies, the interrogator will know it. The greater the background knowledge, the greater the likelihood that valuable information will come out of the interrogation.

Nichols knew just what this theory meant when applied to the arriving detainees. "In order to effectively interrogate somebody," he says, "you need all the circumstances of their capture, you need all of what we call their pocket litter, which is anything that was on them in terms of papers, notebooks, pictures, wallets, passports...cell phones...You need all that stuff—and anything that they say or do or anyone with whom they're affiliated, because then you can give all that to an interrogator." But the "pocket litter" from the captured al Qaeda and Taliban was nearly worthless. "Some guys came with stuff, and some guys came with nothing," he explains. "Sometimes we got plastic bags full of stuff that wasn't associated with a single person. So, you would have captured material, but you wouldn't know who had it. So, it's essentially ineffective...The bottom line is—in order for us to conduct interrogations, you need all that stuff to prepare yourself for—so that the guy that you're talking to, you know, if he knows that you don't know anything, not even his name, or anything, you're not gonna get anywhere." Standard operating procedure, as outlined in FM34–52,[24] which based preparation for interrogation upon a thorough immersion in the background materials of the suspect, just wasn't going to work with these detainees.

When Buikema arrived, Nichols was candid with his fellow Marine Corps officer about the appalling dearth of background information on the detainees. Yet together, the two-man team started to prepare for the interrogations in an effort to comply with Rumsfeld's orders. But just what information JTF 160 or the J-2s would be able to deliver remained to be seen.

On the surface, the SECDEF had ordered SOUTHCOM to design, assemble, and set in motion a viable interrogation operation. But the emphasis on intelligence marked a shift away from JTF 160's work on the ground thus far. The task force's attention to detention, and its avoidance of the intense and unstinting interrogations that the SECDEF felt were imperative, made SOUTHCOM as well as Michael Lehnert look like a hindrance rather than a help for the intelligence missions.

In short, JTF 160 was not the reliable ally Rumsfeld sought in his venture. As a result, a correction was in order. Something outside of JTF 160 was necessary—an intelligence operation and command structure that the secretary of defense could have more direct control over, one that would report to him more directly and understand his purposes more sympathetically.

So while SOUTHCOM did its best to follow the Secretary's orders and shift into high gear in the matter of interrogations, he was already deeply involved in finding an alternate route to interrogations at Guantanamo Bay. But first, he would have to ensure that the same sluggishness that he now perceived at SOUTHCOM and in JTF 160 did not appear in the legal realm.

The legal counterpart to Rumsfeld's push for more serious interrogations at Guantanamo had begun with the Military Order of November 13, 2001, and continued through the War Council's draft memo of January 9, Taft's response memo of January 11, and the Bybee/Yoo memo of January 22. Here, the lawyers and policy makers had identified the points of contention that would continue to divide them: Would the Geneva Conventions apply to al Qaeda and the Taliban? Would the detainees be prisoners of war? Would there be judicial review for the military commissions down at Guantanamo? After the first rounds of legal memos had been exchanged between Washington agencies and offices, the War Council continued to press its case, despite the writing on the wall.

For Taft and his team, as we have seen, the Geneva Conventions were not written in stone; they allowed for flexibility when it came to the actual context in which they were being applied, in interrogation as in more mundane issues such as housing. The lead lawyer for the State Department's legal response to the January 22 memo, David Bowker—the "one with the pen," according to Taft—recalled one meeting where of the War Council's false charges of State Department inflexibility became alarmingly clear.

After the memo circulated, Yoo visited Taft and his team at their offices to state his case for the new legal paradigm that according to him and his War Council colleagues was required by the unprecedented national security risks that the war on terror posed. Taft, however, was unyielding. He had become legal advisor to the State Department only after serving as general counsel to the Department of Defense—now Jim Haynes's job—and deputy secretary of defense in the 1980s. Taft was therefore well-versed in the rules and proto- cols of military law and international law. As a result, he could not understand why Yoo was so insistent on breaking with the Geneva Conventions, why he wouldn't just utilize the flexibility at hand. Taft and his lawyers were still not persuaded that the U.S. government should renege upon its legal obligations to uphold the tenets of the Geneva Conventions. As they reasoned to Yoo and others, "If you're not going to violate the Conventions, then why create the legal space to do so?" As Taft and others explained to Yoo repeatedly, even for interrogations there was more room than the OLC was allowing. There was, in the minds of the lawyers at State, ample room to interrogate, ample leeway within the law. As in a police interrogation, they argued, interrogators could throw a chair against the wall, get aggressive, raise their voice, take away a blanket. But they were still subject to the Geneva Conventions.

Finally, according to Bowker, Taft turned to Yoo and asked, "John, what is it that the administration wants to do? We agree that you don't need to give POW status. The requirements are not satisfied. But there is flexibility within the law, within the Geneva Conventions themselves and how they apply. So why do you need to make this point, that the Geneva Conventions do not apply?" There was a moment of silence in the room. Yoo looked around, poker-faced, and then told Taft: "We have an Article 17 problem."[25]

Article 17 addresses matters of interrogation. It states:

> Every prisoner of war, when questioned on the subject, is bound to give only his surname, first names and rank, date of birth, and army, regimental, personal or serial number, or failing this, equivalent information. . . . No physical or mental torture, nor any other form of coercion, may be inflicted on prisoners of war to secure from them information of any kind whatever. Prisoners of war who refuse to answer may not be threatened, insulted, or exposed to any unpleasant or disadvantageous treatment of any kind.

Such limitations preclude intense forms of interrogation, and therefore posed a "problem" in regard to the program Rumsfeld envisioned if it applied to the detainees. If they didn't want to give more than name, rank, and serial number, Yoo argued (and continues to argue to this day), the U.S. authorities couldn't even take away their toothbrushes.

Yoo's argument placed his earlier memos in context—a point that had been elusive earlier, since the word "interrogation" had never even appeared in the memo trail. Still, his appeal to the legal dissenters in the State Department amounted to asking them to assent to the creation of a legal space for coercive interrogation that was outside the bounds of international law. Bowker claims that State never contemplated that they were being urged to acquiesce to a secret government initiative designed, among other things, to allow the interrogation of prisoners outside of the bounds of international law. But he did conclude that Yoo's interpretation amounted to a violation of Article 2 of the Constitution in that the executive was no longer agreeing to the promise to "preserve, protect, and defend the Constitution of the United States."

The very first overt mention of interrogation in writing came from Powell's office—the result of Taft's responses to the Yoo memo. While Rumsfeld had been down at Guantanamo touring the site (and while someone in the White House leaked to the *Washington Times* the statement that Powell, contrary to rumor, was on board with the newly emerging detention policy), Powell was formulating his official response to the January 22 memo. His memo, dated January 26, took a more functional approach than prior legalist approaches. Powell's argument was that whether or not Geneva applied, many issues remained unaffected. He made the argument about flexibility central to his response. With or without Geneva, "the same practical flexibility in how we treat detainees, including with respect to interrogation and length of the detention," existed. Not following Geneva, the Powell memo argued, "may provoke some individual foreign prosecutors to investigate and prosecute our officials and our troops." In other words, again echoing the debates between OLC and State, the War Crimes Act would prevail whether the United States liked it or not. It was a revelatory memo, naming the real issues at stake. Powell had named interrogation and prisoner treatment as the issue. He had named war crimes as the possible punishment.[26]

Even with both clarity and law on his side, Powell's retort barely caused a ripple. The match—all of it taking place in secret, without public or congressional vetting—was fixed, and those on Powell's side were the losers. On February 7, President Bush declared formally that the Taliban and al Qaeda "do not qualify as prisoners of war," and thus were not entitled to the rights guaranteed under the Geneva Conventions. For the record, the president reiterated, now a month later, the same vague directive that had been given to Lehnert and others as they first landed at Guantanamo: "As a matter of policy, the United States Armed Forces shall continue to treat detainees humanely and, to the extent appropriate and consistent with military necessity, in a manner consistent with the principles of Geneva." Notably, the memo mentioned the nation's armed forces, but no other government actors such as the CIA, one of the agencies that received the memo.[27]

With his February decree, Bush brushed aside international law, both as a system for either regulating U.S. behavior or punishing it. The disregard for international law confused many and astonished others. As Taft would later comment, "Why lawyers, of all people, should want to establish the point that such a lawless regime could legally exist, even as a theoretical matter, much less recommend that one actually be created, is, I confess, beyond me."[28]

Taft was never at peace with the notion of granting the authority to violate the Geneva Conventions. He reasoned that such power would not actually lead to any policies per se. Rather, he—as Prosper had done earlier, and as he persuaded himself to do now—trusted his fellow lawyers to act ultimately as public servants who, when push came to shove, would take the correct and legal course.

Confronted with the unyielding persistence of John Yoo, backed by the War Council center of power in the executive branch, Taft agreed to a compromise. He would sign off on the memo, though he remained completely unconvinced on the point about the Geneva Conventions not applying to al Qaeda or the Taliban, but Gonzales would agree that the memo exempting the United States from the Conventions be classified. In this way, Taft hoped to protect the United States from the calumny of world opinion, thinking it would be "toxic to our foreign policy," and to ride out the evident panic that had over-taken his colleagues at OLC and elsewhere.

Part of Taft's acquiescence was based on his own experience inside the Pentagon. He knew the military well. As Taft puts it, "I had confidence in the military." He knew how essential following the Geneva Conventions was to officers and enlisted men. He knew that they would comply with Geneva if told to do so, as Lehnert was in fact determined to do.

The naïveté of Taft, like that of Prosper before him, was based on another factor as well. It did not occur to them that something more nefarious could be brewing behind the legal antics of their colleagues: that, for example, the request for there to be no judicial review of the Guantanamo detainees and the military commissions could be about protecting illegal activities on the part of the U.S. government.

Laying the legal foundation, of course, was only one form of preparation. Organizational preparation was important as well. For effective interrogation, you need a strong and centralized structure of operations. Informal interro-gations, more aptly called interviews, were already taking place constantly during the in-processing of the arriving detainees and during the visits of the various sunglass-sporting visitors—DIA, FBI, CIA, Secret Service, INS, and the Naval Criminal Investigative Service (NCIS). Some sort of organizational structure, some sort of coordination was needed to avoid the spectacle and waste of separate interrogation units redundantly asking the same questions, many of them not very sophisticated or knowledgeable—for example, "Did you know Mullah Omar?" or "Will you admit that you are a fighter?" As one study of military interrogation explains, "control over the operations and adminis-tration of a strategic interrogation program should be direct and unambigu-ous. This authority should be exercised exclusively by a single office" able to "cut across areas of responsibility for combatant commands."[29]

Toward that end, Rumsfeld needed to think beyond the organizational and legal structures already in place.

JTF 160 was clearly not designed for supervising, even administratively, such a complex intelligence effort. Instead, a new entity was needed. So the military chain of command began to discuss the possibility of a second military unit at Guantanamo. This unit would be titled JTF 170 and its purpose would be to coordinate the various intelligence-gathering efforts at Guantanamo.

There were numerous pros and cons to establishing such a unit. On the pro side, it could theoretically reduce competition between the intelligence agencies, a necessity for the effective use of information. It could also give some coherence to the questioning of detainees. Rather than different actors with different questions and different agendas, there could be streamlined, coordinated interrogations. And presumably it would improve the Pentagon's chances of getting the kind of information it needed.

But for all of the positives, there were negatives looming in the very idea of a separate intelligence unit. Most notably, the creation of a separate entity solely for intelligence gathering would violate a central tenet of military protocol— namely, the imperative of maintaining unity of command and unity of effort. The concept of unity of command harkened back to the beginnings of organized warfare, with both Sun Tzu and Clausewitz holding it as a central rule in their respective tomes. In modern times, General Eisenhower had made unity of command a preeminent part of his articulated theory of war.

Beyond the interference with command efficiency, there were other problems with deciding to set up a separate interrogation effort. The first was the matter of the purposes for which the information would be used.

From the very beginning of the discussions about intelligence gathering, all the parties overlooked a persistent discrepancy. While Donald Rumsfeld and others equivocated about information and interrogation, custody and the like, there was a deeper and more important confusion that was being papered over and generally left outside of discussion—the discrepancy between information to be used for trials before military commissions and information for strategic and operational ends.

Guantanamo had been set up in the fall as the military commissions were being vetted by the legal and policy communities. The debates in Congress and in the press were all about whether or not the president's military commissions, as his lawyers envisioned them, would allow sufficient legal protections for the detainees. When applied to the detainees in Afghanistan and on their way to the United States, processes designed to elicit "information" had nothing to do with preparing for trial but were solely for strategic purposes—to prevent a future attack.

But as the detainees arrived at Guantanamo and settled into place, the day-trippers who came to interrogate them were following two competing agendas. In theory, the FBI was there to help build cases against the detainees as well as to find out details of planned attacks or operatives of note. The CIA, like the DIA, was there to detect and stop future attacks. But the overlap and blurring of missions meant that the overall purpose of information gathering was murky at best. This lack of clarity played an essential role in the way Guantanamo was transformed from a detention camp into an interrogation facility.

The problem wasn't merely the lack of expertise within JTF 160 or at SOUTHCOM, over which General Jackman had lamented. The deeper problem was that the military commissions seemed to have disappeared as a priority in the first weeks of Guantanamo. Bob Buehn remembers scouring the base in search of a suitable site for a courthouse and finding a nice piece of level ground. Day after day, week after week, he awaited orders to begin the building process. But none came, and over time he began to realize that the courthouse was not going to materialize. Likewise, concern for legal processes was hard to detect in the methods applied by the miscellaneous agents who arrived on an erratic schedule to interrogate the detainees. Nor did the language of the Pentagon and its officials attempt to hide this fact. The mission now, with no official public notice of the change in purpose, had become one of interrogation for "combat support," not for the purpose of bringing the terrorists to justice.

There were still no substantive signs of military commissions. In fact, on February 1, the Pentagon set up CITF, the Criminal Investigation Task Force, for the purpose of arranging the military trials. A joint task force, CITF was comprised of agents from the criminal investigative agencies of the services: Criminal Investigation Division (CID) for the Army, Naval Criminal Investigative Service (NCIS) for the Navy, and the Office of Special Investigations (OSI) for the Air Force. The chain of command for CITF went through CID and thus the Army, and ultimately to Haynes in the Office of the Secretary of Defense.[30] Meanwhile, in Washington, lawyers were becoming deeply involved in conversations about the procedures for running the commissions. Military lawyers had been given some indication of what the Pentagon's rules for the new commissions would be, and were worried. In a prolonged discussion with OSD, their protests echoed those of Lehnert and JTF 160. They did not want to be put in the position of violating protocol, not to mention the law.

In particular, the Army was concerned that the detainees would not have access to civilian lawyers and that this would compromise the process, and with it the Army. As the Army's Judge Advocate General, Maj. Gen. Thomas J. Romig, wrote in a memo to Jim Haynes: "There is no greater proof of the government's confidence in the fairness of its proceedings than to open them to participation and scrutiny of any qualified attorney that an accused individual can secure."[31] The pushback from the Army and others in the administration meant that there would be no agreed-upon policy for the first several months of 2002.

The substitution of one agenda for another, or rather for two others—interrogation for detention and interrogation for military tribunals—was critical to the future of Guantanamo. It wasn't just a matter of Rumsfeld's insistence upon information. The turnabout also reflected the realization early on that the kind of information needed for bringing anyone to trial was simply not available. General Lehnert remembers reviewing the detainees' files with Nichols sometime in the first weeks of Guantanamo. Nichols had shaken his head in disbelief, telling the general that there was no way he could foresee building any sort of legal case given the sketchiness or total absence of incriminating evidence.[32]

When Tim Nichols confided in General Lehnert that he didn't think the evidence existed to try these guys, he may have had a lingering suspicion about something else. He, along with others, had begun to doubt just how dangerous these detainees might be. One nonagenarian detainee, one dying prisoner, and "Wild Bill," the noisily masturbating schizophrenic, all sharpened doubts. Skepticism continued to pile up. When Staff Sergeant Arthur Parra phoned a friend back in Afghanistan to ask about Wild Bill, the friend knew just who he was talking about—the man who had apparently already been considered crazy in the theater of battle. Tim Nichols got a similar story from his contacts in Afghanistan.

There is no way to pinpoint an exact date on which the members of JTF 160 fully acknowledged that most of the detainees at Guantanamo just did not seem to be the worst of the worst, although Lehnert confesses to knowing in the first weeks that the major portion of his prisoners were not particularly dangerous or hardened terrorists. And the same kind of doubts spread to the matter of intelligence. For his part, Tim Nichols broke it down into three categories. Some were likely to have "some moderate intelligence value. A larger group had less than moderate intelligence value. But most had none." The largest group, in Nichols's estimation, clearly had nothing of substance to offer and should not have been there at all.[33]

A wide swath of JTF 160 staff shared Lehnert's and Nichols's early doubts about both the guilt of and the danger posed by the detainees. In a series of interviews that the Marine Corps conducted in the first week of March, the attitude toward the detainees and the mission itself had lost much of the vengeful energy that fueled the mad rush to build X-Ray in the first place. In place of fear and distrust, empathy and a sober assessment of who these detainees were not began to find a home. Saif's presence may have in some ways encouraged the change in attitude, as his conversations with the detainees had humanized them in a way that had been impossible under the no-talking regulations that existed when the camp first opened. So, too, Lehnert's frequent presence and his emphasis on responding to the needs and complaints of the detainees may have chipped away at the aura of unknowable evil that the detainees had arrived with.

As the soldiers began to lower their guard a little, they recognized many similarities between themselves and the detainees—young men, some seemingly at the outer fringes of the socioeconomic spectrum, who had looked forward to the danger and camaraderie and purpose of battle. Accordingly, when interviewed in early March 2002 by Marine officers documenting the events at X-Ray, the officers and enlisted men interviewed expressed more concern about the preferential treatment accorded the detainees than about any dangers posed by those in their custody.

At the higher levels of command, the intelligence value of the detainees was coming under question. According to one investigation, former Secretary of the Army Thomas White echoed Nichols's observation when he told investigators a third of the population didn't belong there.[34] According to Rear Admiral Donald Guter, in the spring of 2002 a senior Army intelligence officer told him "that we're not getting anything because there might not be anything to get."[35] The presence of the elderly and infirm was circumstantial evidence that Guantanamo might have been as much a dumping ground for bodies that were in Tommy Franks's way as a detention center for carefully selected individuals with some intelligence value to offer or who posed a danger.

Sensibilities and guesses aside, it was unclear in early February just what kind of information the detainees might possess. As secretary of defense, Rumsfeld felt that it was his duty to go the extra mile and find out what they knew. His desperation for even minimal information was clear. "The faster we can interrogate these people and identify them," the safer Americans would be, the Secretary said.[36] Having captured them and transported them, it was perhaps hard to admit so early on that so many mistakes had been made. If they did have valuable information—even their names—to offer, Donald Rumsfeld was determined to get it out of them. He would shatter china if that's what it took to get things rolling in that direction.

On February 16, SOUTHCOM received the execute order for an intelligence mission. The combatant command was ordered to stand up a new unit, JTF 170, which was to coordinate U.S. military and government agency interrogation efforts in support of Operation Enduring Freedom. Essentially, Guantanamo was given the mission of interrogation for the entire global war on terror. And with the execute order, the transformation of Guantanamo from a prison camp into an interrogation facility had begun.

According to Jackman, the idea of JTF 170 was a "recipe for disaster," an affront to the philosophy of unity of command. JTF 160's mission had been downgraded, and therefore the unit would face an even more difficult struggle for adherence to law. Similarly, Taft and his team were never again consulted on the issue of Guantanamo and the legal status of the detainees.

Lehnert, meanwhile, stood in the middle of the brewing storm. He was to continue his role, but now there would be a parallel command with a vastly more important responsibility—from the point of view of the Pentagon—than that of care and custody. Lehnert's team would now be supporting not the operation in the Afghan theater but the interrogation operation of JTF 170. From soldiers to handymen, from players in the war on terror to lackeys, his troops, as well as the detainees themselves, faced a new challenge in the form of JTF 170.

To complete the transformation of Guantanamo and of JTF 160, the newly created unit still needed its own commander. It would have to be someone with firsthand knowledge of intelligence gathering through interrogations. Someone whom the Pentagon and the secretary of defense could trust. Someone who was not averse to tossing protocol aside to get things done. And above all, it should be someone holding a higher rank than Michael Lehnert.

10

A Political Animal

He told me what he wanted; not how to do it.

— Maj. Gen. Michael Dunlavey

On Friday, February 15, six weeks into the Gitmo operation, Michael Lehnert ferried to the leeward side to greet the day's planeload of Washington VIPs. The group of executive-branch officials was arriving for what was becoming known as the standard "windshield tour" of the detention facility.

One of those who stepped onto the tarmac and into the bright midday sunlight that day was Pierre Prosper, the newly appointed head of the diplomatic mission attached to the Guantanamo detainees. His principal job would henceforth be traveling to the detainees' countries of origin and making arrangements for the return of some of them as either relocated or released detainees. He looked around at the others on his flight. This particular group included Elliott Abrams (known for his criminal conviction for withholding information from Congress about the Iran-Contra affair), who, along with John Bellinger, legal adviser to the National Security Council at the White House, had assumed the joint directorship of the interagency group that Prosper once ran. Also on the plane was Lincoln Bloomfield, like Prosper from the State Department. Prosper's eyes also lit upon someone he did not recognize. Energetic, blustery, and dressed in army fatigues, the middle-aged man projected himself as someone with a purpose. Not unfriendly, but supremely self-confident, he introduced himself as "the new head of the intelligence operation down here."[1]

Press coverage during the preceding two weeks had softened somewhat. The persistent criticisms of Guantanamo had been toned down. At the beginning of February, media outlets were reporting that the facility was settling down. The New York Times described a tea party following a successful surgery on the detainee whose eye had to be removed. In the words of the report, it was "a formal ceremony that marks an informal easing of tensions here as the American captors and their prisoners begin to see each other in human terms." Overall, the article concluded, "some of the tension of the early days

[is] dissolving into familiarity, if not entirely with each other, at least with their roles and routines."[2]

Signs of this newfound stability were visible elsewhere as well. Even Carrico, as he was later to reveal in interviews, had begun to see the prisoners as "calm and cooperative," and basically more compliant. "I think they understand that they're going to be treated humanely," Carrico explained. "I think when they got here, there was a real question. As we've proved to the world that we are treating them humanely, I think they have become more at ease."[3]

Several memoirs of this period, written a year or more afterward by some of the first detainees interned at X-Ray, also indicate that a sense of ease had settled over the camp in early February. Asif Iqbal, detainee #87, recalls that during this time, the MPs and the detainees began to talk casually to one another about their mutual situation—just as Carrico had feared. The guards even began confiding in the detainees. According to Iqbal, for example, the guards revealed that they had been told that the detainees were "wild animals." The detainees also learned, in Iqbal's words, that the guards had been warned that we were ready to "kill them with our toothbrushes at the first opportunity, that we were all members of al Qaeda and that we had killed women and children indiscriminately."[4] The detention atmosphere had evolved; the guards now felt safe enough with their captives to acknowledge that they were not the monsters the soldiers had been led to expect.

Having become increasingly confident of his achievements, Michael Lehnert was not fully conscious of the larger project being developed and implemented at the time. Nor did he realize that the short visit of this new head of intelligence would mark the beginning of the end for his plan for a humane and professionally run detention facility at Guantanamo. The "looky-look" and soon to be commanding presence at the camp would strain to the breaking point the equilibrium Lehnert had managed to effect, bringing to a head the incompatibility between smoothly managed detention and urgent interrogation.

In the words of Galen Jackman, Major General Michael Dunlavey was a "political animal."[5] His career had been meteoric in nearly every period and context of his life. His strategic savvy and personal maneuvering were noteworthy. Like Haynes and Rumsfeld, with whom he would work closely, he was a product of ROTC, having attended Notre Dame. His mixture of aggressive ambition and talent evident even then, he had been commissioned after two years of ROTC rather than after the usual four years.

Assigned to infantry school, he was transferred to intelligence training, serving in Vietnam in 1970–71 as a combat intelligence officer, operating as part of III Corps between Saigon and the Cambodian border. He later liked to brag that he had interrogated 3,000 suspects there.[6] He received three medals for his service in Vietnam: two bronze stars and the Vietnamese Gallantry Cross.

Returning to civilian life, he attended the University of Buffalo Law School and settled down in Erie, Pennsylvania, first working for the district attorney and then shifting to private practice. In 1999, he was elected county court judge for Erie. Despite the demands of his profession and a family of four children, Dunlavey's commitment to the military remained central to his life.

His rise in the Army Reserves began in the 1970s and was just as impressive as his earlier military and legal careers. From the late 1970s to the late 1990s, he racked up promotion after promotion. In 1977, he became a major. In 1985, at 38, he rose to become the youngest full colonel in the Army. In 1993, he was appointed deputy commanding general of INSCOM, the Army Intelligence and Security Command at Fort Belvoir, Virginia. And in 1997, he was assigned to the Pentagon, to work for Lieutenant General Claudia Kennedy, the senior intelligence officer on duty there. Dunlavey shuttled back and forth from Erie to the Pentagon weekly to work on budgetary and personnel issues. Or so he claimed in an interview with his local paper, which added that Dunlavey could not fully describe his duties. "He does work extensively with the FBI, the CIA, and intelligence officers from other branches of the military," the paper reported. "He travels worldwide."[7]

Dunlavey's dedication did not go unrewarded. In 1995, he earned his first star. Two years later, he received a second star. Then, in 2000, as a major general, he was named mobilization assistant to the director of the National Security Agency (NSA), who at that time was Michael Hayden. The job was significant even in peacetime, when it involved supervising all reserve personnel attached to the NSA. Known as "cryppies" for their decoding skills, these reservists attended monthly weekend drills and went on active duty once a year for a two-week stint, usually to NSA headquarters. If "wartime" ever came, Dunlavey was slated to retain this position and oversee the mobilization of all the reserves tasked to work alongside NSA personnel.

Like other military units after the end of the Cold War, the NSA had been seriously downsized during the 1990s. The result was that on-call reserve units became essential to NSA's ability to respond to a crisis, and even a reserve major general could be an important player. Dunlavey wasn't modest about his new prestige, boasting to the press that he held "the highest-ranking position for any reserve intelligence officer in the military. . . . "[8]

Following the attacks of September 11, Dunlavey took a leave from his judgeship, assuming full-time the position of mobilization assistant to the director of NSA. He threw himself enthusiastically into the alternate life track for which his reserve work had prepared him.

The Pentagon had turned its attention and expectations to its signals intelligence arm, the NSA, in the immediate aftermath of 9/11. By September 2001, the NSA had become the largest spy organization in the world, at least according to Jim Bamford, an historian of the agency. The chief purpose of "the most sophisticated, pervasive, and secret of organizations" since its inception in 1952 was to use electronic surveillance and code breaking in order to prevent a surprise attack—a vital mission of the U.S. military in the war on terror.[9]

By the year 2001, as a result, Dunlavey had developed active ties with some of the principal players in the national security network in Washington. His work at INSCOM had given him not only an understanding of the NSA but also a familiarity with its personnel, including Michael Hayden. He also had some acquaintance with Homeland Security Director Tom Ridge. Both Pennsylvania lawyers, they had crossed paths in the political as well as in the professional realm. Dunlavey had thrown a victory luncheon for Ridge when he was elected to the governorship in November 1994. It was another link connecting Dunlavey to the innermost circles of executive power. His skill at playing the promising cards he had been dealt over the years was never in doubt.

For the intelligence command at Guantanamo, it was difficult for the Pentagon and the military intelligence hierarchy to imagine anyone with better military and civilian qualifications. In the military realm, Dunlavey's skills included not only combat intelligence operations, which he often said included interrogations, but also signals intelligence and communications. In addition, he came out of the reserves, and Washington was decidedly loath, given the uncertainties of the ongoing war in Afghanistan and the impending war with Iraq, to assign an active duty general to the position, given the shortage of personnel and the escalating requirements that the military was anticipating.

But Dunlavey's background as a lawyer and judge was of equal significance. His legal skills became an immediate weapon in the debate that was brewing in D.C. Having requested and received legal blessing for its detention and interrogation policy from the War Council, the administration probably considered itself able to speak with authority and swat away civil-liberties concerns when and if the potential illegality of American detainee policy became an issue.

Dunlavey's familiarity with the way the policy debate was being framed in Washington could help him parry the growing criticisms on grounds of constitutional and international law. The administration knew that it was entering uncharted waters, and Dunlavey had the requisite intelligence savvy to be the point man on legal matters at Guantanamo. His background as a conservative prosecutor and judge, moreover, meant that he shared a common idiom and frame of reference with the War Council. As the man on the ground for the Office of the Secretary of Defense (OSD), Dunlavey could talk directly to Haynes about detention, interrogation, and surveillance, sharing assumptions about how far statutes, treaties, and constitutional principles could be reasonably stretched, reinterpreted, and circumvented in a time of national emergency.

The effect of Dunlavey's appointment did not end there. It had a symbolic appeal as well. He was also able to receive visiting law-enforcement officials and impress them as a recognizable colleague. Rather than meeting a military officer, foreign investigators from police departments and prosecutors' offices abroad would now be interacting with a man of the law. As one visiting police investigator from Europe recalled about his meeting Dunlavey at Guantanamo, "He was a judge. It was impressive."[10]

But Dunlavey's legal expertise paled when compared to his intelligence qualifications for the job at hand. He did not have a background in international law, any more than John Yoo had been an expert on the laws of armed conflict when he sat down to write his controversial memos. But Dunlavey was adept at moving from one area to another while retaining or even improving his previously acquired status. For instance, he capitalized on his military experience to give him a leg up in the civilian sphere. He had campaigned for his judgeship in a close race as a veteran and reservist, stressing that he held "the highest rank in the Army Reserves," and that his experience with Vietnam battlefields made him the "only candidate who has had to make decisions of life and death of those in my charge."[11] There was nothing especially cynical or manipulative about this pulling of rank. In his every endeavor, Dunlavey's prime moral and emotional identification was with military intelligence. This is no doubt why Rumsfeld sent him to Guantanamo.

Several days after his trip to Guantanamo, Dunlavey found himself in the office of the secretary of defense. Deputy Secretary Wolfowitz and others were present. This, according to Dunlavey, is when he was briefed on the purpose of his mission. "The SECDEF needed a common sense way to do business."[12] Rumsfeld also, according to Philippe Sands, encouraged Dunlavey "to report directly to him, on a weekly basis, bypassing SOUTHCOM and the usual chain of command." When someone suggested that Dunlavey should report to SOUTHCOM, Rumsfeld, at least according to Dunlavey, blurted out, "I don't care who he is under. He works for me."[13] Three years later, when interviewed by the DOD for a report on detainee abuses at Guantanamo, Dunlavey boasted of taking his instructions from a still loftier authority. "I got my marching orders from the President of the United States."[14]

Whoever issued the orders, Dunlavey himself had a crystal clear and unwavering sense of mission: to obtain what Rumsfeld and those around him were urgently seeking—namely "intelligence now." Moreover, the SECDEF wasn't going to micromanage the business. He left it to Dunlavey's expertise and experience to figure out what it would take to extract vital intelligence from the closed-lipped worst of the worst. "He told me what he wanted," Dunlavey recalled, "not how to do it."[15]

Initially, there was no public announcement of Dunlavey's appointment. Very few knew who he was or what exactly he would be doing. Carol Rosenberg astutely guessed that he was the head of the new interrogation effort when she first saw him surveying the base, unnamed and unidentified. But no one would confirm this to her officially.[16]

It was Dunlavey who ultimately announced his role, and he did it in the same style with which he introduced himself to his fellow passengers on his first trip to Gitmo. He informed them that all of Guantanamo would one day be under his control. To meet Dunlavey was to learn, first thing, that he worked for the most important people in Washington. Dunlavey conveyed the sense to individuals at SOUTHCOM, to Lehnert, and to others that he was "personal friends with the Secretary of Defense" and "buddies with Tom Ridge."[17] At Guantanamo, he missed no opportunity to reiterate that he had Rumsfeld's ear. Some suspected that he really reported to Stephen Cambone, at that time the Principal Deputy Under Secretary of Defense for Policy. Others mentioned Haynes; still others said it was Tom Ridge. But Dunlavey worked hard to create the impression that although he reported officially to SOUTHCOM—to the chief intelligence officer (J-2) there, Brigadier General Ronald Burgess—he had a back channel to Rumsfeld himself. Day by day, he established his bona fides by repeatedly mentioning his relationships with key figures in OSD, a piece of bravado which those listening at Guantanamo did not know how to assess, but which few had the confidence to doubt.

Dunlavey's assertions about his own power and prestige were backed up by the fact that his rank in the reserves outstripped the ranks of the other officers in the normal reporting chain of command. General Burgess—though he had a strong intelligence background and a year later would become the J-2 for the Joint Staff—was only a one-star. So, too, as we have seen, Gary Speer, the Acting Commander at SOUTHCOM, held only an equivalent two stars. Dunlavey had no one above his rank to report to at SOUTHCOM. Once again, it became clear that by removing the four-star general Peter Pace from SOUTHCOM to make him the vice chairman of the Joint Staff, Rumsfeld had—inadvertently or not— given himself a means of delegitimizing the normal chain of command.

For the remaining weeks of February and into March, Dunlavey flew back and forth between the States and Guantanamo, gradually consolidating control of his new command. His job was to coordinate the various intelligence efforts being made by the anonymous polo-shirt men who came and went. At this stage, as Tim Nichols noted, the techniques and approaches being applied to the prisoners were not standardized in the least. Perhaps Dunlavey could set up a coherent system for conducting interrogations. Perhaps a less haphazard and more disciplined approach would help extract the information that was being so desperately requested from above.

As a first step, JTF 160 was unceremoniously instructed to turn over the data that had already been amassed on the detainees, beginning with the various packages that had arrived aboard the planes with the detainees. According to Lehnert, Dunlavey said "Just bring them over." Nichols appealed to General Burgess at SOUTHCOM for a chance to keep the documents, but Burgess supported Dunlavey's request. Lehnert agreed to release the documents, but he didn't want an informal handover without a clear bureaucratic structure in place capable of recording accurately the chain of custody. He required a signature of receipt for each file that was turned over. Dunlavey was initially reluctant but eventually relented. Lehnert appointed Tim Nichols to oversee this by-the-books process of transferring the material seized from the detainees.[18]

That he insisted on this bureaucratic formality was telling. Lehnert complains about "the bureaucracy" as much as any Marine engineer devoted to getting things done. But he also has a high regard for keeping things transparently legal, especially when his command is involved. And although it was good common sense to document the transfer of the detainees' dossiers, Lehnert's insistence on following process also revealed a strain of distrust on his part toward Dunlavey's preference for shortcuts over formalities. When

I asked him years later why he had organized the transfer of documents and materials in this highly legalistic way, Lehnert told me that he had simply wanted to make sure that the material wasn't tampered with. "For future prosecutions," he explained, he wanted "to avoid a situation where someone said we didn't know what happened to the paperwork."[19] Although he went along with Lehnert's chain-of-custody rules, Dunlavey himself—despite his training as a lawyer and his command's law enforcement mission—was too intensely focused on the immediate extraction of actionable intelligence to worry excessively about procedures designed for hypothetical war crimes trials to be conducted in some unspecified future year.

As Dunlavey established his presence at Guantanamo, Lehnert's suspicions were confirmed. Dunlavey was eager to take as much control as possible, hoping to dominate the 160 as well as his own unit, the 170. Among other things, Dunlavey wanted access to the members of Lehnert's command staff who had information about the detainees, beginning with Saifulislam.[20]

It was understandable that Dunlavey would think Saif had special information about the detainees. After all, he was in contact with them every day. He spoke with them, heard their thoughts. According to General Lehnert, Saif, and Tim Nichols, Dunlavey thought it imperative that Saif cooperate with the intelligence authorities and share whatever he learned of a personal nature from the detainees. He pressured Saif directly, letting him know that he expected the chaplain to give him information.

To say that being put in this position made Saif uncomfortable would be an understatement. His boyish good nature, his openness to the detainees, and his commitment to the ethics of a religious leader made this an untenable request. But he did not have the kind of psychological armor necessary to stand up to Dunlavey. Instead, Dunlavey, multiple ranks above him, frightened him.

The JTF had gone out of its way not to ask Saif for this kind of information. As Tim Nichols explained it, although Saif was helpful in explaining what was on the minds of the detainees in terms of how the detainees thought generally and what they were thinking about their detention, he was not considered a source of intelligence. As Nichols explained the distinction, "[W]hen we were trying to figure out why certain things were happening, you would talk to him and he would go, 'Well, this is the way that they think.'" But, Nichols continued, "I didn't want to use the chaplain as an intelligence tool....He wasn't a gatherer for me."[21]

It is likely that Saif had access to details about the detainees beyond their living conditions. He spoke to them about their families and about their circumstances, but neither he nor the detainees have ever indicated that they spoke about more than that. He counseled them and he represented them to Lehnert, as we have seen. And at times, he told me, he chose not to tell Lehnert everything he knew. But Lehnert's trust in Saif led to the assumption that if Saif did in fact know something of value, he would have found a way to pass it on.

Lehnert decided to ask Saif directly about what he would do if placed in a potentially compromising situation. "What if you learned of an attack that was being planned? What if you uncovered a plot?" Lehnert asked, referring to the possibility of an attack on the base itself. Saif reassured the general, insisting that, though he valued the confidences of the detainees, he would behave appropriately when it came to threats that would cause loss of life or harm to individuals. Lehnert had covered his legal and moral bases. He had asked, and in asking, confirmed his expectation that Saif would be a loyal sailor first and a chaplain second. Given the closeness of their relationship, Lehnert trusted Saif to do the right thing.[22]

Lehnert informed Dunlavey in no uncertain terms that Saif was not there to help with the interrogation effort.[23] For his part, Saif was greatly relieved to have someone stand up for him. Still, he was aware of the fact that some of his fellow soldiers as well as others higher up in command saw him as a possible collaborator. (Ironically, the detainees saw him as a likely spy as well as a tool of the military.) And in fact, each of the Muslim chaplains who would serve at Guantanamo would be suspected of becoming too close with the detainees. Saif took shelter under the protection of Lehnert, who maintained that the chaplain's role was not to be a spy.[24] Still, it was hard for Dunlavey to accept the fact that there was such a readily available source of information and that the chaplain could so nonchalantly stonewall requests for intelligence from the nation's security services. Saif knew that at some point, as yet undetermined, Lehnert and his team would be leaving Guantanamo. And he feared that he might have to stay, given the dearth of Muslim chaplains in the services. But he would jump that hurdle when he came to it.[25]

The conflict over Saif illustrated the pervasive problems of the parallel command structure. Technically, Lehnert did not have the authority to give Dunlavey orders. Nor was Dunlavey, technically, obliged to defer to Lehnert's decisions. As Lehnert explained the parallel structure to me, "He may have had two stars. And I had [only] one star. But he had no tasking authority over me. I had no tasking authority over him. He was the supported commander... I was the supporting commander."[26]

The idea that the American personnel at Guantanamo served a variety of not always compatible values (such as security, humanity, medical ethics, and so forth) made little sense to Dunlavey, for whom one value—national security—trumped all other concerns. It was in this spirit that Dunlavey went to talk to the psychiatrists at the medical center whom Al Shimkus had brought in to attend to the detainees' mental distress.[27] Just as he had consulted Saif, so Lehnert conferred with the experts before making a decision about the propriety of psychologists brought in to attend to the mental health of the detainees being for interrogation purposes. The psychiatrists let him know that they had deep reservations about sharing their information. They were there to aid the detainees, not to enable and improve interrogations. As Shimkus explained, getting involved in extracting intelligence compromised their professionalism. It was quite simply "unethical."[28] Lehnert informed Dunlavey of his decision. The psychiatrists would remain solely under the command of JTF 160.

Beyond seeking access to the potential sources of information on the base, Dunlavey sought to introduce new techniques into the interrogation process. He approached Lehnert with one such plan. His idea was to have men wearing black hoods conduct frighteningly intimidating raids on the cells, dragging away one or more of the detainees. The purpose of these unexpected bust-ins was to scare the detainees and thus intimidate the others into talking. Lehnert turned Dunlavey down. And he similarly refused his request to use pushing and shoving during interrogations.[29]

At X-Ray, in the meantime, the interrogations were not being filmed. Therefore, to prevent abusive treatment of the detainees inside the interrogation rooms, Lehnert relied on the system he and Carrico had devised early in the mission. They required that a guard be in the interrogation room at all times. Lehnert recognized that this was not a foolproof guarantee of decency inside the huts. The guards, after all, could be complicit with any interrogators who might want to use coercive means to get information from the detainees. But it was the best he could do. Here, as elsewhere, Lehnert never gave up his concern for the possibility that the young soldiers, sailors, and Marines could be roused into anger, something he was always on the lookout to deter.

With two people in charge, there was essentially no one in charge. Technically, that person could have been the Acting CINC at SOUTHCOM, Major General Gary Speer. But, in fact, for reasons of personality and rank, there was no unifying commander. The weakness at the top of the SOUTHCOM piece of the chain of command, with Speer as a two-star and the J-2 General Burgess as a one-star, fueled Dunlavey's conviction that he was equal or superior to those he ostensibly reported to.

Both Dunlavey and Lehnert recognized the stalemate created by the parallel commands of JTF 160 and JTF 170. Neither man had the power that he would have liked. And so they drew the lines carefully between their respective spheres. One night, Lehnert remembers taking a six-pack over to Dunlavey's quarters to discuss their different commands. There, in the cool night, they clarified the terms of the standoff. Dunlavey would not interfere with the detention effort, and Lehnert, reciprocally, wouldn't interfere with interrogations. This informally struck bargain meant that Lehnert had to refrain from certain actions he might otherwise have taken, as he expected Dunlavey to do in return.[30]

Subordinates within JTF 160 interpreted the improvised Lehnert-Dunlavey pact to mean that they should simply keep away from Dunlavey's operation. It was don't ask, don't tell. As Pat Alford described it, "My direction to my staff was, you will have absolutely nothing to do with an interrogation process. You don't ask about it. You don't get involved with it."[31]

At such a small and geographically isolated facility, however, it proved impossible to prevent unshielded contact between the two commands. Besides, Dunlavey's brashness and arrogant disrespect for others exacerbated the sense of conflict on the base. "Cowboyish," according to Tim Nichols,[32] he paraded around the base, in General Jackman's words, like someone who envisioned himself to be "a star player on the world stage."[33] Dunlavey asserted his presence after hours as well as at work. JTF 160 chief of staff Charles Brule described Dunlavey as a "fun-loving person" who "enjoyed having a drink with the troops."[34] In Migdalia Hettler's words, the JTF 170 commander "liked to party." This pleased some, but made wary those who considered such behavior "inappropriate."[35]

The standoff between JTF 160 and JTF 170, a direct result of Rumsfeld's cavalier disregard for—or intentional dismantling of—the unity of command, was essential to Dunlavey's success at building an independent mission, one that was basically inscrutable to outsiders and that very quickly began to subvert Lehnert's own, more transparent command.

Lehnert likes to describe the rivalry between the two commands in military terms. He sees it as Clausewitzian friction, as if it were a normal part of military engagement.[36] But it wasn't that. It was neither battlefield friction nor a bureaucratic turf war. It was about discovering an enemy within one's own ranks. And in this case it turned out to be an adversary with powerful links to the weightiest public officials in the country.

Dunlavey's ceaseless attempts to subordinate Lehnert's detention effort to his own interrogation agenda were to be expected. That was his job. But there was a more subtle—and more potent—dimension to what he was doing at Guantanamo. He was injecting uncertainty into the camp. His presence, like some subtle poison introduced into drinking water, could have a widespread effect. Where Lehnert had managed to create an accepted set of rules and expectations, Dunlavey introduced the unexpected. Where there had been one commander who insisted that things be done his way, with respect for the Geneva Conventions, there was now a countervailing voice with new ideas, some of which seemed to encourage disregard for procedure and law. Dunlavey had begun to subvert everything Lehnert stood for—his focus on established protocol, his adherence to the U.S. Constitution and the Geneva Conventions, his allegiance to the traditions of the uniformed military, and his sense of his own command responsibilities.

Details aside, Dunlavey was challenging the very atmosphere that Lehnert had been struggling against all odds to create. And the reason was not difficult to discover. The stability that Lehnert had worked so hard to introduce was, to Dunlavey, the last thing that would lead to fruitful interrogations. As the official military manual itself explained, the uncertainty and instability that resulted from "extreme disorientation," "a foreign environment," and the sense of having "no control" were key to an effective interrogation process. Stability and safety—psychological and physical—allowed for the return of "established values" and personal "mores." And then, as the army's manual warned, "much of an individual's susceptibility to interrogation is gone."[37]

From Dunlavey's perspective, then, Michael Lehnert had inadvertently done precisely the opposite of what interrogators would have wanted him to do. He had implemented policies aimed at restoring to the detainees a sense of coherent selfhood and self-worth, based on their own cultural values and mores. He had tried to make their strange new environment seem *less* foreign. He had given them a sense of control by enabling them to express their discontent and to seek comfort in familiar items, foods, and religious practices.

Lehnert's approach to detention, in other words, was violently at odds not only with the theory of penal detention embraced by Terry Carrico—a theory Lehnert's position allowed him to override if he so chose—but with the doctrine of interrogation that Dunlavey brought into Guantanamo. Having fought for a detention regime as opposed to a prison colony, having fought for lawful treatment though essentially given a free hand to do otherwise, Lehnert would now have to fight a rearguard battle for humane treatment in an atmosphere where national security concerns, and prevailing military doctrine, dictated the opposite.

It was only a matter of time before the tensions gathering force in JTF 160 would dominate the atmosphere of the camp. By the end of the month, the spirit of coherence and relative calm that had defined the first half of February began to falter. Eventually, the handful of individuals assigned to JTF 170 would grow to 200 men and women. But although they remained a small fragment compared to the 2,000-plus personnel who worked for JTF 160, JTF 170 had succeeded in upending the respect for order, stability, and protocol that Lehnert had worked tirelessly but futilely to establish.

And then, quite suddenly, the tense atmosphere that had marked the relations among American military factions began to spread to the prisoners in their cages. From now on, it turned out, the detainees would be fully active participants in the battle over the destiny of the camp.

11

Towels into Turbans

The simple fact that the general got there so quickly and in person...had

a much greater impact than we could possibly imagine.

—Nizar Sassi, Guantanamo Detainee #325

"15, 17, 14, No B, L, D"[1] was scribbled by hand on a large piece of canvas taped to the wall above the press desk. The sequence telegraphed an ongoing human drama in numbers and letters. To an outsider, it might have resembled some sort of enigmatic code. But everyone on the island base—officers, staff, the press, and even the detainees—knew exactly what it meant.

The numbers and letters referred to the first hunger strike at Guantanamo Bay, Cuba. Posted on the wall of the press office at the airfield where reporters and photographers gathered to file their stories, the code appeared daily during the strike on a poster-size piece of canvas that Rosenberg had made by unraveling one of the military burn bags used for disposing of government documents. Each letter signified a meal—breakfast, lunch, and dinner; each number, the count of detainees who continued to refuse food. The tally required no words.

The original hunger strike at X-Ray took many by surprise. According to Tim Nichols, it came "out of the blue." Not only had the troops and the guard force settled down into a recognizable routine, but the detainees, as we have seen, had developed some degree of trust in the newfound stability in the camp. Even the abuses of an overzealous guard force—the arbitrary punching, the shoving of prisoners' faces into the ground, the verbal assaults, and all the other methods of asserting their authority—had become commonplace and predictable. Still, for the most part, recognizable routines were being established under Carrico's and Lehnert's confident command. Violent excesses by U.S. personnel, though few, were grounds for reprimand, if not ejection from inside the wire.[2] One interpreter, for example, was removed from his post because of his inability to keep his temper in check.[3]

Although he appreciated the relative predictability that had begun to settle over the camp, General Lehnert was not among those surprised by the
prisoners' revolt that occurred during the first two weeks of March 2002. Signs
of stress were mounting as the month progressed, intensifying tensions—not
just among Lehnert's own troops, but also among the detainees. Lehnert worried daily about the mental condition of young men who were beginning to
realize fully what it meant to be trapped in a legal black hole. For all they knew
at this point, they could be held incommunicado at the camp for the rest of
their lives without ever being informed of a specific reason for their detention
or provided with a serious chance to argue that their seizure and transfer were
based on misinformation and mistaken identity.

Lehnert had visited with the detainees and tried to reassure them, but there
was no visible sign that a legal process was about to begin.[4] And while Lehnert,
who had some experience rescuing 20-year-olds from bouts of depression,
could try to buoy the detainees' hopes, he couldn't encourage his wards with
scenarios that as yet had little plausibility to them. There were still no military
commissions scheduled. There were still no lawyers with whom the detainees
might confer. There were no charges being leveled, and no criteria for release
available to share with the detainees.[5]

Lehnert responded to Washington's evident and continuing policy of
unclarity and silence by turning to logistical challenges. He might not be able
to settle the question of what would be done with the detainees, but he could
move forward on building a more permanent camp. Indefinite detention itself
might be a form of psychological torture, but at least the physical conditions
could be improved. How long, after all, could the detainees be kept in this
temporary situation, without running water, without flush toilets in their cells,
without privacy, and exposed to the sun?

Improving these conditions was something that Lehnert knew he could do
well and quickly and with minimal supervision from above. Despite the verbal
agreement he had received from Rumsfeld more than a month earlier about
the need to go ahead with Delta, Congress and DOD had yet to appropriate the
money for building the new camp.[6]

Frustrated and convinced that JTF 160 was sitting on top of a powder keg,
Lehnert decided to do everything he could with the resources at his disposal
to move things along. He had earlier assembled a team of Navy Seabees and
SOUTHCOM engineers and drafted a 1391, the necessary form for any build-
ing appropriation, specifying the work schedule and the preliminary budget.
The form had been submitted to Congress on February 1. It would have to be

approved by both Congress and the Pentagon.[7] The newer, larger facility was to be constructed at Radio Range, which had held the migrant camps in the 1990s. Located approximately five miles to the south of Camp X-Ray, the piece of land chosen for the new facility overlooked the ocean. In fact, Camp Delta had been on the drawing board since the very first days of the detainee operation. With the engineering plans in place, Lehnert and Brown & Root simply awaited the go-ahead. But plans, site selection, and the impatience of the command staff to begin the project did not suffice to propel it forward. For that, funding had to be approved and orders had to be issued.

Week after week, throughout February, Lehnert waited for approval. But he heard nothing. Feeling like he was balancing on a tightrope that could send him and his mission plummeting into free fall at any moment, he pushed incessantly to find out what the delay was all about. He also tried to raise public awareness of the importance of building the new facility, which would have walls and ceilings, some degree of privacy, and running water, and, because it was designed from the ground up as a prison, would require a much smaller guard force than the converted open field at X-Ray. While the requisite paperwork apparently languished unattended on Rumsfeld's desk,[8] Lehnert took every opportunity to mention to the press the need to begin construction at Radio Range. He even took the media out to the site at one point to show them the bulldozers ready and in place.[9] Washington, he implied, was somehow unaware of the need to start building a replacement for the obviously inadequate Camp X-Ray.

While sending distress signals, Lehnert simultaneously began work on those facets of the Camp Delta project that technically did not need budgetary approval and for which he could scrounge up the manpower and materiel. He could, and did, assemble the prefab container-style huts that would house the troops at the new site. He bulldozed the ground in preparation for the full-scale building effort when and if it began. He also oversaw the building of several model cells, constructed in accordance with Bureau of Prisons standards and approved by himself as well as Dunlavey. But still the green light to start constructing Camp Delta was not being given. Yet another symptom of Washington's negligence, this delay added to Guantanamo's atmosphere of precarious stability. The difference between order and disorder now hinged not only on the detention policy but on the construction effort as well.

Throughout February, Lehnert and his command staff could not be sure what was to come. This sense of limbo that Washington for some reason seemed bent on intensifying had repercussions inside the wire as well. Word spread rapidly to the detainees themselves, despite their insulation from the world. The name of Donald Rumsfeld was known to them, as were the secretary's attitudes toward them. Detainee #61, Murat Kurnaz, reports that the Red Cross informed one of the detainees that the United States was planning to hold them permanently. A detainee who Kurnaz refers to as "Salah" further told him that "Donald Rumsfeld believed we could be kept in these cages indefinitely and without a trial."[10] News and information circulated within the camp by other channels as well. Guards and other members of the task force were by no means uncommunicative. Day by day, the detainees were given to understand that they had no future at all. They had been left in Allah's hands, abandoned, unprotected, and lost to the world.

The first to notice the change in the camp's atmosphere was Saifulislam. February 23, 2002—a month to the day from when he arrived—marked the Muslim holiday of Eid al-Adha, the festival of sacrifice that commemorates Abraham's willingness to sacrifice his son Ishmael, as the Koran tells the story. Celebrated by prayer and the sharing of meat, Eid al-Adha comes at the end of the hajj, the annual pilgrimage that devout Muslims must make to Mecca at least once in their lives. It was the first major Muslim holiday to occur after the arrival of the detainees at X-Ray and, as such, it riveted the attention of the detainee population. As with any group of men removed from their families, the holiday brought to mind what they were missing. For the more religious, it reminded them that they were missing not just loved ones, but the hajj itself.

One week earlier, Saifulislam had begun to call attention to a new and worrisome melancholy spreading among the prisoners. He attributed their despondency to the coming holiday. "There is anxiety being played out at the moment," Saif told Rosenberg. "This is the first time that they are not able to celebrate the way they are used to."[11] But Saif added that, although the detainees wouldn't be able to slaughter a sheep as was the custom for the holiday, a special meal was being prepared for them in honor of the holiday.

Food was a general problem at X-Ray, and not only during religious holidays. It was a topic, as Saif said at the time, that was "as important as the five-times-a-day prayer call and his one-on-one spiritual meetings with the prisoners."[12] Despite frequent boastings to the press and to visiting VIPs about the command staff's attentiveness to the dietary preferences of the detainees, and despite measurable weight gain among the inmates, most of the detainees later recalled the food they were given at the time with palpable disgust, citing pitiful MRE rations and food that was inedible to them. Lack of salt and spice made meals additionally unpalatable. Captain Shimkus worried about the nutrients they were getting. Froot Loops, for example, which was part of their meal rations, could not sustain a prisoner. Nor could it satisfy a detainee's appetite.[13] Carol Rosenberg cited a diet of 2,700 calories per day.[14] The food issue, like everything else at Guantanamo, was an experiment in the making, waiting upon information about an unknown culture, upon better communicative rapport with individual detainees, and above all, upon decisions from above.[15]

Perhaps the melancholy that Saif detected had other, less obvious causes as well. The eleventh and last shipment of detainees bound for X-Ray had arrived on Friday, February 15, bringing the total number at the camp to 300. Camp X-Ray was now filled almost to the brim. The remaining 60 or so cages would remain empty, available in case the Pentagon wanted to transfer any high-value detainees there, or perhaps for another purpose. Outside of the detainee population, the U.S. presence seemed to have stabilized itself as well. Lehnert's expanded team and Rumsfeld's proxy, Dunlavey, were now in place. And though everyone knew that Lehnert's JTF 160 wouldn't remain there forever, news of their replacement still hadn't come. With no further detainees set to arrive at this facility, with the camp's personnel established and in place, and with plans for building a new facility languishing, it began to seem to prisoners and staff alike that this improvised state of limbo was not temporary, but permanent.

Inside their cages, in their seventh week of captivity at X-Ray, the detainees' gloom was deepened by these signs that a transitory phase was turning into a permanent condition. The constant sunlight, the swarms of insects, the all-too-frequent sight of snakes slithering easily into the cages, and the cramps and pains from so little movement made visible the captors' indifference to the human fate of the detainees in the present or the future.[16]

To be sure, the detainees were adapting in their own ways to the new routine. They had learned to use the correct hand signals to get access to a toilet. They had learned to keep their hands outside of their blankets at night, and to back away from the doorway when the guards entered their cages to transfer them to interrogation. Surgeries had become a regular event at the facility. The first of several amputations had taken place on February 7. Surgeons had also performed neurosurgery and thoracic surgery, not to mention the much-celebrated eye surgery. But the growing incidence of disease and depression worried Saif. The detainees were simultaneously enraged and heartbroken, excruciatingly lonely, scared, and lost. In later years, the detainees would regularly request copies of the book *Don't Be Sad*, a compilation of aphorisms and lessons from the Koran and the Hadith counseling ways to fight depression.[17] But at this point in time, they were just learning to cope.

On the American side, managing the turbulent emotions of the guard force seemed to get harder with each passing day. According to the detainees' memoirs, this was a period when random acts of abuse occurred with greater frequency. Lehnert was aware that the tension that was beginning to pervade Camp X-Ray stemmed not only from the psychological state of the guards but from that of the detainees as well. He and Carrico knew that small arbitrary acts of detainee violence, normal to any prison situation, could trigger an abusive overreaction on the part of the guards.

Even as the growing unease gathered momentum, JTF 160 continued to try to address the detainees' complaints one by one. But, as with the provision of Froot Loops, their solutions often only created more problems than they solved. The decision about how to move the detainees more quickly was a case in point.

Medical personnel had brought to the command staff's attention the fact that the detainees were beginning to show bruises and cuts on their ankles. The wounds, some of them suppurating, were caused by the shackles. In transport, a walk of several hundred yards, the shackles chafed against their ankles as the detainees could take only short step after short step, leaving cuts and bruises.[18] So, according to Lehnert, Terry Carrico made the decision to place prisoners on gurneys to make the journey easier and more efficient.[19] But even as he praised the solution, Lehnert saw the new problem that it raised: transfers by gurney were likely to be seen as transporting prisoners that had somehow been rendered incapable of walking. Lehnert suspended the policy after several days, and soon thereafter JTF started moving prisoners in golf carts, which are still used for transport to this day.

The increasing anxiety of the detainees and the evident sense of change and tension in the direction of the operation meant that it was only a matter of time until some sort of incident occurred. Out at Radio Range, one could drive by and see the idle bulldozers. The symbolism was hard to overlook. Camp X-Ray was ready for something—anything—to happen to break the logjam, the continual sense of being in limbo.

Sitting on the floor of his cell in Charlie Block, detainee #61, Murat Kurnaz, heard a wail pierce through the daytime din of the camp. Immediately, he fathomed the source of such a plaintive cry. It could only be one thing— desecration of the Koran. "[O]therwise the prisoner wouldn't have howled like that." Kurnaz looked in the direction of the noise to try and detect the cause of the "long, tortured cry," but all he could see was the "guard trampling on something."[20]

It was the third weekend in February, the beginning of Eid al-Adha. The Koran had been an issue from the beginning of Camp X-Ray, a point of negotiation, a symbol of the religious rights of the detainees, a testament to American tolerance. By this time, JTF 160 had instituted the use of surgical masks, hung from cell walls, for cradling the Korans. These aseptically clean, improvised Koran-holders addressed two concerns. First, they lifted the Koran up from the floor and allowed the detainees to keep them where scripture demanded—at the highest point in the room. Second, they kept the holy book out of range of accidental or intentional boot-kicks by the guards.

The guard who had been in the detainee's cage at the time of the incident denied that he had abused the holy book. When he went to close the door, he told Lehnert, the Koran had fallen from its nest and onto the floor.[21] That is when the detainee began screaming for all to hear. Other detainees remember the incident differently. Housed in the same block of cells as the detainee who alleged the abuse, Rhuhel Ahmed recalls, "I saw a guard walk into a detainee's cell, search through the Koran and drop it on the floor. The detainee told him to pick it up and put it into its holder. I remember the guard looked at the Koran on the floor and said 'this' and then kicked it."[22]

Others saw the incident from close up as well. All accounts reported the bedlam that afterward broke loose. "Everyone started shouting and banging the doors," Rhuhel remembers.[23] The wailing from the cage of the detainee spread throughout the cell block as the guard continued, in plain sight, what looked to the detainees like abuse of the Koran. Murat Kurnaz described the chaos and the noise: "It was as though lightning had struck in a zoo. Some of the prisoners tried to kick down the cage doors, others shook the fencing, trying to tear or bite their way through the chain links." The guard sprinted from the cage. According to Kurnaz, the Immediate Reaction Force (IRF) came in to settle things down, shooting pepper spray into eyes and employing physical force to remind the prisoners just who was in charge. The uproar eventually quieted down. But this was not the end of the trouble.[24]

Three days later, on Tuesday, February 26, a second incident occurred while a detainee was engaged in his midday prayers. Fortunately for Steve Cox and JTF 160, the press had not been informed of the earlier incident, the reporters having already retreated to the leeward side to file their stories. The hot sun baked the camp relentlessly. As had happened a few days earlier, the camp was transformed within a moment to utter chaos. Once again, the spark was religious. One of the detainees had wrapped a towel around his head, forming a makeshift head covering as is required when praying.[25]

Putting anything on the head was a violation of Camp X-Ray rules; a weapon could be hidden there, and for this reason headdresses were forbidden. Immediately, the violation was noticed by a camp guard, who stormed into the cage and removed the turban. According to several reports, the guard kicked the detainee's Koran for good measure.[26] Some also report seeing the guard punch the detainee. Whatever the truth of these charges, at this point the compound erupted into a medley of screams and rattling cages. This time, the prisoners were not satisfied with terrifying the guard who had allegedly committed religious sacrilege. Screaming and kicking, the detainees thrust every one of their comfort items out of their cages. En masse, they suddenly began to toss out whatever they could, first their toothbrushes, then their plastic flip-flops. Even their sleeping mats found their way to the ground outside, fitting with some effort through the three-inch slot between the cell door and the wire mesh walls. The wildness spread from block to block. Phrases in Arabic rang out angrily, echoing as in a call and response among the detainees. Overlooking the debris-strewn passageways between the cell blocks, the guards in the towers pointed their guns at the detainees. In an instant, the camp had been transformed into a veritable garbage dump. The persistent yelling and spitting that accompanied the outburst continued even after the cells were completely emptied of belongings.[27]

Immediately alerted to the disturbance, Lehnert quickly surveyed his options. His gut reaction was to wait out the riot, to view it much like a parent would view his child's tantrum, and to let the angry energy dissipate on its own. He repeated what he had come to tell himself: If he had been left to rot in a cage without any hope for the future, he, too might succumb to uncontrollable rage.

Lehnert also considered prison riots a normal part of incarceration. Outbursts occurred and then faded into the past. His instinct was therefore to wait and let the detainees vent. Moreover, he felt baited, and immediately vowed not to take the bait. The detainees, to his mind, were spoiling for a fight, one that could lure the guards into an unjustified or brutal show of force. Lehnert wanted to avoid being drawn into this kind of confrontation. The detainees, after all, were locked up and without any serious means of attack.

For all of these reasons, Lehnert was averse to a response of any sort. Once the riot was all over, he reasoned, the command staff could decide what to do—whether to return the comfort items, whether to punish some of the detainees, whether to institute new policies.

Terry Carrico was of a different opinion. In keeping with his own theory of detention, any signs of non-cooperation needed to be nipped in the bud. Noncompliance, let alone outright resistance, had to be crushed. Punishment at the first sign of trouble was the remedy. "If you accept unacceptable behavior then it becomes acceptable," he said. "When you're running a prison camp you have to always have control." Otherwise, "it's just going to manifest [itself elsewhere] and they're going to take it one step further and one step further and one step further."[28]

The ICRC weighed in on Lehnert's side.[29] They agreed that it was wisest to let the tantrum exhaust itself. The detainees would likely cool down by themselves, without the intervention of the Immediate Reaction Force (IRF) or other displays of irresistible force.

As the commanding general, Lehnert had his way. There was to be no response while the riot raged. The IRF could amass at the periphery of the camp, showing its potential, as it often did. And according to press accounts, the full-scale outburst lasted only 45 minutes before it began to simmer down. The camp was quiet by late afternoon.

Steve Cox was having lunch when he received word of the disturbance at the camp. He knew the press well enough to know that he had problems.

On the leeward side, Bob Franken heard about the rioting almost immediately. He remembers phoning the SOUTHCOM and JTF 160 public affairs officers, William Costello and Steve Cox, and demanding confirmation of the news. "To their credit," Franken recalls, they brought the media back to the other side of the bay.[30] But by the time the reporters arrived, the detainees had quieted down for the most part. The incident nevertheless engendered distrust between the press and their minders. After all, the JTF had not alerted the media despite the fact that the media had demanded that the JTF inform them about what was happening. Furthermore, JTF had ferried journalists back to leeward before lunch, while the riot was raging. "You hid this from us. You let us sit over here and eat lunch," Cox recalled them complaining. "You put us on the boat and you got us out of the way."[31]

The handling of the outburst was a testament to the organizational and improvisational capacities of JTF 160. All the elements of Lehnert's camp, the medical team, the JTF's intelligence unit, the guards, Saifulislam, and the ICRC, had worked together to prevent the provocation from escalating. Together, Lehnert and Carrico—along with their men, who kept their heads and followed orders—had quelled the skirmish. Their good results also indicated that Lehnert's basic rule, that the guard force was to be restrained until signaled otherwise, was a sound one.

Yet alongside the success at managing a potential disaster, an ominous new element had been introduced into Camp X-Ray. Some of Lehnert's most enlightened policies had been turned against the JTF. With his decision to cater to the religious needs of the detainees—the diet, the prayer beads, the Korans, and more—Lehnert and his troops had created vulnerabilities that angry inmates were learning how to exploit. If the JTF needed to praise itself for its religious tolerance, then proving to outsiders that the military command was not as tolerant as it claimed became a tactical goal of the detainees. If it mattered so much to the command staff to pat itself on the back over such a policy, it mattered to the detainees to subvert the policy, to reveal the hypocrisy of American tolerance and generosity toward men who, likely in most cases, had been wrongfully imprisoned.

As darkness fell that night, February 26, few thought that life was about to return to normal at the camp. The second outbreak in a week suggested that more might be brewing. Lehnert knew that repeated protests of this sort, intensifying in scale, would lead eventually to more pressure on him to employ force as a countermeasure. He knew, too, that the conditions giving rise to the protest—a growing sense of despair and hopelessness and an increasing state of tension between the guards and the detainees—were unlikely to abate in the coming days.

Sure enough, before the ink was dry on the newspaper stories, Terry Carrico's warnings about the negative consequences of a policy of leniency and tolerance seemed to be confirmed. Just as Lehnert, too, had worried, the detainees had learned how to strike at what mattered most to JTF 160: the idea that, in matters of care and custody, if not law, they were following the Geneva Conventions.

On Wednesday, February 27, the day following the massive protest, the detainees announced to their guards that they were on a hunger strike. Many refused breakfast. By lunchtime, the authorities were counting: 59 skipped lunch, 109 skipped dinner. The next day the numbers rose: 107 skipped breakfast, 194 skipped lunch.[32] At this rate, the entire camp would be on strike in short order. Suddenly, and without much warning, JTF 160 had been hurled back into the predicament that they had all worked so hard to overcome. Once again, they confronted a new situation without knowledge, without rules, and without available expertise. Now, they were again compelled to improvise in a void of policy and know-how.

But the command staff was adept by now at reacting to the emergency of the moment at Guantanamo, and quickly launched into tackling this new problem. The medical officers and Saif had to answer the initial questions. What, they needed to determine, did this coordinated protest mean? What exactly was a hunger strike? How long could it last? At what point did it become life-threatening? What, if any, were the available means of medical intervention? "You've got this group of clinicians that's used to dealing with a very healthy population [i.e., military personnel and families]. And now we're faced with this hunger strike. And this is one of the things that boggles my mind, you know. We really didn't have anybody who knew a whole lot about people starving themselves to death."[33]

The Washington brass displayed no more interest in this problem than they had in the other logistics of Guantanamo. They were "remarkably unconcerned," said Lehnert. In Rumsfeld's words, the hunger strikers were on a diet to get press attention.[34]

Without direction or help from Washington, Al Shimkus and Pat Alford and the rest of the medical staff began to educate themselves about hunger strikes. "So we started doing research. We got into the books. We got into the Internet. And surprisingly the only thing we could find about groups of people starving themselves to death were some of the experiences in Africa with the refugee populations. With the Hutus [and the Tutsis]."[35] Better-known cases were a guide as well. Al Shimkus explained to the general that, biologically speaking, individuals could survive a long time without eating, much longer than the general had assumed. In fact, while fasting begins to harm the body after several days, a person can last up to 60 days or so without food. The IRA's Bobby Sands had lasted 66 days. Mahatma Gandhi fasted several times, once for 21 days, but never more than that. Still others have been known to linger for over 100 days. The medical team contacted the Bureau of Prisons, which verified Shimkus's report. Absorbing everything they could readily find, the medical officials concluded "from the literature [that] we could pretty much predict that death would occur between Day 45 and Day 60. If you don't eat."[36]

Scrambling to ascertain the facts and outline the worst-case scenarios, the command staff told themselves that they had a little bit of leeway, given the relatively healthy condition of most of the detainees. In the weeks since the detainees had arrived, many of them had put on noticeable weight, which the constant weighing of the detainees had documented.

Weight gain, in truth, had not been especially difficult to achieve. The relatively high caloric content in the food and the general lack of movement and exercise made it easy.[37] In addition, the change from a winter climate to a tropical one added to conditions where putting on pounds was relatively effortless. As a result, some of the detainees had visibly beefed up by this time. Many others remained scrawny and underweight, however, possibly affected by the brief fast than some Muslims choose to observe in the days leading up to Eid-al-Adha,[38] although, in cases of religious fasting, JTF 160 made sure that food was provided before sun up and after sun down—the only times when meals are permitted during a fast.

But there was a flip side to this coin. The detainee hunger strike had undermined the Pentagon public-relations claim that the detainees were being treated humanely—proved in part, they claimed, by weight gain. From all accounts, Lehnert himself had been particularly focused on the weight of the detainees and saw to it that they were weighed at least weekly, which provided defenders of the camp numbers to cite as statistical proof that the prisoners were well cared for.

The detainees were leveling an attack against the U.S. military regime where it mattered. It was as if they had been listening to the press briefings. As Shimkus put it, "For a regime fixated already on weight gain, this was the perfect challenge. This mattered to JTF. We took body mass readings regularly."[39] Galen Jackman was particularly articulate about the detainees' aim. He pointed out that the hunger strikers' protest was one that the military command had to care about. "I'm not gonna eat anything" was an effective sally in the battle of symbols that had come to define JTF 160.

In fact, the hunger strike posed a major challenge once again to the entire approach Lehnert had insisted upon from the start. Lehnert had insisted on letting the detainees communicate with one another. He had insisted on religious tolerance to an extreme. He had focused on providing food as a sign of proper care and custody. Yet the hunger strike, like the outbursts precipitating it, had exploited these measures. The detainees had clearly communicated with one another to do just what critics of the less punitive measures would have predicted—namely, to form a concerted agreement about striking out at JTF 160. It was as if Carrico's theory of detention and the Pentagon's theory of the danger posed by the detainees had now coalesced. Clearly, they were plotting and dangerous, a threat even in their cages.

Not only were the detainees proving that they were the dangerous lot that many had suspected all along, not only were they now proving false every assertion about the camp's progress and stability, not only were they exposing Lehnert's camp as vulnerable, but the strike was providing Carrico's sensibilities a vote of confidence as well. The hunger strike also threatened to do exactly what Dunlavey feared most—having the detention effort harm the interrogation effort. If there was ever a sign that detention and interrogation could not really be separated, the hunger strike was it. Not only would the ill-health of the detainees compromise their ability to be interrogated, especially if they were in the hospital, but according to Iqbal, the detainees had made a pact among themselves, to carry the hunger strike over into the realm of interrogation as well. "[W]e had all agreed not to speak at our next interrogation as part of the protest," he said.[40]

Lehnert was unnerved by the hunger strike. "The hunger strike bothered me a great deal," he later recalled. Nor was he quite sure at first how to handle it. "You don't want to give it too much attention...because then it'll cause everyone to go on a hunger strike. But at the same time...I was very concerned about the physical aspects of it."[41] He was in constant need of medical reassurances from Shimkus, asking him repeatedly how many days they could go without food. Even in his press relations, the hunger strike appeared to have changed him. As he quipped during one session: "How many of you didn't have breakfast today? Does that mean you're on a hunger strike?"[42] In addition to abandoning his typical frankness with the press, Lehnert kept the press out for a day and a half after the strike had officially begun.

As always, the international community was watching and eager for news. And Lehnert's petulance did not last long. Day after day, the media reported numbers of striking detainees at each meal. The burn bag chart in the press tent charted the strike's progress. Frequently, JTF 160 passed on information about their understanding of the medical implications of the strike and the possible need one day for intravenous feeding. Memories of the riot kept them to their original obligation to report frequently to the press. "They learned their lesson," Franken summed it up. "They were, in fact, really pretty assertive to give us information." One strategy was to have Al Shimkus speak directly to the press. As Cox recalled, "Al Shimkus was amazing, calm, clear-headed, laying it all out for us all"—for Lehnert, the staff, and the press.[43]

Lehnert seemed to sense at some level that his strategy of accommodation had inadvertently fueled the strike. The detainees were acting like individual human beings with rights. Nothing could have spoken more directly to his intentions. Yet, his success was also his failure. By accommodating, even bolstering the sense of human dignity among the detainees, he had stoked the fires of disruption.

But Lehnert did not conclude that a change of strategy or policy was necessary; indeed, at no time did he seem to think that his approach should change. As he explained to General Speer at SOUTHCOM and to visitors from OSD who came down to inspect the strike conditions, it would always be crucial to stave off hopelessness, to provide grounds for a sense of a better future. He had learned during the Sea Signal days with the Haitian and Cuban migrants that detainees needed to believe that a process was in motion that would prevent them from being in limbo forever. "They have that feeling of hopelessness because they don't know their status."[44]

Even as he continued to explain the strike as an outgrowth of the hopelessness resulting from Washington's seemingly directionless policy, Lehnert began to doubt his own conviction that his nonpunitive and personally attentive approach would ultimately be proven an effective tool of management for his prison. The hunger strike was not just an isolated piece of business to attend to; it was a challenge to his entire view of the world. And he intended to rise to the occasion.

Lehnert's options in responding to the strike were limited. He could have capitulated to Carrico and instituted harsh measures, such as taking away comfort items, most of which had been returned after the riot. After all, Carrico had virtually predicted that a worse event would follow the short uprising that occurred the day before the strike started. He could have called in a guard force to be present inside the wire at all times, with their dogs and riot gear serving as a perpetual threat. He could have taken a number of individuals into isolation and scared the others with such tactics. Or he could have changed his mind and learned to see compassionate treatment as a strategy that would lead to more trouble within the camp. But for him the choice was clear: the only rational extension of Lehnert's philosophy was to try to talk to the detainees, to hear their complaints, and to try to address them.

Contemplating these avenues of response, Lehnert chose to react to the hunger strike by doubling down on the bet he had made with himself. He would do this in a way that satisfied his professional oaths and his personal conscience. He would end the strike his way. Rather than compromise, he would go full out.

To do this, he would rely upon the team of close allies he had brought into his inner sanctum, regardless of rank. His earlier decisions to structure his command team with individuals who would not normally be brought into command-level policy discussions, notably Shimkus and Saifulislam, proved immediately helpful. The two of them joined Meier, Buehn, Carrico, and Nichols as a core team of advisors for the strike. The mechanism established for running a camp that demanded novel decisions each day was there for Lehnert in the face of this emergency as well. So, too, the rapport—the result of the mutual respect that had been built between the task force and the ICRC—was an important resource. According to Lehnert, the Red Cross responded with irritation at first, advising Lehnert that if he wanted to resolve the situation, he should just "let them all loose." But they quickly pitched in, adhering to their organizational mandate to alleviate suffering and trauma, not to change the overall situation. After that, they spoke to Lehnert more constructively, trying to help him devise strategies to end the strike.[45]

On the matter of his philosophy, more even than regarding his command structure, Lehnert trusted himself. The implicit accusation lingering over the episode was that Lehnert's behavior had led directly to this unfortunate state of affairs. Had he not "coddled" the enemy, had he understood the first thing about prison regimes, had he understood that tough authority and full control were the only way to maintain order, then none of this would have happened.

For starters, he broadened and deepened his contact with the detainees. On the first afternoon of the strike, February 28, as the lunchtime numbers of self-proclaimed hunger strikers nearly doubled in size, General Lehnert addressed the detainees directly, his first public address to them as a group. His tone was conciliatory but respectful of the detention effort. Lehnert's goal was to be "firm but not confrontational." In every word, he conveyed the sensibility that in their situation, he would react similarly. You can "turn your towels into turbans," he announced over the public address system. (Saif provided simultaneous translation.) But if you do, he added, we reserve the right to inspect them at will, to look for concealed weapons. He urged the detainees to please cease their protest, and conveyed as best he could the desire to accommodate their grievances. Consulting with Saif ahead of time, he addressed the strike not by asserting the command's authority but by appealing to the sensibilities of the detainees. He referred to suicide by starvation as violating the Koran.[46]

In the short term, his strategy worked. His words had an immediate impact. By dinner, only 88 were still on strike, and by the next morning another 15 had agreed to eat.

But it was not to be so easy. There were other forces at work within the camp: the persuasive words of those who were encouraging the hunger strike.

The leaders and agitators whom Nichols had tried to identify by watching from the towers had a counter-influence that was strong. And over the course of the next several days, the numbers began to rise again. Nichols worked with interpreters to try to identify the leaders, to see who was talking to whom and to what effect, and to understand the structure of command for the strike.

Lehnert, meanwhile, pursued his own strategy. He talked to the detainees personally, individually and in public. In order to further figure out what to do, Lehnert began to visit the detainees. At night or in the daytime, he would come into the camp, settle himself on the ground beside a hunger striker, and listen. His legs crossed, his cap removed, Lehnert listened. Detainees in adjacent cages saw and could sometimes even hear what was being said as Lehnert asked for explanations, confessed to sympathy for their predicament, and made promises for the future.

Lehnert's visits made a strong impression on the detainees. In the words of Nizar Sassi, detainee #325, the general "listens, and shakes his head from time to time."[47] As Kurnaz remembered it, the general came to the camp and "talked with one of the English-speaking prisoners. The prisoner refused to stand up in the general's presence. The general took his cap off and sat on the ground in the corridor in front of the cage." Kurnaz expressed surprise and confusion at Lehnert's behavior. He first saw this gesture as a sign of submission on the part of the enemy. "At that moment, I realized that we were not utterly powerless. We could bring them to their knees if we all went on hunger strike!" But almost immediately, a second thought occurred to him. "Was he trying to signal that he wasn't on the job, that he wanted to speak to the prisoner as a human being?"[48]

Other detainees had the same question, marveling at the general's show of humility and compassion. On one occasion, Lehnert was seen to be literally begging a detainee to eat. Frustrated and inconsolable, Lehnert sat outside the cell of this detainee who refused to budge. To the shock of the onlooking detainees, the general wept, the unmistakable flow of tears cascading down his face. To Shafiq Rasul, the moment was a revelation. It let him and others know, as Sassi would later write, that the absurdity and unfairness of the situation was impossible to escape, even for the general in charge.[49]

Lehnert was committed to engaging with the detainees, one-on-one. He was going to get to the bottom of their discontent, to open negotiations, and to resolve the strike through discussion. His conversations with the detainees offered promises in return for ending the strike. "Then he begins speaking. He promises that changes will be made. Orders will be given to improve respect for religious practice."[50] He would, he assured them individually, punish the guard who had provoked the strike. He would allow the wearing of "towels" turned into "turbans"; more importantly, he would order prayer caps for the detainees. Sassi describes one interchange between the general and a Saudi who was participating in the hunger strike. Lehnert listened to the Saudi's list of grievances, which included "the quality of the food, the daily acts of violence, [and] the iron foot shackles that injured our ankles" during transport from one place to another.[51] Lehnert agreed to address each and every one of the detainees' concerns. But in exchange, they were to end their strike.

He would do more, if that's what it took. And in one case, it required more, much more than either protocol or even leniency would have suggested.

One of the striking detainees seemed like a lost case. His wife had been pregnant when he was captured, and he had no idea whether the child had been born, whether his wife was all right, whether they knew where he was. All he knew was that her due date had passed. Lehnert thought that if he knew that he had a child, the detainee would regain the will to live. Giving his private cell phone to Saif, he asked the chaplain to call the detainee's wife. The woman answered. Saif spoke to her, telling her he was there with her husband who wanted to know how she was, and then he asked about the baby. Within seconds, Saif shouted out, "It's a boy! It's a boy!" The message was unmistakable. There was a future. The detainee now had a reason to live. He ended his strike.[52]

Despite his reaching out to the detainees, and doing so successfully, Lehnert nursed residual doubts about his own approach. "I wondered if I was just enabling them," he later confessed.[53] And, for that reason, he sought other avenues toward ending the strike. He turned to Saif for help formulating new strategies. Saif thought that it would be worthwhile to obtain a fatwa stating that suicide violated fundamental tenets of Islam, but he sensed that the detainees just didn't accord him enough respect as an imam to accept his interpretation with any conviction. Determined to help Lehnert, Saif contacted another imam to see if he could obtain a religious ruling that might seem persuasive to the detainees. Lehnert wholeheartedly endorsed the plan. Saif remembers calling upon Dr. Taha al-Alwani, a founding member of the International Institute of Islamic Thought in Virginia, and explaining the situation at X-Ray. Saif asked the imam if he would consider drawing up a fatwa announcing that Islam forbade hunger strikes in unambiguous terms.[54] The imam agreed and sent Saif a fatwa as he had requested. According to Saif, however, this first fatwa included a number of angry insults hurled at the detainees for the harm they'd caused America. After Saif explained that this was not what he'd had in mind, the imam issued a less confrontational fatwa against hunger strikes and Saif presented it to the detainees. It was relatively successful. According to Saif and Lehnert, a large number of detainees gave up the strike when presented with the religious ruling.

Saif had other ideas about how to use insight into the detainees' situation to end the strike. They told him about the peer pressure that made them reluctant to eat even if they wanted to, so he suggested that Lehnert move prisoners thought to be wavering to other blocks. But according to Saif, it was hard to turn against the group. It amounted to betrayal. As one hospitalized detainee told Saif when the chaplain offered him peanuts, "I'm not doing it for me. I'm doing it for the cause of everybody." For those fasting, the idea was that "everyone would benefit" even were the detainee to die.[55]

Still, Saif pursued the idea that incentives in the form of food could be helpful in ending the strike. Although Lehnert and others had prided themselves on the halal meals provided for the detainees, and although the detainees were gaining weight, the detainees themselves found the food both atrocious and in short supply. As Iqbal told it, "the food was very limited and insufficient." So much so that during the hunger strike, some of the detainees who didn't fast greedily ate the portions of those who were fasting, grateful to fill their stomachs.[56] Saif suggested bringing in customary breakfast foods—eggs and salt instead of bagels—and offering chocolates.[57]

But Carrico and Tim Nichols had a different, less gentle and accommodating, approach, one that emphasized threats, punishment, and the removal of incentives and in which the identification of the strike's leaders also played a role. Carrico may have been right about the riot that preceded the hunger strike; punishment, Lehnert acknowledged, could be a deterrent. In his second speech to the detainees as a group, given on March 8, he addressed the camp again, making it clear that he would penalize those who refused to suspend the strike. He would take away their comfort items, however limited they were, including their sleeping mats, their toothbrushes, and their all-too-limited exercise privileges. The one thing he refused to take away was the Koran, a policy that, persisting into later periods of the camp, unintentionally guaranteed that detainees would identify the inviolability of their persons with religious scripture.[58]

Lehnert also agreed with Carrico that isolating the leaders of the strike was essential for ending the strike. Together with Carrico and his guard force, and with information provided by Tim Nichols and by interpreters, the task force focused on the ringleaders, who, they concluded, were cajoling others into prolonging the strike. The 60 cellblocks that had been left vacant, located in the most distant part of X-Ray, were an ideal new home for the apparent leaders of the strike, those most adamant about never giving in. Lehnert moved about 15 of them to the remote but still visible section of X-Ray.

This tactic, combined with persuading the more compliant strikers to end their strike, seemed to work.[59] Without the intense peer pressure exerted by those fervently dedicated to the strike, most of the remaining strikers ceased their protest and agreed to eat. By the middle of March, two weeks after it had begun, the strike had subsided to a manageable level. The numbers dwindled to the low teens, with two or three hospitalized, and would stay at that level for the remainder of the month and beyond. But for Lehnert and others on his staff, the full-blown strike was effectively behind them. What remained was a remnant of detainees, approximately a dozen, who were steadfast in their refusal to eat. For Al Shimkus and Michael Lehnert, force feedings via intravenous tubes loomed on the horizon as a likely possibility.

Lehnert never stopped trying to use reason, rather than force, to get the detainees to end their strike. Part of what continued to motivate Lehnert was his unshakable conviction that there was method to the seeming madness of the detainees—that they had a valid reason to starve themselves. "I would not associate somebody who was on a hunger strike "with the most hardcore cases," Lehnert explained. "It could just have been an individual who really honestly believed he didn't deserve to be there" or simply someone of relative inconsequence. The growing suspicion that very few of the detainees were significant terrorists contributed to his feeling that those who were on strike might very well be those who were merely hapless youths who were in the wrong place at the wrong time rather than hardened terrorists with the will to plot lethal terrorist attacks on the United States.[60]

Several former detainees have told memorable stories about Lehnert's visits during the hunger strike, stories that illustrate his willingness to deal with the detainees as individuals, his attempt to provide hope that they would eventually be heard, and his insistence that in return for recognition of their concerns, they end the strike immediately. Some detainees' memoirs single out Lehnert's personal reaching out as the sole expression of respect in a world where they were otherwise stripped of all human dignity, during the strike as in normal circumstances. Others also noticed Lehnert's efforts. "It's fair to say that we do see a responsiveness by the camp authorities that we'd like to see mirrored by the Bush administration," commented

Alistair Hodgett, a spokesman for the human rights organization Amnesty International.

As Lehnert continued his strategy of trying to end the strike, person by person, individual case by individual case, others adopted his approach. Shafiq Rasul reports that even interrogators, in at least one instance, turned their sessions into opportunities to hear grievances. Just after the onset of the strike, Rasul says, representatives from MI-5, the British domestic intelligence service, arrived at the camp, and during this interrogation, an American Army colonel approached him. Together, and with Rasul in the room, the two officers discussed what was happening in the camp. According to Rasul, the American Army colonel tried to apologize to the British detainee, assuring him that the perpetrator—the one who had kicked the Koran—had been removed. "We apologize for what that Sergeant did. He's been taken out of the camp," the colonel told him repeatedly.[61]

Despite all these efforts, the strike proved difficult to end. Even as the number of active hunger strikers dwindled, Lehnert remained concerned about the possibility of losing one of the prisoners to suicide. Repeatedly, he would query the medical staff about their medical opinions, especially those that downplayed the need for worry. And he prepared for the possibility of force-feeding, an eventuality that would force Lehnert—along with Shimkus—to weigh his respect for the autonomy of others against a firm opposition to suicide. "If I have a choice between letting somebody die and force feeding them, I will go with force feeding them."[62] Lehnert decided that he would order hospitalization and compulsory nutrition after 30 days—the point at which, according to Alford, the chemistry of your body is completely "out of whack."[63]

When all was said and done, the hunger strike—which at first seemed to offer proof that Lehnert's whole approach to the camp was wrong—became his way of proving just the opposite, that he was indeed right. He handled the strike in accordance with the policy he had set in motion on day one. In keeping with the spirit of the Geneva Conventions, he insisted that the detainees, whatever they had done, were human beings and needed to be treated as such. He insisted, in word and deed, that they were essentially to be treated as prisoners of war. While the arrangements he put in place during January and February pointed in this direction, it was the hunger strike in the first half of March that allowed and even compelled Lehnert to put his humanitarian policy into effect. He became the chief negotiator with the detainees, as well as the director of other efforts. He used himself as the ultimate test of whether or not the approach he believed in would work. And he succeeded. He spoke to the detainees as a group, he spoke to them as individuals, and he commanded others to attend to their individual and collective responses.

Some might have accused Lehnert of exhibiting too much sympathy with the detainees. Even today, when hearing him talk about the hunger strike, a listener is struck by his sense that their cause was legitimate. He continually remarks, as mentioned, that if he had been treated as they were, he would have reacted similarly. In this regard, Lehnert replicated at a higher level the process of emotional and moral identification that had begun to develop between the detainees and some of the guards. Lehnert had become more and more convinced that many of the detainees were not even remotely in the running for the "worst of the worst," that there were numerous cases of mistaken identity. For the honor of the military and his country, the best he could do was to keep the psychological situation from deteriorating even further. During the hunger strike, this meant showing the detainees that there were law-abiding, compassionate Americans who believed that the presumption of innocence applied to foreigners too.

Essentially, Lehnert had defined the battle between the detainees and the camp authorities as a battle over hearts and minds.[64] In Galen Jackman's words, Lehnert had "worked his way through the options that he had . . . [trying] to get at the essence of why they were protesting."[65] And on these terms he won. The detainees were moved by the palpably genuine attention that Lehnert showed them. Even Terry Carrico recognized the lesson that had been learned. Carrico remembers himself as being on Lehnert's side in this way. When I asked him, "Do you know what ended the hunger strike?" Carrico responded, "I think it was just a matter of someone talking to them. And telling them that things were going to get better."[66]

But try as he might to address the problems that plagued the detainees, there was one issue that Lehnert couldn't raise, and that was the lack of legal progress. For those at Guantanamo, the fact that CITF—the Criminal Investigation Task Force, whose job it was to prepare for the military commissions—existed, or that there was a battle raging among lawyers in D.C., meant little or nothing. Not until later in the month would a conclusive document be released on the military commissions.

This reality was not one Lehnert could erase by his own action. No amount of chocolate or cigarettes, no special ethnically sensitive culinary spices, no

variety of prayer beads, could change the fact that the military commissions—
and thus any sense of hope on the part of the detainees—still lay far off in
the future. The detainees, especially those from European and other Western
countries, knew just what this meant and could share their sensibilities with
their fellow prisoners. They had all been consigned to a lawless limbo. From
the looks of things, moreover, no one cared, or at least no one could effectively
interfere, not even the ICRC.

Still, Lehnert had put up the good fight and, for the moment, won. The way
the strike was handled was a triumph of major proportions for the idea that
treating the detainees as human beings could bring about calm and a resolution to the conflict. The problem was that, contrary to Lehnert's sense of
the world, stability was not necessarily the desired goal for Guantanamo Bay's
detention facility. In this respect—the value of stability—detention and interrogation were at loggerheads with one another, the former bent on creating
an equilibrium, the latter on inducing a destabilized environment. Temporary
détente between the two was permissible. But the outright victory of the detention values over those pertinent to interrogation was not.

In any case, even the detainees noticed Lehnert's success. They saw his
embrace of the Geneva Conventions as tantamount to his own revolt. In Sassi's
words, "the general, it seems, took off his officer's cap with all its insignia,
and threw it to the winds."[67]

Given his success and the defiance it conveyed, it should have surprised
no one that no sooner had Lehnert's success at managing the camp revolt
displayed itself on the horizon than the tide began to turn. By the time the
numbers of those on strike had diminished to a mere handful, Michael
Lehnert was notified that his post at Guantanamo, along with that of the JTF
160 contingent from Camp Lejeune, would be over by the end of the month.
A replacement was being selected. Going forward, he was informed, there
would be two new commanders at the base: one for intelligence gathering and
interrogations, one for the care and custody of the detainees. What he didn't
know at the time was that the status of the interrogation command would
come to dominate the tenor of the camp, and that the rank and experience
of the interrogation command would come to outstrip that of the care-and-
custody command. Moreover, with Lehnert and his Camp Lejeune officers
and enlisted men out of the way, the memory of the hunger strike, and thus its
lesson—that treating the detainees as human beings could lead to a manageable state of affairs, pending movement of some sort in Washington—would
vanish as well.

12

Bowing Out

I don't think this mission's going to go away.

—Lt. Col. Timothy Nichols

In the third week of March 2002, U.S. Army reservist Brigadier General Rick Baccus's phone rang. Baccus, head of a National Guard military police brigade in Warwick, Rhode Island, was looking forward to being called to active duty, but he was surprised when the call came not from his local bosses but directly from the National Guard bureau at the Pentagon. Even more surprising than the break from protocol was his assignment. On that cold day in mid-March 2001, Rick Baccus was named the new commander of JTF 160 at Guantanamo Bay. General Lehnert's successor was soon on his way to Cuba.

Brigadier General Baccus was displeased by this seemingly inconsequential breach of standard operating procedure. Immaculately dressed and groomed, with a cleanly shaven head, steady eyes and a soft, thoughtful face, Baccus is a devotee of protocol and precise policy guidelines and directives. He packed his bags for Guantanamo with little preparation in terms of either experience or temperament for the challenge that lay ahead.[1]

In March 2002, despite his respect for order, his career was setting out on a path that would turn his understanding of life and the military topsy-turvy. Taking a leave from his civilian job running the Veterans Cemetery for the state of Rhode Island, he received perfunctory briefings at SOUTHCOM, at FORSCOM, and in D.C., where he was also given some public affairs training. By the end of March, he would assume his new command.

The choice of Rick Baccus spoke volumes about the Pentagon's evolving plans for Guantanamo. This time, the powers that be had selected a commander with even less experience in running a prison than Michael Lehnert had had. They did this even though the lack of penal expertise had been a cause for much concern from the day the JTF first landed on the island. They chose a commander without detention experience even though Camp Delta was slated to open within five weeks as a formal prison compound. From the point of view of Al Shimkus and Terry Carrico, questions about prison policy were becoming more rather than less important. As Baccus told a CNN interviewer years later, "my only experience in prisons prior to [Guantanamo] was…in a lockdown at the Adult Correctional Institute in Cranston, R.I."[2] He had been called in as liaison to potential military backup during a riot at the prison. But for much of his career, he had served in the administrative services. As head of a military police brigade, moreover, Baccus would be bringing along troops with police backgrounds but little prison knowledge or know-how.

A reservist and guardsman, rather than a career officer or combat soldier, Baccus did not have the same prestige or authority as General Lehnert. Still, in deploying him to Guantanamo, DOD avoided depleting its active-duty soldiers, who were needed in Afghanistan and in the run-up to the invasion of Iraq. Less obviously but more importantly, Baccus's personality was no match for the confidence and determination of Michael Dunlavey. Baccus has a quiet way about him—attentive but not forceful, reticent rather than active.

This personality imbalance between Baccus and Dunlavey was magnified by the issue of rank that defines military relations. Baccus was a one-star general; Dunlavey had two stars. And while Michael Lehnert was not about to take a backseat to a two-star reservist, particularly one who entertained contrary ideas about the rule of law and the military's treatment of prisoners, Baccus would have no choice. As he made clear to Baccus, Dunlavey wanted Baccus to report to him.[3] And if a single chain of command had been set up, that subordination would have been normal and formalized. But the OSD, for reasons of its own, wanted a dual command, two structures working side by side with different missions.

Lehnert sensed the direction toward which the Pentagon was trying to move by making Baccus his replacement. Baccus made a quick day-visit to Guantanamo right after he was called up, and then arrived just days shy of the change of command. Under normal conditions, the handover would have taken place over a two-week period. During the first week, the replacement force would shadow the original team in a process the army refers to as a "right-seat ride." In the second week, they would swap seats, the old team accompanying the new team. But as with so much else at Guantanamo, this handover did not follow the usual script.

Lehnert may have wondered whether the unnecessary suddenness and brevity of the handover was deliberate. Perhaps the authorities did not want him to convey too much tactical and logistical information to the new commander. Certainly, a cursory briefing would weaken Baccus's position vis-à-vis

Dunlavey, who had been shuttling back and forth for nearly a month by the time of Baccus's first visit.

Whatever OSD had in mind, Lehnert decided on his own, given the short time available, not to overwhelm the new commander with too many details about the challenges that would confront him once he took over. Addressing himself to Baccus with his usual directness, Lehnert described the general tensions besetting the operation with candor but without any rancor. There was no need to share his reservations about Dunlavey. Nor was there any reason to confess any disappointment he might have had about the Pentagon, which, after initially failing to provide operational guidance, had ultimately adopted strong-arm techniques to commandeer the entire camp for the purposes of extralegal interrogation. Instead of forewarnings, Lehnert offered his replacement some constructive advice: "I told him to stay in his lane," Lehnert remembers, using a customary military phrase, the same that Carrico had employed when referring to Saif's interactions with the prisoners. "I told him that... it would probably be tough for him." He cautioned Baccus about the essential incompatibility of JTF 160 and JTF 170 and suggested that he would likely be asked to do things he would want to resist doing. He recommended that Baccus decide ahead of time what he would do if asked "to do something that in his view was either unethical or illegal."[4] But, in general, he left the specifics for the new commander to uncover for himself.

Leaving Dunlavey aside, Lehnert warned Baccus about the passions of the troops. These young men and women had been encouraged to see the detainees as evil incarnate, and were primed to explode with vengeful anger if not watched and managed. Lehnert also emphasized the public relations burden that fell to the commander of JTF 160. "The whole world is watching," he told Baccus.

Last but not least, Lehnert expounded on the vision that had motivated his own command at Guantanamo. Despite the president's decree that the Geneva Conventions need not apply, and the continued insistence from above that the detainees were the "worst of the worst," Lehnert told Baccus that the key to performing this mission well was hewing to the Geneva Conventions as closely as possible and recognizing that "these are human beings we have here." Finally, Lehnert recommended that Baccus seek advice from Shimkus and Buehn along the way. They, Lehnert assured Baccus, were "men of integrity" and would be able to help assess and maneuver through the kinds of conflict that would inevitably arise given the implicit contradictions built into the Guantanamo mission.[5]

From Baccus's quiet, polite, unaggressive demeanor and the fact that this mission was many levels above any position that the new commander had held before, Lehnert likely surmised that Dunlavey would quickly have his way. The safeguards that Lehnert had tried to build into the detention operation seemed headed for collapse under his successor. But there was little he could do about it beyond direct and indirect warnings, unpersuasive assurances, and the generous acknowledgments that he gave to those he was leaving behind.

Lehnert told himself that this was how things happened; this was military theory and military practice rolled into one. The U.S. Marine Corps set things up and then withdrew, leaving the aftermath to the latecomers who were tasked with the longer-term effort. And while his every instinct may have told him that the tenuous stability and respect for law and order he had worked day and night to preserve would unravel given the new personalities in charge, not to mention the new and dysfunctional dual command structure, he pushed such apprehensions out of his mind to focus on the next task at hand.

Above all, he was concerned about those he was leaving behind: Al Shimkus, Bob Buehn, Terry Carrico, and last but not least, Saifulislam.

When it came to Shimkus and Buehn, the leave-taking was unproblematic. Both were senior officers, able to handle most situations that came their way. Professionals, each would continue to adhere to a code of honorable conduct and legality and would know how to do so without making waves. Lehnert's farewell to them included the expectation that they would all keep in touch. Just as they had been posted together in Newport a decade earlier, so their paths might well cross again. Taking their last runs together, the three reminisced about what they had gone through and what they had accomplished. With Guantanamo's first hunger strike now essentially over, they felt they had steadied a boat that had been on the verge of capsizing. Lehnert thanked them for having been such gracious and generous hosts. He did not speak to them directly about the basic conflict that had marked the detention facility's first two months. But they were all aware of what had been at stake and of the resistance they had offered—and of the pride they felt for these efforts. They had stayed true to the mission: the care and custody of the detainees.

Lehnert left the debriefing of Terry Carrico to Bill Meier. Carrico would assume Bill Meier's post of chief of staff to the new commander of JTF 160, Rick Baccus. Lehnert later noted that the departure of his JTF 160 would leave Carrico to step into his "comfort zone." Responsible for the long-term detention of prisoners, the U.S. Army would be assuming its rightful authority, as had been planned from the beginning.

Saying good-bye to Saif was a more complicated story. Because he had no official connection to the Camp Lejeune contingent, Saif's deployment was open-ended. But the subject that most deeply colored Lehnert's last conversations with the chaplain was what would happen to Saif in his absence. Once Lehnert handed over the command to Baccus, he would no longer be able to run interference for the chaplain. Saif would be vulnerable to the new regime.

Saif and Lehnert discussed this situation as thoroughly as discretion allowed. Aware of the potential difficulty of the situation that awaited him on the other side of Lehnert's departure, Saif was anxious about staying behind. Lehnert had protected Saif not only from Dunlavey and the OSD, but from all those who considered Lehnert's traditional approach to military detention to be potentially dangerous. So what pressures might now be brought to bear on the frightened chaplain? Both men knew that a whisper of distrust had accompanied discussions about Saif since his arrival. Foreign-born, speaking languages that the jailed but not their jailers understood, in constant contact with the detainees, and above all, a Muslim, he could be a natural target for the soldiers' pent-up anger and suspicion. Lehnert told Saif to "be careful" and urged him to call if he encountered difficulty. Lehnert said that he would do what he could.

The well-meaning offer could hardly have been reassuring to Saif, who knew how defenseless he would become as soon as Lehnert departed. He vowed to let Meier know, at the first opportunity, of his desire to leave Guantanamo—the sooner the better.

Having said his good-byes, Lehnert turned his attention to two additional pieces of business.

First, he wanted to address the detainees as a group one more time.

Lehnert had come to enjoy the camp addresses that he had delivered during the hunger strike. On March 20, Rumsfeld provided Lehnert with the excuse he needed for a final address to the detainees. On that day, the SECDEF announced guidelines for military tribunals, filling in the details of the president's November 13 Military Order. The trials would be partly open; they would be open to the public, "except proceedings closed by the presiding officer." The press, for example, could be excluded at the discretion of the judge, or the sound could be turned off in the listeners' gallery. Sessions could be closed in the name of national security. Further, an accused detainee would not be able to examine all of the evidence being used against him, and evidentiary standards would be relaxed to allow the introduction of information that would normally be excluded in civilian courts or courts-martial, including hearsay evidence and forced confessions. In contrast to the November 13 Military Order, there would be an appellate process to a special review panel, with final review by the president, but no independent appeals to the federal courts would be allowed. Moreover, the death penalty could still be obtained, but now with the votes of only two-thirds of a full seven-person panel, a requirement that would change periodically as the number of people on the panel changed.[6]

At the same time that the new rules were released, the Pentagon announced its plan to keep under lock and key not only those detainees who were neither tried nor convicted but also those who, after being tried and acquitted under the procedures governing military commissions, were still considered a threat to U.S. national security.[7] The new military order, according to the SECDEF, ensured a process that would be "fair and balanced." Although the Secretary didn't say so directly, there was no doubt that it was the detainees at Guantanamo who were targeted by these new rules.

Right away, the legal debate was revived between those siding with the administration and defensive about the concessions it had made and those who insisted that the new protocols fell short of justice by, for example, contemplating proceedings without the right to independent appeal. But General Lehnert wasn't concerned with the legal nuances, or even with what would eventually happen. He was concerned with the here and now, as he had consistently been, and in particular with the state of mind of the detainees. Having weathered the storm of the hunger strike, he was desperate to provide them with any sign of positive movement that would take them out of limbo and give them a legal process, any legal process. Eager to do this sooner rather than later, he addressed the detainees on the 21st and told them about the announcement of the military commissions. It was going to happen, he assured them. Finally. He had already walked through X-Ray, together with Baccus, introducing him to several of the detainees, letting them know that he was about to be replaced. Now he had something to give to the detainees in addition to a replacement. He had hope to offer them—in the form of hearings that would, it seemed practical to assume, end their perpetual limbo.

The detainees stood in their cells, listening to Lehnert's departing words.[8] Lehnert advised them as best he could. "Cooperate fully," he told them. Trying his best to paint a picture of a rosier future, and knowing it was his last chance to do so, Lehnert spoke about the new facility to which the detainees were about to move, a complex with plumbing and electricity, and with privacy as well as air-conditioning. He told them that for Ashura, a Shia holiday, the fast would be respected by providing food before sunrise and after sunset. And

Lehnert told them yet another piece of news—that Saif's wife had given them a cookbook they could use to prepare more ethnically and religiously suitable meals.

Lehnert's urge to throw goodwill the way of the detainees, as if to encourage them to hold on just a little bit longer, amounted to a sad farewell. He made no mention of the death penalty, nor did he allude to the Pentagon's intention to keep some of them at Guantanamo without trials. Keen to raise their sinking spirits, he had tailored the truth. Seeing the military commissions as the one avenue to legality at Guantanamo, Lehnert tried to convince himself along with the detainees that the commission processes could change things. They could introduce not just legality, but hope for an end to the limbo into which the detainees had been thrust.

Finally, before he left, Lehnert needed to have one last word with the press.

Alongside the anger of the troops and the despair of the detainees, the presence of the press was a third source of pressure on JTF 160. Every member of Lehnert's command team whom I interviewed, when asked what the most difficult part of the mission had been, answered, usually without hesitation: the media. The lack of experience with the press, its constant presence, and the attention of the public, domestic and international, were daily facts of life from the day before the detainees' arrived.

Now, in preparation for his departure, Lehnert had one last chance to address the press corps. Although he privately winced at the constant presence of the press, his relationship with the journalists covering Guantanamo had remained cordial and polite. Overall, guided by Bill Costello at SOUTHCOM and Steve Cox at Guantanamo, Lehnert had successfully avoided a major incident with the news media, something which would prove much more difficult for Baccus, who would eventually find himself at odds with members of the press corps, including both Carol Rosenberg and Bob Franken. Lehnert had managed to make a persuasive case that the detainees were fairly treated even during the hunger strike.[9]

There had been moments of conflict, however, that did not augur well for Lehnert's legacy. He had, in February, tossed out a photographer for taking pictures of the transport of detainees to and from the interrogation huts on gurneys. The dismissal was based on the principle of adherence to the Geneva Conventions, but it seemed also to have to do with the fact that the gurneys conveyed an undesirable image of the way detainees were being treated. The photos displayed a major faux pas on the part of JTF 160, a wrong decision that was quickly reversed. Always focused on the visuals, Lehnert had made an example of the banned photographer, unwilling to see her as a potential ally as he had Carol Rosenberg. So, too, he had treated the press without much respect when he tried to deny the significance of the hunger strike by likening it to the reporters' own decision to skip breakfast. He had, on these two occasions, violated his own allegiance to transparency, falling instead into the doublespeak of the administration.

Now, he called one last press briefing. But as prelude to that meeting, there was one relationship he wanted to address directly—the one with Carol Rosenberg of the *Miami Herald*.

Two days prior to Lehnert's scheduled departure, a new kind of flag flew over the airfield. Up early as always, Rosenberg noted the flag with her usual curiosity. She had never seen this one before and couldn't find it by searching on the Internet. It was salmon-colored and it bore two insignia: a star and a palm tree. Predictably, Rosenberg asked about the flag. She got no answer, and the next time she looked, it had been taken down. Rosenberg's further attempts to find out about it were fruitless.

Two days later, General Lehnert met the press for his final briefing, hosting them for the first time in his office. On the ride over to the windward side, Rosenberg, who often vetted her questions first with Cox, asked if she could ask about the strange flag. She was surprised by Cox's quick assent. "Yes, ask about that," Cox told her, smiling. As they entered Lehnert's office, she saw the flag draped over a table. Immediately, she piped up with her question. "General Lehnert, the flag that's over there. Can you tell me about it?" "We'll get to that," the General responded. But Rosenberg refused to wait. She was insistent, not wanting to be sidelined and then forgotten. "Okay," Lehnert said. "We can start with that." He paused. "The thing is, Carol, it's yours. It's your flag." He paused again. "We had it made for you." Rosenberg laughed, still wanting to know what it was, and displeased with what seemed to be a glib remark. She had no choice but to allow the general to proceed with the rest of the briefing.[10]

When the briefing ended, Lehnert still hadn't returned to the topic of the flag, and Rosenberg knew better than to push any harder. She was disappointed but it was just one more piece of absent information among many down at Gitmo. As the press left the office, Lehnert called after her. "Carol, you've forgotten something." She turned. "Your flag. You've forgotten your flag." The star signified the flags she had persistently tracked, even at the wee hours of the morning, and the palm tree presumably signified her home base, Miami. Shocked, never quite understanding the role she had played, Rosenberg took the flag with her. It had been made especially for her, under the direction of Michael Lehnert. The unspoken message was this: Keep doing what you're doing. *Please.*

That night, the Pentagon officially announced that Michael Dunlavey would be commanding the JTF 170.

The next morning, March 28, was the day of departure for JTF 160. Michael Lehnert awoke with a sense that he'd done what he could to prepare for his leave-taking. It had been 100 days since he had first received the phone call announcing his deployment to JTF 160 at Guantanamo. It had been 81 days since the JTF had arrived at the base, full of foreboding.

Much had been accomplished. The ICRC had arrived, despite the Pentagon's initial refusal to invite them. Although Saifulislam would leave in another month, a slot for a Muslim chaplain had been created. The Joint Task Force concept had worked, with minimal rivalry between the troops and none that undermined the functioning of the camp or the larger base. Most of all, to the extent possible within the mandate of the care-and-custody mission of JTF 160, Lehnert's directive to follow the Geneva Conventions had been generally obeyed. And those who wanted to circumvent the law had been resisted and temporarily thwarted.

The rotation of command was to be the first of six prior to the summer of 2008.[11] General Gary Speer, along with Generals Jackman and Burgess, flew in from SOUTHCOM for the ceremony, bearing gifts. Jackman presented Lehnert with a coffee mug that he continues to use to this day, and Speer gave him the military's traditional testament to a job well done—a military coin naming the mission or the unit served. Then it was time for Lehnert to deliver his closing words. Addressing the assembled officers and others outside the Pink Palace, Lehnert spoke as if hoping to cast a spell that would outlast his words. He reminded the assembled, Dunlavey and Baccus standing there among them, that the honor of the country was at stake. He reminded them that becoming like the enemy was more akin to defeat than success.

The change of command went unnoticed by the *Washington Post* and the *New York Times*. Ironically—given the slow progress of the commissions, which had damaged JTF 160's ability to manage the detention—both papers were too focused on Rumsfeld's and Haynes's policy announcements about military commissions to pay attention to a seemingly routine rotation of command at the base itself. Even the *Miami Herald* did not devote much space to fact of the change of command from Lehnert to Baccus, preferring to focus on Dunlavey, who had elected to speak to the press that day "for the first time."[12]

But it was, in the evolution of Gitmo toward shame and disaster, a genuinely momentous occasion.

That morning, Bob Buehn, Al Shimkus, and Michael Lehnert took their final run together, a truncated version of their usual Sunday route. They ran along Sherman Avenue but not down to Windmill Beach. As they neared the top of the steepest part of the street, Rick Baccus joined them, conspicuously fit and in shape. The symbolism was hard to miss. The first JTF 160 had carried the mission up the most treacherous of slopes but had not quite succeeded in mastering the challenge. And now, in the midst of the escalating conflict, Rick Baccus was stepping in. Only, the group would now be moving forward without Michael Lehnert. With Baccus now leading JTF 160, it would be a treacherous climb to the summit and beyond.

Meanwhile Dunlavey was essentially biding his time, knowing that Lehnert's departure was imminent. As if to signal his expectations for the new regime, he presented Lehnert with a book—a history of the Guadalcanal campaign, the successful series of battles that turned the tide in the Pacific theater during World War Two and in which the Marines played an indispensable role. It was a thoughtful gesture. It acknowledged Lehnert's love of history and gave homage to the successes of joint forces. Most of all, it was a nod to the Marines who had played a major role in the battle. It was Dunlavey at his best. Confident about the future without Michael Lehnert, he tried to be generous and charming on the personal level.

From McCalla Hill, outside the Pink Palace, Lehnert and his Marines went directly to the leeward side and the waiting commercial jet. Climbing aboard, few if any were regretful over their leave-taking. Many heaved a sigh of relief that they had completed the mission without greater confrontation and violence.

Behind on the tarmac, on the base, and at X-Ray itself, a stillness prevailed. No one felt the emptiness and the uncertainty of the future at Guantanamo more than Saifulislam. Yet he was consoled by the parting gift that Lehnert had left him, a pen carved out of wood found on the base. Lehnert had made it himself. He had presented Al Shimkus and Bob Buehn with pens from his lathe as well, reminders to all, perhaps, that when they signed things, his support—and his conscience—would be with them.

That afternoon, Bob Buehn returned to his office. Under normal circumstances, he might have indulged in some thoughtful reflection on Michael Lehnert's JTF 160. But this day, he had another, more immediately pressing concern at hand. That evening, a country rock group, the Charlie Daniels Band, would be entertaining the troops and the families on the base. And, in fact, Charlie Daniels himself was coming by the office to introduce himself. Larger than life, with his signature white hair and beard, his Southern-style cowboy sound, and his incomparable fiddle playing, Daniels drew the attention of officers and enlisted personnel, reservists and regular troops alike, distracting them from the daily chores and difficulties that had come to define Guantanamo and its ever-present tensions.

Daniels was known for his unbridled anger over the events of 9/11. In October 2001, he had even pulled out of Country Music Television's annual television show, where he was customarily one of the stars. The organizers had asked him not to perform his newest single, entitled "This Ain't No Rag, It's a Flag"—a patriotic call for retribution for 9/11—on the grounds that it might offend some viewers. Daniels's response was to withdraw from the program. As he explained later, "I don't think this is a time for healing. I feel that this is the time to rub salt in the wounds and keep America focused on the job at hand."[13]

That night, the Charlie Daniels Band played to a full house of 500 at the Windjammer Ballroom, in the heart of town, about two and a half miles down the road from Camp X-Ray. Bob Buehn enjoyed the break from the tension of the daytime routine that had come with the JTF. Debi Buehn, too, enjoyed the concert immensely. For many, it was a high point in the Guantanamo deployment. One Marine Corps reservist stood in awe as Daniels played six songs on the Marine's guitar. Daniels played to the crowd, changing the words to his best-known song, "The Devil Came Down to Georgia," to fit the event. "The Devil Went down to Gitmo," the band crooned, "He was looking for some Taliban." The crowd "went wild with applause."[14]

Among the songs that the band played was the one that the promoters at Country Music Television had worried about, "This Ain't No Rag, It's a Flag." Released during the summer of 2003 on his album *Freedom and Justice for All*, the song was a clarion call to patriotism, an unveiled reference to the attacks of 9/11, and an embrace of revenge. The enemy, described as "a dirty little mole," needed to be hunted down "like a mad dog hound" to "pay for the lives you stole."

According to Daniels, this song captivated his Gitmo audience, as did one other song, "America," which celebrated the American spirit. Others on the base agreed that the concert had been successful in reminding the audience of just what America stood for. "Charlie is a good symbol of America," one fireman on the base told the Associated Press.[15]

It was the perfect unwriting of the Lehnert script. As Daniels explained in his soapbox web posting "Poor Ole' al Qaeda," "These people behave like animals, therefore they have to be treated like animals. Put in cages where they can be watched and monitored twenty four hours a day . . . given food and water and a place to sleep which is about all they had in those holes in the ground in Afghanistan." Daniels would later speak and write with conviction about U.S. policy at Guantanamo. "The truth is that these scum bags are not only being treated humanely, they are probably better off healthwise and medically than they've ever been. . . . "[16]

The air still ringing with the memories of the Daniels concert, a new era was launched at Guantanamo Bay Detention Facility, embodied in the insistent chords of the band. Perhaps it was not by coincidence that, as Shafiq Rasul remembers, the afternoon of Lehnert's departure was punctuated by the beating of a detainee that caught everyone off guard with its brutality. Something new was definitely in the air. And though no one at Guantanamo Bay knew it yet, the war on terror had taken a step forward that day. Abu Zubaydah, one of the masterminds of 9/11, was captured on the 28th and was now in U.S. custody,[17] though there was no mention of plans to bring him to Guantanamo.

With a new spirit in the air, a new cast of commanders, and the possibility of information coming from outside of Guantanamo, the detention facility could be truly transformed into the interrogation center that the Pentagon had in mind.

Before he left, Charlie Daniels gave Bob Buehn the violin bow he had played with during the Gitmo concert. In less than 24 hours, Buehn had received two gifts that he would keep forever—the fiddlestick he continues to cherish, as the gift of a celebrity and American musical icon, and the pen Lehnert had made for him, a reminder of a friend whose commitment to justice rather than vengeance he had helped uphold for the first 100 days of the camp. For Buehn, both were reasons to smile. Like Buehn, the newly constituted JTF would try its best to keep itself aloof from the conflicting messages of the dual command—that of Dunlavey and that of Baccus, that of interrogation and that of detention. But there were forces out there—Dunlavey's aggressiveness, for instance, and the unseen but ever present hand of Washington—that would make it impossible for any task force or commander, no matter how strong of heart, to uphold Lehnert's legacy.

When Lehnert and his team pulled out of Guantanamo, the building of Camp Delta began, and by late April the new JTF 160 began to move the prisoners into their new quarters, which stood on the same ground that the migrant camps for Cubans and Haitians had once occupied.

Unlike X-Ray, which had been along the main road and sported open cages, Camp Delta was invisible. Located far away from the center of town, approximately three miles down the road from X-Ray, Radio Range's 600–700-acre patch was out of the way, tucked away miles off Sherman Avenue, "up and over the hill." It was more out of sight from the Cuban guard towers than X-Ray had been. And it was even more hidden from the sight of those who dwelt on the American side of the island than those on the Cuban side. Residents of the Villamar housing complex had been able to see the lights of X-Ray, and even to hear the morning call to prayer. For Radio Range, there was no such proximity to residents of the base, or to anyone else not directly involved in the work of Delta. People would seldom go by it on their way anywhere. Further institutionalizing the separation from the rest of the base, a gate was built to divide the rest of the island base from the new compound.

Eventually, Delta's isolation would be complete, for both the staff and the detainees. It was created to be a self-contained community, and over the next year it would become just that—a place where the soldiers who worked inside the wire could find anything from a bar to a movie theater. The complex would eventually sport a chapel, an auditorium, restaurants, a recreation area, and a gymnasium. For those who had lived on the island since before the arrival of JTF 160, it was as if the new detention facility didn't exist.[18]

Lehnert had fought hard for the building of this new prison city as an antidote to the primitive conditions of X-Ray, which had bordered on the inhumane. Now the new, stronger structures were in place, solid, with walls and proper ceilings, and impervious to the winds of a hurricane. But, in an ironic twist, the changes that occurred inside these new structures were a far cry from what Lehnert would have envisioned, or tolerated, within their walls.

The once excessively visible camp was now cloaked in invisibility. Unlike X-Ray, Delta was out of sight and hidden. And what went on beyond its gates would now be done behind closed doors.

Guantanamo's physical transformation was mirrored in the nature of General Rick Baccus's command. Where Lehnert had relied upon tact and diplomacy, as well as a measure of trust, Baccus substituted rules and regulations. Baccus embraced his own tendencies toward control and order, and lived up to the Army's reputation for bureaucracy, by putting pen to paper. Within a day of assuming his new post, the reservist general from Rhode Island began to issue policy letter after policy letter, as if doing so could ease the tense atmosphere into which he had stepped. "All of a sudden we had more written orders than you could shake a stick at. We were drilling things that we had been doing for months. . . . " said the medical administrator Pat Alford.[19]

Ranging from fraternization and pornography to dress code, the letters revealed Baccus's strategy of using memos to mitigate the overpowering sense that things were out of his control.[20] But it was more than just a retreat to paper. For in these policy letters, Baccus shifted the attention of JTF 160 away from matters relating to the detainees.[21] Instead, as Ray Fannaro, the Command Sergeant Major of JTF 160 under Baccus, later explained, "it was always soldiers first."[22] When he did focus on the detainees, Baccus insisted that his policy decisions began with the needs of his troops. He allowed the detainees "to do what they would normally do in their religious observances" not primarily out of a sense of moral obligation to the detainees but because to his mind it was something that was good for the troops. This way, he reasoned, "they're not spitting on my MPs or throwing urine at them or feces or anything else they can find, and creating havoc in the camp."[23]

This too, became his rationale for the use of dogs and a restrained use of the Immediate Reaction Force. The soldiers risked being hurt every time they had physical contact with the detainees. Every time the Immediate Reaction Force entered the cells, it posed a danger to the troops. After all, the detainees weren't about to go anywhere, so employing excessive force could only cause unnecessary harm to the soldiers.

Similarly, Baccus developed an attitude toward isolation that was anchored to what best promoted the safety of his soldiers. He insisted that isolation lasting more than 30 days—and thus extending beyond the legal limit—required SOUTHCOM's approval. He reasoned not out of human rights concerns for the detainees but out of his belief that the psychological deterioration that the illegal isolation would cause would in turn induce anger among the detainees, an anger he feared would be directed against the soldiers.[24]

Reasoning this way, Baccus pulled back from some of Lehnert's firmest policies. Like Carrico, Baccus did not approve of guards—let alone himself—talking to detainees. The new physical reality made his sentiments easy to reinforce. For, once inside Delta, the prisoners did not have a way to communicate easily either with each other or with the guards, as they were separated from one another, closed off behind doors and glass windows. Likewise, when it came to Saifulislam, Baccus sought to use him more as a window into the prisoners' behavior than as an interpreter for Muslim culture and religious practices.

For Lehnert, this would have been putting the cart before the horse. "I wasn't worried about the soldiers. They could take care of themselves."[25] The last thing that would concern him was the safety of his Marines or regular army soldiers. On the contrary, he trusted the strength and expertise that came from their training. It seemed to be different when it came to the reservists who by now made up the majority of JTF 160 force.

No one felt the change more directly than the detainees themselves. They sensed the change of emphasis with a sense of panic. Psychologically, the move to Delta was an immensely destructive blow. Though it is hard to imagine preferring life in cages, many remember the days of the wire mesh cells as the good old days. In the new cells, they couldn't communicate with anyone. They were essentially in isolation, especially when compared to their cages, where at least they could see and interact with other human beings, prisoners and guards alike.

Their new cells were smaller than the cages of X-Ray, and far more isolating for the detainees. True, the new cells had walls, a proper ceiling, and a tiny sliver-like elongated window, along with stainless steel toilets and sinks at the proper level for ablutions for their feet, as well as beds that came out sturdily from the walls. The prospect of lizards and insects scurrying through their cells at all hours had vanished. Furthermore, there was running water, and lights for each cell. The medical facility had already been open and running at Delta already for a while. And the new interrogation rooms were equipped with air-conditioning, carpets, and the ability to tape the sessions—something the huts at X-Ray had not had.

Above all, their new walls and their shining new toilets and beds were all too suggestively permanent.

These individual detainees, and the 500 who would follow, had been moved out of a physical limbo. But they were not moving toward a future. They were here to stay—without charge, without lawyers, without process, without a trial. Encased in concrete, they had been buried alive.

Postscript: The Banality of Goodness

"While we are struggling mightily to try to find out what happened in Abu Ghraib,
they are beheading people....We are nothing like our enemy..."
—Alberto Gonzales

The U.S. military has made a fetish of reminiscence. After nearly every operation, the memories are stored. Interviews are taped, photographs are archived, and relevant documents are stamped and shelved. Sometimes videos appear, useful for recruiting purposes as well as for documentation. The military calls these histories "Lessons Learned."

The lessons to be learned from JTF 160's experience at Guantanamo are vast and varied—and ultimately sad. And they speak far beyond the 45 square miles of the southeastern tip of Cuba.

By May, the move to Delta was complete. The detainees were no longer in plain sight. And Michael Dunlavey's parallel command had begun to take over virtual command of the camp. Within weeks, Dunlavey was pushing to extend his command to the medical facilities, to the chaplain's office, and into the daily lives of JTF 160 troops. Starting at the top, he expressed his desire to have Rick Baccus report to him.[1] Shimkus found himself battling against requests to use the services of the psychiatrists whom he had hired to attend to the mental health of the detainees. His use of the psychiatrists was to diagnose and treat the psychiatric problems that detainees were experiencing. Dunlavey, it appeared, wanted advice from the psychologists about how best to get information from individual detainees. After refusing to comply, the chief medical officer heard from his staff that the office files had been rifled through.[2] Meanwhile, Saif was subjected to the pressures against which Lehnert had effectively protected him. It was left to Baccus, ineffective in so many ways, to defend Saif against Dunlavey.[3] Baccus, for his part, stumbled periodically onto JTF 170's intrusions into his command, finding, for example, on a walk through Delta, that JTF 170 had ordered the lowering of temperatures in one of the cell blocks, an order which he quickly reversed.[4] The ICRC continued to offer some protection against lawlessness but was now there periodically rather than permanently. And the press, while still there exerting its own form of pressure in the name of accountability, was unable to see much of what was going on.

It was only a matter of time.

As the tenor began to change at Guantanamo, Washington provided additional help. Specifically, the Office of Legal Counsel now put the final—and fateful—touches on the policy that had begun with the Military Order of November 13, 2001. On the first of August 2002, the Office of Legal Counsel, over the signature of Jay Bybee, the departing head of OLC, issued a memo legalizing what amounted to torture. Attributed to John Yoo as well as to Bybee, the memo redefined the nature of torture. Anything other than "pain . . . of an intensity akin to that which accompanies serious physical injury such as death or organ failure"[5] fell outside the category and did not constitute torture.

With this memo, a mission and a policy that had begun as a discussion of battlefield detention and military tribunals had officially been transformed into an interrogation mission. And for that mission, the basic rules of conduct had changed. Not surprisingly, there were still no defense attorneys at Guantanamo, nor was there much discernible progress toward the military commissions. Detention, originally the handmaiden to the battlefield effort and simultaneously the alleged partner of the military commissions, now had the legal backing to become the stepchild for interrogation outside the law. According to Baccus, interrogations picked up speed in August, taking place around the clock.

As the administration in Washington provided legal cover, Dunlavey escalated the course toward harsh interrogation techniques not just by defying professional detention policy but also by signaling a tolerance for lowered standards when it came to off-duty behavior. Baccus's policy letters were ineffective against the parties at which Dunlavey was on occasion a participant, indicating to the troops that Baccus was not entirely in control and that the rules need not always apply. Baccus's emphasis on deterring his troops' consumption of alcohol and guarding against sexual activity thus took on new significance.[6]

But it was a losing battle. In an environment removed from the world, rife with tension and pent-up patriotic anger, these parties stood as a possible spark for the kinds of passions that General Lehnert had done his best to restrain.

The summer of 2002—with its attempts to undo Lehnert's policies, the persistent battling between the two JTF commands, and the nighttime parties—constituted the transition from the 100 days of General Lehnert to the days of interrogation via enhanced interrogation techniques that would follow late in the year.

On August 2, the day following the issuance of the torture memo, Congress confirmed the appointment of General James "Tom" Hill to be combatant commander at SOUTHCOM. Finally, the acting CINC Gary Speer—who for nearly a year had stood in without the requisite rank or support staff to run what had become one of the more difficult commands in the military—could leave the command that was expressly over his head in terms of military protocol.

General Jackman remembers informing Hill immediately of the problems that were mounting at Guantanamo. "The first thing that I told him," Jackman recalls, "was that there are two things that demand your attention right now. You've got to demand that there be one JTF. And you have to get rid of the two reserve generals and bring in an active duty general."[7]

But if Hill understood the weaknesses and potential danger inherent in the disunited command structure, and the personalities of Baccus and Dunlavey, he did not seem to have control over the timing when it came to changing things. Not until mid-October did General Hill pull Baccus out—a dismissal clouded in silence—and when he did, without giving Baccus advance notice, Hill left Dunlavey in charge by himself for a period of several weeks, from October 11 to November 4.

On the very day that Baccus packed up and left, October 11, a new memo appeared over the signature of Dunlavey's lawyer, Lieutenant Colonel Diane Beaver. Under increasing pressure to get information from the detainees and concerned with getting information particularly from Mohammed al-Qahtani, the so-called twentieth hijacker, the Pentagon had issued a list of 18 new techniques, outside of those allowed by the military interrogation manual, that could be used during interrogations.[8]

These techniques were divided into three categories. The first group, Category I, included yelling and techniques of deception. Category II techniques included sensory deprivation, prolonged isolation for up to 30 days, the use of stress positions and 20-hour interrogations, hooding, the removal of clothing, and the use of phobias such as fear of dogs, among other things. Many expressly violated the Geneva Conventions. Category III pushed the

standards even further toward illegality, including techniques such as water-
boarding and the use of threats of death for the detainee or his family.⁹

Under tremendous pressure, Dunlavey's lawyer, Diane Beaver, had been
asked to assess these techniques on legal grounds. Her memo to Dunlavey
concluded that the techniques were legally permissible, even those in
Category III.¹⁰ "It was not my job," she says in her defense, "to second-guess
the President."¹¹ Her hope, she later claimed, was that at SOUTHCOM or
somewhere else up the chain, someone would review and annul her work.¹²

When Hill received Beaver's memo, he sent it down to Manuel Supervielle. It
was now more than 10 months since Supervielle had stepped into this look-
ing-glass world in which with each step he took the ground he recognized
seemed to erode. He had watched as Article V hearings were summarily dismissed, as the Geneva Conventions were set aside, and as his own efforts to
protect the rule of law were ridiculed by his superiors. Now Supervielle pro-
crastinated over the latest manifestation of an operation at Guantanamo that
continued to move away from recognizable legal ground—Diane Beaver's
memo.

Nearly two weeks later, he still hadn't addressed her briefing. As a result,
he was called into the office of Brigadier General Ronald Burgess, the J-2, or
director of intelligence, for SOUTHCOM. Burgess had just gotten off the
phone with Jim Haynes, he told Supervielle. Apparently, Beaver's memo had gone
to the Pentagon as well as to SOUTHCOM, yet another sign of the dual chains
of command at work within Dunlavey's JTF. Haynes, it seems, was incensed,
wanting to know why JTF 170, which reported to Burgess, had not yet implemented the enhanced interrogation techniques approved in Beaver's memo.

Called on the carpet for his delay, Supervielle explained his disagreement
with the memo, dismissing it as irresponsible at best and incorrect as to the
law at worst. Supervielle remembers explaining to Burgess that certain techniques in Category II probably violated laws even if the United States were not
beholden to Geneva. He further opined that Category III techniques were illegal under U.S. criminal law. As an intelligence professional, Burgess, according to Supervielle, was not as opposed to the use of these techniques as was
the lawyer, but more to the point, Burgess seemed unwilling to get involved in
any pushback against Washington. What do you expect me to think about your
objections when Washington has said that it's okay? Supervielle remembers
him asking. If Supervielle wanted to register his objections, he would have to
speak to Hill on his own, without Burgess.¹³

Hill did not have the luxury of taking himself out of the loop as Burgess did. When Supervielle explained his legal objections to the Beaver memo, he advised his commanding general to send the memo back down to Guantanamo, to tell JTF 170 that it was a "no go." Hill decided instead to pass the matter up the chain of command.

When he sent his memo to General Myers, the chairman of the Joint Chiefs, Hill acknowledged the failure of accepted techniques in eliciting information from "some detainees." Concluding that the "first two catego-ries . . . are legal and humane," he admitted that he was "uncertain about all the techniques in the third category" and put that matter in the hands of the lawyers at DOD.[14]

With legal sanction and the power of his unified command position behind him, Dunlavey, Rumsfeld's man at Guantanamo, stepped into the role of Commander JTF GTMO with gusto. In theory an amalgamation of JTF 160 and JTF 170, JTF GTMO was finally positioned to become the interrogation center that Donald Rumsfeld had wanted from the very start. Dunlavey was on board with an interrogation policy that considered the Geneva Conventions too antiquated for the needs of the war on terror. As Dunlavey explained it, "Mr. Rumsfeld wanted to know who they were and what they knew. He wanted me to 'maximize the intelligence production.' No one ever said to me 'the gloves are off.' But I didn't need to talk about the Geneva Conventions, it was clear that they didn't apply. The President said they should be treated humanely. But Geneva didn't apply."[15]

Despite his evident desire to be the commander of JTF GTMO, Dunlavey was relieved of command on November 4, 2002. He was, therefore, not able to implement the new techniques that had been approved. That would wait on one more memo—written by Haynes, approved by Rumsfeld[16]—and one more appointment—that of Dunlavey's successor, General Geoffrey Miller. The following year, 2003–04, many of the patterns that had been aborted dur-ing Lehnert's regime came to fruition at JTF GTMO.

It took a full six months for Dunlavey and those who followed to fully break the back of what General Lehnert and his 160 had endeavored to build—a custody regime that adhered to international law and, beyond that, consid-ered the detainees to be human beings deserving of fair and just treatment.

Still, by the time General Dunlavey departed in November 2002, Michael Lehnert's efforts to hold back the forces of the extralegal and the illegal, and to insist upon upholding the tenets of military professionalism, had effectively been erased.

One curious fact about the discussions over Beaver's legal memo was the Pentagon's insistence, through Haynes, on legal documents to back up what were essentially considered policies that had already been approved from above and were waiting to be implemented. From the first issuance of the Military Order to the last Rumsfeld memo, the paper trail was relied on as a necessity for setting policy and claiming it to be legal. Similarly, though behind-the-scenes processes led to the Military Order and to subsequent memos influenced by the War Council, the need for aboveboard interagency processes remained important. And in their legitimacy lay their power, as JTF 160 so powerfully demonstrated.

As for legal documents, so for interagency processes. Whether they were seeking immunity—which was a strong factor in all of the memos—or just finding a way to institutionalize the radical reforms they had in mind, the fact was that the administration, for all of its secrecy, redefinitions of law, and subversion of process, tried its best to create what it saw as the "correct" legal avenues. For that, they needed a paper trail.

In Beaver's case, the muscle and pressure of the Pentagon was enough to get the job done. She complied. By contrast, Powell and Taft, like the generals at SOUTHCOM—all occupying much higher positions than Beaver—took the option of behind-the-scenes protest and then withdrawal, rather than compliance.

But for JTF 160, an instinctive understanding of the power of those who implement policy as opposed to those who create it led to another path: that of pushback, and ultimately defiance. The Pentagon had assumed JTF 160 would carry out their policies despite the fact that those policies began with a rejection of law. They were wrong. And as it turned out, without the compliance of the soldiers on the ground, the strength and power of authority could only go so far. Lehnert and his command staff had found their own ways to keep the process within the law. But they were easily replaced with individuals who proved powerless to resist the pressures from above.

Without fanfare, without verbal articulation, but with their attitude toward management and operations, JTF 160 turned what was a hoped-for lawless zone into a potentially lawful one. But no matter what, it could not have lasted.

In March of 2003, the United States invaded Iraq, and an entirely new population of detainees came into U.S. custody—this time in a place where there was no question about the status of the Geneva Conventions. Iraq was a sovereign country and as such subject to the restrictions and protections of international law.

From the earliest days of American detainees in Iraq, the lessons of Guantanamo were ignored and its problems repeated. Weak commanders, competing commands, and a lack of policy guidance provided a suitable environment for questionable detention operations. At Abu Ghraib, reservist Brigadier General Janis Karpinski found her detention effort subservient to the demands of the interrogation regime.[17] In addition, at issue in Iraq were a paucity of skilled prison guards and a general absence of policy guidance.[18] As Lieutenant General Ricardo Sanchez says about Abu Ghraib, referring to a time one and a half years after Lehnert's command at Guantanamo, "When circumstances on the ground required the need for establishment of standards and guidance for soldiers in a variety of areas (such as detention and interrogation procedures, among many others), we immediately acted. I made repeated requests to higher headquarters for help. But when the Pentagon refused to help us with interrogation procedures, I issued the guidelines myself."[19] In the words of the Schlesinger Report on DOD Detention Operations, "Interrogation policies...were inadequate or deficient." And there was a notable "absence of specific guidance from CENTCOM."[20]

It was the same story. In the absence of policy, ad hoc lawless behavior could easily, even predictably, occur. Professionalism and unity of command, two of the basic tenets that had guided Lehnert's command of JTF 160, had been a deterrent at Guantanamo. Now, both were pushed aside at Abu Ghraib as well—in full knowledge of the likely consequences.

Structurally, politically, and legally, the pattern of a policy void as a threshold to illegal behavior—the pattern that would erupt at Abu Ghraib—had been created, tinkered with, and adapted on the Caribbean island base.

But the most lasting legacy of Guantanamo's JTF 160 has not been the governmental perversions of policy that succeeded in eroding time-honored principles of military protocol and international law. The most lasting legacy of the early Guantanamo is the image of the slight, dark-skinned men in orange jumpsuits, chained and bent over on their knees, goggled and deafened, dehydrated and soiled, unaware of where they were or why they were at Guantanamo, and destined not to be told unless the Bush administration yielded to a whim to tell them. This was an image, paradoxically, from Michael Lehnert's time. And it is one he never succeeded in erasing from public memory—or from his own. It was the hand that was dealt to JTF 160 and through them, to the United States as a whole.

Backing away from that image has been impossible, not because Lehnert and his 160 didn't try, but because no amount of tinkering could fix a policy that was determined to be cruel and inhumane. Today, when the men—many of them still children, actually, when they arrived at Guantanamo—are seen weeping[21] or are reported to be banging their heads on the tables and walls out of despair, or when three detainees, ages 21, 28, and 30, are found dead of suicide after five years of imprisonment and others are found hanging but still alive,[22] it is all to be expected. This may even have been the intention from the beginning. The plan may have been primarily to teach the world a lesson; Americans can be as cruel as others. Americans can turn their backs on law and reciprocity among nations as well as any tribally organized dictatorship can. Americans can dehumanize other human beings by a reliance on fear and the human impulse toward vengeance.

One can only wonder what might have happened had the military protocols established under Lehnert been able to continue as U.S. policy. Certainly, the reputation of the United States would not have been as damaged as it has been by the unabashed pushing aside of law. A more pressing question perhaps— how the United States would have fared in terms of national security—also yields a disturbing conclusion. For all of the time, effort, distortions of law, and allocations of funds put into Guantanamo, after seven years, the only result has been two convictions. David Hicks pleaded guilty and was returned to Australia in 2007, where he served out a nine-month term. And in 2008, there was conviction of Salim Hamdan, a driver for bin Laden against whom there was such scant evidence that his sentence was only five and a half years.

This is hardly a record of judicial successes, or something for the most powerful and reputedly advanced nation on earth to take pride in. And the cost has been extraordinary in terms of wasted resources, political energy, and distractions from effective national security. Nor has the informational value of the detainees panned out. While 14 "high-value detainees" were moved to Guantanamo in 2006, among them masterminds who likely had valuable information, the later reason for Guantanamo's existence—the need to get information—turned out to be essentially flawed by the capture and detention of individuals who had little to no useful information to give.

It will take decades for Americans to recapture a sense of themselves as a country of good-hearted, knowledgeable people, confident in their ability to distinguish the dangerous from the ineffectual and defiantly convinced that the way of law and justice is the right way and, in fact, the only safe way. Maybe, going forward, the 100 days of Michael Lehnert and JTF 160 will serve as a model for Americans when they decide to reconnect with what has distinguished the United States at its best throughout history—not only its embrace of the rights of its own citizens but also its confidence in decency, honor, and compassion.

Michael Lehnert insists that once he left Guantanamo, he scarcely gave the detention facility a further thought. That's the way it is in the military. You move on. You focus on your new mission.

But his distraction was only temporary. Even though he was preoccupied with the deployment of his unit to Kuwait, in anticipation of the invasion of Iraq, Guantanamo stayed on his mind. And it has stayed on his mind to this day, gathering momentum with each inquiry into prisoner abuse and each accusation of illegality at the hands of the military. And even by the fall of 2002, he had begun to worry about the legacy of Guantanamo, a facility which he had started.

As Bob Buehn recalls, when the change of command from Baccus to Dunlavey occurred, Michael Lehnert was definitely paying attention. On the day following the change of command to Dunlavey, Lehnert sent an e-mail to Buehn, his former deputy. Lehnert made the usual pleasantries about family and work. He raised a question or two about Buehn's role in the new JTF GTMO. Before signing off, he asked Bob to send his regards to two people, Al Shimkus and Carol Rosenberg, signaling to Buehn that, in the absence of Saif who had departed months before, they were the two who had shared the conscience of law and morality.

In the subject line of the message, Michael Lehnert hammered home the point he had raised more subtly with the mention of Shimkus and Rosenberg. Here, preserved for the future should anyone care to look, was his epitaph to all that had gone before and to all that he feared would come.

His words, as his command had been, were deceptively simple, easily overlooked, and starkly prophetic.

"What goes around comes around."

Notes

Preface

1. Many of these later stories have been expertly told. See, for example, Philippe Sands, *Torture Team: Rumsfeld's Memo and the Betrayal of American Values* (New York: Palgrave Macmillan, 2008); Jane Mayer, *The Dark Side: The Inside Story of How the War on Terror Turned into a War on American Ideals* (New York: Doubleday, 2008); Tim Golden, "The Battle for Guantánamo," *The New York Times Magazine* (September 17, 2006); Clive Stafford-Smith, *The Eight O'Clock Ferry to the Windward Side: Fighting the Lawless World of Guantanamo Bay* (New York: Nation Books, 2007).

Chapter 1

1. Author interview with Capt. Robert Buehn, January 14, 2008. See also Angus Phillips, "Seeking Solace in the Long Run," *Washington Post*, October 29, 2001.

2. Carlotta Gall, "Prison Sealed Off as U.S. Picks Inmates to Interrogate," *New York Times*, December 30, 2001. Rumsfeld later said, "We want to capture or kill the senior leadership.... We want to catch and imprison the remainder." Lally Weymouth, "Go After Them and Destroy Them," *Washington Post*, December 16, 2001.

3. Author interview with Pierre-Richard Prosper, July 1, 2008.

4. Hearing of the White House group from the *Washington Post*, Armitage asked Prosper to approach Gonzales's group, which he did. Author interview with Pierre-Richard Prosper, July 1, 2008.

5. In Prosper's words, "We knew right away that we would retaliate against the Taliban and al Qaeda. There would be prisoners." Author interview with Pierre-Richard Prosper, July 1, 2008.

6. The interagency group included the general counsels of all the major departments and agencies—the White House itself, the National Security Council (NSC), the Office of the Vice President (OVP), the State Department, the Office of the Secretary of Defense (OSD), the Chairman of the Joint Chiefs of Staff (JCS) and the intelligence agencies. Following the launch of Operation Enduring Freedom, the retaliation against the Taliban for having harbored bin Laden and al Qaeda in Afghanistan, they had met regularly to discuss matters related to the laws of war, to detention, and to fighting nonstate enemies within the bounds of the Constitution, due process, congressional statutes, military law, and international treaties.

7. The order, intentionally recalling Proclamation 2561, which President Franklin Roosevelt issued during World War II, acknowledged that there would be prisoners in the "state of armed conflict" that the terrorist attacks of September 11 had launched. According to the government, the president had authority to issue the Military Order and

create military commissions owing to the enactment by Congress of the Authorization for Use of Military Force Act (AUMF). This Act had authorized the president "to use all necessary and appropriate force against those nations, organizations, or persons he determines planned, authorized, committed, or aided the terrorist attacks that occurred on September 11, 2001, or harbored such organizations or persons," which, according to the government, legitimized the use of military commissions as one aspect of waging war. This argument was to some extent adopted by three dissenting justices in *Hamdan v. Rumsfeld*, 548 U.S. 557 (2006).

8. Subsequent debate would surround these issues and the addition of two new 1977 protocols to the conventions, Protocol I relating to the Protection of Victims of International Armed Conflicts and Protocol II relating to the Protection of Victims of Non-International Armed Conflicts.

9. Jennifer Elsea, "Terrorism and the Law of War: Trying Terrorists as War Criminals Before Military Commissions," CRS Report for Congress, December 11, 2001. Some of the differences in the two documents are worth noting from a historical point of view. The Military Order exempted the president and the secretary of defense from any opposition, legal or otherwise. President Roosevelt's proclamation had recognized that his authority could be restrained by the attorney general and the secretary of war; President Bush's order specifically rejected such limits on his authority. According to the Military Order, it was unclear just who could be apprehended and tried under the Military Order, though the assumption was that it would be only noncitizens.

10. Karen DeYoung, *Soldier: The Life of Colin Powell* (New York: Vintage, 2007), 36. Author interview with Pierre-Richard Prosper, July 1, 2008.

11. Chris Mackey and Greg Miller, *The Interrogators: Task Force 500 and America's Secret War on al Qaeda* (New York: Back Bay Books, 2005), 124.

12. Andy Worthington, *The Guantanamo Files: The Stories of the 759 Detainees in America's Illegal Prison* (Ann Arbor, Mich.: Pluto Press, 2007), 23–24.

13. "Al-Qaeda Prisoners Could Be Taken to Guam," *Global News Wire*, November 23, 2001.

14. Author interview with Pierre-Richard Prosper, July 1, 2008.

15. Author interview with Pierre-Richard Prosper, July 1, 2008. See also Michael J. Strauss, "Leasing Guantanamo Bay: A Guide to Territorial Arrangement," unpublished manuscript, 2007.

16. Steven Kleinman, "The History of MIS-Y: U.S. Strategic Interrogation During World War II," unpublished thesis, Joint Military Intelligence College (2002), 9.

17. Author interview with Pierre-Richard Prosper, January 16, 2008.

18. Author interview with Pierre-Richard Prosper, July 1, 2008; Michael J. Strauss, "Leasing Guantanamo Bay."

19. The request itself showed a degree of naïveté about the law, as even in outer space, treaty law applied at the time of these discussions.

20. Author interview with Capt. Robert and Debra W. Buehn, September 29, 2006.

21. Author interview with Capt. Robert and Debra W. Buehn, September 29, 2006.

22. Author interview with Capt. Robert and Debra W. Buehn, September 29, 2006.

23. Capt. John Pomfret, *The History of Guantanamo Bay, Vol. II*. U.S. Naval Base Guantanamo Bay Cuba, 1964–1982.

24. Author interview with Capt. Robert and Debra W. Buehn, September 29, 2006.

25. Author interview with Capt. Robert and Debra W. Buehn, September 29, 2006.

26. Author interview with Capt. Robert Buehn, February 8, 2007.

27. Author interview with Migdalia Hettler, February 9, 2007.

28. The funds for the initial construction at Guantanamo came from Navy funding lines and were later supplemented with other funds. An initial concern about the lack of funding made Buehn's staff jittery, but they persevered nevertheless, filling out order forms, projecting supply shortages, and waiting for the hypothetical "maybe" to flip into "all systems go." Author interview with Admiral Jan Gaudio, January 29, 2007; interview with Capt. Robert and Debra W. Buehn, September 29, 2006.

29. Author interview with Capt. Robert Buehn, February 8, 2007.

30. Michael J. Strauss, "Leasing Guantanamo Bay: A Guide to Territorial Arrangement," unpublished manuscript, 2007, chap. 4.

31. Author interview with Admiral Jan Gaudio, January 29, 2007.

32. Author interview with Northeast Gate tour officer, February 14, 2007.

33. Author interview with Capt. Robert Buehn, January 9, 2007.

34. Author interview with Capt. Robert and Debra W. Buehn, September 29, 2006.

35. Author interview with Capt. Robert Buehn, January 9, 2007.

36. Perhaps the most celebrated of these commuters among the resident community was Mr. Mack (short for McPherson), who planned and managed the entire numbering system for the buildings and facilities on the base and created the detailed map that listed these addresses.

37. Author interview with Capt. Robert and Debra W. Buehn, September 29, 2006.

38. Many Haitians at home also had HIV and therefore by law could not be granted entry to the United States. Ultimately, the federal courts upheld the Clinton administration's decision to ignore the international law principle of non*refoulement* (nonreturn) and to repatriate the HIV-infected Haitians to Haiti despite the threat of persecution; Nicola White's "The Tragic Plight of HIV-Infected Haitian Refugees at Guantanamo Bay" (*Liverpool Law Review* 28 (2007): 258, 263) explores the implications of this decision with respect to international human rights law. The *Miami Herald* assembled a time line of the Haitians' battle in the courts during the first migrant crisis, which it published under the title "Chronology of Rulings" on February 2, 2002. The Haitian Refugee Center in Miami sued on their behalf.

39. The Cubans at the camp were well educated and in relatively good health. As a result, their chances of successfully integrating into life in the United States were fairly good. The Haitians, by contrast, were understandably desperate about their future prospects. By far the smaller group, the Haitians also posed a much harder

challenge. They feared being sent back to Haiti, and their despondency cried out even to the young American troops guarding them. Nevertheless the military assessed this second migrant experience as a success. No one died; no diplomatic crisis ensued. And the improved handling of the detained seemed to have inspired "democratic" behavior in the camps; "Controversial Operation Sea Signal Draws to a Close," *All Things Considered*, National Public Radio, January 19, 1996; William Booth, " 'Gitmo' might not be Haitians' Club Fed, but gets 'A' as Asylum," *Washington Post*, September 1, 1994. In the end, the U.S. government's position in the second crisis, as determined by the Clinton administration's attorney general, Janet Reno, was that the Haitians would be repatriated unless there was a real and reasonable fear of prosecution. The Cubans were determined by Attorney General Reno to be admissible to the United States unless they had been convicted of serious offenses either in Cuba or during their stay at the camp.

40. Author interview with Capt. Robert Buehn, January 9, 2007. These refugees, officially called "migrants" so as not to entitle them to rights accorded to refugees, continue to dream of living in the United States. The State Department takes the Cuban migrants right back to the Northeast Gate and hands them over to the Cuban Army unless the legal standards for asylum are met. The few who qualify as asylum-seekers live together in a small camp reserved for them on the leeward side of the base, while the State Department tries to find willing third-country homes for them.

41. Author interview with Capt. Robert and Debra W. Buehn, September 29, 2006.

42. Author interview with Capt. Robert and Debra W. Buehn, September 29, 2006; author interview with Capt. Albert Shimkus, October 12, 2006.

43. Author interview with Capt. Albert Shimkus, October 12, 2006.

44. Author interview with Admiral Jan Gaudio, January 29, 2007.

45. Michael J. Strauss, "Leasing Guantanamo Bay: A Guide to Territorial Arrangement," unpublished manuscript, 2007, chap. 2.

46. For cases tried in the U.S. courts, see *USA v. Ronald Lee*, 906 F.2d 117, 1990; *USA v. Michael Chambers*, 940 F.2d 653, 1991. For the Haitian refugee case, see *Sale v. Haitian Ctrs. Council*, 509 U.S. 155 (1993), reversing *Haitian Ctrs. Council v. McNary*, 969 F.2d 1350 (2d Cir. 1992); and *Haitian Refugee Ctr. v. Baker*, 789 F. Supp. 1552 (SD Fla. 1991), reversed by the appellate court in *Haitian Refugee Ctr. v. Baker*, 949 F.2d 1109 (11th Cir. 1991). For a good overall discussion of the Haitian cases, see Brandt Goldstein, *Storming the Court: How a Band of Law Students Sued the President—And Won* (New York: Scribner, 2005).

Chapter 2

1. Quoted in Tom Ricks, *Making the Corps* (New York: Scribner, 1998), 181.

2. Fabiola Santiago, "New Sign of Guantanamo Despair: 'Suicide Gestures,' " *Miami Herald*, February 6, 1995, online ed. Available through the Miami Herald Online Archives.

3. Author interview with Dr. Dan Dean, May 18, 2007.

4. Author interview with Col. Dave Gurney, January 3, 2007.

5. Victor H. Krulak, *First to Fight: An Inside View of the U.S. Marine Corps* (Annapolis, Md.: United States Naval Institute Press, 1999), 3.

6. Ricks, Thomas E., *Making the Corps* (New York: Scribner, 1998), 30.

7. Ricks, Thomas E., *Making the Corps: 61 Men Came to Paris Island to Become Marines, Not All of Them Made It* (New York: Pocket Books, 1998), 19.

8. Author interview with anonymous Marine, August 27–29, 2007.

9. U.S. Department of Defense, United States Atlantic Command, *Migrant Camp Operations: The Guantanamo Experience* (Hampton, Va.: OC, Inc., 1996), iv–v; *Sea Signal* (film), Department of Defense, 1996.

10. Carol Morello, "Patience Fades in Guantanamo Refugee Camps," *The Philadephia Inquirer*, September 11, 1994; "Controversial Operation Sea Signal Draws to a Close," National Public Radio, January 19, 1996.

11. U.S. Department of Defense, *Migrant Camp Operations*, 25–27; Morello, "Patience Fades."

12. Author interview with Maj. Gen. Michael Lehnert, March 28, 2007.

13. Morello, "Patience Fades."

14. "Controversial Operation Sea Signal Draws to a Close," National Public Radio, January 19, 1996.

15. U.S. Department of Defense, *Migrant Camp Operations*, iii. See also David Bentley, "Operation Sea Signal: U.S. Military Support for Caribbean Migration Emergencies, May 1994 to February 1996," National Defense University, *Strategic Forum*, May 1996.

16. Office of Force Transformation, "Elements of Defense Transformation," Office of the Secretary of Defense, October 13, 2004.

17. Bush, George W. "Acceptance Speech: Republican National Convention, 2000," First Union Center, Philadelphia, August 4, 2000; Bush, George W., "A Period of Consequences," The Citadel, Charleston, S.C., September 23, 1999.

18. U.S. Department of Defense, *Quadrennial Defense Review Report, 2001* (Washington, D.C.: GPO, 1991), IV; Donald Rumsfeld, "Transforming the Military," *Foreign Affairs* 81 (May/June 2002): 31.

19. Midge Decter, *Rumsfeld: A Personal Portrait* (New York: HarperCollins, 2003), 121–131.

20. Author interview with Col. Wiliam Meier, August 28, 2006.

21. Those who were there merely to observe and report back included representatives from SOUTHCOM, from the Joint Staff, from FORSCOM, and from Joint Force Command.

22. Author interview with Major Scott E. Packard, March 7, 2002.

23. The Piedmont Consortium consists of Duke University, the University of North Carolina at Chapel Hill, and North Carolina State University.

24. U.S. Department of Defense, Office of the Joint Chiefs of Staff. *Joint Publication 1: Doctrine for the Armed Forces of the United States* (Washington, D.C.: GPO, 2007); U.S. Department of Defense, Office of the Joint Chiefs of Staff. *Unified Action Armed Forces (UNAAF)* (Washington, D.C.: GPO, 2007).

25. Author interview with Maj. Gen. Michael Lehnert, January 8, 2008.

26. See, for example, U.S. Department of Defense, "DoD News Briefing—Secretary Rumsfeld and Gen. Myers," Washington, D.C., December 27, 2001.

27. Author interview with unnamed source.

Chapter 3

1. Author interview with Sgt. Marc L. Coudriet, April 20, 2007.

2. Lt. Col. Timothy L. Miller, Marine Corps interview, March 8, 2002.

3. Author interview with S. Sgt. Robert Farabee, April 22, 2007.

4. Author interview with Maj. Marc Coudriet, April 20, 2007.

5. A group of 12 individuals from SOUTHCOM, including one lawyer, was temporarily dispatched to Guantanamo to assist with the setup. Known as the deployable joint task force, or DJTF, this unit was intended to give an extra boost in the early days of the operation and to strengthen ties between the field officers and the chain of command in the days to come.

6. In place of an execute order, a working order was being repeatedly, almost obsessively, rewritten and amended at the Pentagon. Author interview with unnamed source.

7. Author interview with Col. Manuel Supervielle, September 6, 2007.

8. The Defense Logistics Agency helped with the ordering. The largest agency within DOD, as its brochure boasts, "DLA provides wide-ranging logistical support for peacetime and wartime operations, as well as emergency preparedness and humanitarian missions." Its services are used not only by the military but also by the civilian agencies as well, and its personnel are deployed around the globe.

9. SEA stands for South East Asia, as these huts were designed originally for use in the Vietnam War.

10. Marine Corps interview with Cmdr. Louis V. Coriello, March 7, 2002.

11. Marine Corps interview with Cmdr. Louis V. Coriello, March 7, 2002.

12. Author interview with Sgt. Marc L. Coudriet, April 20, 2007.

13. Author interview with Col. Terry Carrico, April 4, 2007.

14. An early protest by Kate Martin at the Center for National Security Studies summed up many of the arguments that would define the debate on the Hill. According to Martin, the Military Order violated the separation of powers, created an unacceptably broad category for those who could be tried, exceeded the USA Patriot Act's limits on conditions and time allowable for the detention inside the United States of suspected terrorism suspects who were aliens, and was unconstitutional in its attempt to suspend the writ of habeas corpus—the right of the accused to challenge their detention. Martin warned as well that there were international implications to

the Military Order. If authorized by Congress, the "creation of such commissions would have to be consistent with the international legal framework established by the United Nations charter and subsequent instruments..." Kate Martin, "Lawfulness of Executive Order Establishing Military Commissions," Center for National Security Studies, November 19, 2001.

15. Michael Chertoff, testimony before the Senate Judiciary Committee, November 28, 2001.

16. Alberto Gonzales, Op-Ed, "Martial Justice, Full and Fair," *New York Times*, November 30, 2001.

17. Pierre-Richard Prosper, testimony before the Senate Judiciary Committee, December 4, 2001.

18. John Ashcroft, testimony before Senate Judiciary Committee, December 6, 2001.

19. Secretary Rumsfeld, prepared testimony before Senate Armed Services Committee, read by Paul Wolfowitz in Rumsefeld's absence, December 12, 2001.

20. Jim Haynes, testimony before Senate Armed Services Committee, December 12, 2001; Secretary Rumsfeld, prepared testimony before Senate Armed Services Committee, read by Paul Wolfowitz in Rumsfeld's absence, December 12, 2001.

21. "Does the Department of Defense," Levin asked, have "the authority to develop appellate procedures...outside the chain of command, in other words, outside of the secretary and the president?" Where, Senator John Warner (R-VA) wanted to know, was the Justice Department in all of this? He questioned the "degree to which the attorney general and his colleagues are being consulted on this."

22. Author interview Pierre-Richard Prosper, January 16, 2008.

23. Colin Powell, Draft Decision Memorandum for the President on the Applicability of the Geneva Convention to the Conflict in Afghanistan, January 26, 2002.

24. Karen DeYoung, *Soldier: The Life of Colin Powell* (New York: Vintage, 2007), 369. According to DeYoung, quoting one of Powell's senior aides, "his feeling was that you don't go in there demanding things...instead you play the game with the cards you are dealt."

25. Jack Goldsmith, *The Terror Presidency* (New York: W.W. Norton, 2007), 22; Sands, *Torture Team*, 16; Jane Mayer, *The Dark Side* (New York: Doubleday, 2008), 66, 80–82.

26. Chitra Ragavan, "Cheney's Guy," *U.S. News & World Report*, May 29, 2006.

27. Vanessa Blum, "Pentagon's Law Man," *Legal Times*, December 10, 2001.

28. John Yoo, *War by Other Means: An Insider's Account of the War on Terror* (New York: Atlantic Monthly Press, 2006), 32.

29. Timothy Flanigan, "Restoring the Powers of the Presidency," speech at University of Virginia Law School, March 5, 2002.

30. Memorandum from John C. Yoo to Patrick F. Philbin, December 28, 2001, in Karen J. Greenberg and Joshua L. Dratel, eds, *The Torture Papers* (New York: Cambridge University Press, 2005), 29–37. As John Yoo would write in explanation years later, the understanding of the lawyers in the Department of Justice was that the Supreme Court had set a precedent—presumably in the *Eisentrager* case—for the fact that habeas corpus

would not extend to prisoners held outside the United States. John Yoo, "The Court's Gitmo Ruling a Judicial 'Power Grab,' " *Wall Street Journal*, June 17, 2008.

31. William J. Haynes II, Testimony before the Senate Armed Services Committee, December 12, 2001.

32. The idea of exempting captured persons from known legal categories—in this case prisoners of war—became the defining theory of imprisonment for the Bush administration in the war on terror. In place of accepted categories, prisoner treatment that was "consistent with the Geneva Conventions," though not legally required to conform to them, became the basic legal paradigm for legal reforms that would follow. Paul Wolfowitz, press briefing, December 18, 2001.

Chapter 4

1. Angela Bennett, *The Geneva Convention: The Hidden Origins of the Red Cross* (Stroud, U.K.: Sutton Publishing, 2005), 186.

2. "Congress, through Article 21 of the UCMJ, has 'incorporated by reference' the common law of war." *Hamdan v. Rumsfeld*, slip opinion No. 05–184, p. 38 (2006).

3. "A Survey of United States Detainee Doctrine and Experience Since World War II," USAWC Strategy Research Project, U.S. Army War College, Carlisle, Pa. (2006), 5–7.

4. Charles W. Sanders and Charles W Sanders, Jr., *While in the Hands of the Enemy: Military Prisons of the Civil War* (Baton Rouge: Louisiana State University Press, 2005), 1.

5. William Marvel, *Andersonville: The Last Depot* (Chapel Hill: University of North Carolina Press, 1994), 238.

6. Author interview with David Bowker, February 6, 2008.

7. John Yoo and Robert Delahunty to Wiliam J. Haynes II, "Memorandum Re: Application of Treaties and Laws to al Qaeda and Taliban Detainees," in Greenberg and Dratel, *The Torture Papers*, 38–79.

8. William H. Taft IV to John C. Yoo, "Your Draft Memorandum of January 9," January 11, 2002, available at http://www.cartoonbank.com/newyorker/slideshows/01TaftMemo.pdf (accessed on November 11, 2008).

9. For the discussion of the inclusion of spies, saboteurs, and irregular combatants, see "Convention (IV) relative to the Protection of Civilian Persons in Time of War, Geneva, 12 August 1949," Commentary, Part I: General Provisions, Historical Background and General Remarks, *International Humanitarian Law—Treaties & Documents*, available at http://www.icrc.org/ihl.nsf/WebList?ReadForm&id=380&t=com (accessed on November 7, 2008); see esp. commentary on articles 4 and 5. See also Jane Mayer, *The Dark Side*, p. 83.

10. Taft, "Your Draft Memorandum."

11. Taft, "Your Draft Memorandum."

12. Taft, "Your Draft Memorandum."

13. Tim Miller, Marine Corps interview, March 8, 2002.

14. Tim Miller, Marine Corps interview, March 8, 2002.

15. Author interview with Manuel Supervielle, August 20, 2008.

16. Author interview with Maj. Gen. Galen Jackman, July 21, 2007; author interview with Manuel Supervielle, March 15, 2008.

17. Author interview with Col. Manuel Supervielle, September 6, 2007.

18. Author interview with Col. Terry Carrico, April 4, 2007.

19. Author interview with Capt. Robert and Debra W. Buehn, September 29, 2006.

20. One biographical fact that sheds light on why he might have acted as he did is a story that Supervielle tells about his paternal grandfather, Manuel Fernández Supervielle, for whom he was named. Manuel Supervielle takes tremendous pride in pointing out that his grandfather stood up to General Batista after the coup of 1933. Manuel Fernández Supervielle offered to defend the military officers whom Batista threatened to court-martial and execute. With Supervielle's brave defense, none were executed and most served only two or three years in jail. Author interview with Manuel Supervielle, April 16, 2008.

21. Author interview with Col. Manuel Supervielle, March 15, 2008.

Chapter 5

1. Katharine Q. Seelye, "A Nation Challenged: Detainees; For America's Captives, Home Is a Camp in Cuba, with Goggles and a Koran," *New York Times*, January 20, 2002, available at http://query.nytimes.com/gst/fullpage.html?res=9A06E3DA143BF933A1575 2C0A9649C8B63 (accessed on November 7, 2008).

2. Katharine Q. Seelye, "A Nation Challenged: Prisoners; First 'Unlawful Combatants' Seized in Afghanistan Arrive at U.S. Base in Cuba," *New York Times*, January 12, 2002, available at http://query.nytimes.com/gst/fullpage.html?res=9A06E3DA143BF 933A15752C0A9649C8B63 (accessed on November 7, 2008).

3. Author interview with Major Pietro Scarselli, April 20, 2007.

4. Alex Rodriguez, "Base gets 1st load of prisoners—20 land in Cuba after perilous start," *Chicago Tribune*, January 12, 2002.

5. Author interview with Col. Terry Carrico, April 4, 2007.

6. Seelye, "A Nation Challenged."

7. Author interview Capt. Robert and Debra W. Buehn, September 29, 2006.

8. Author interview with Capt. Robert Buehn, February 8, 2007.

9. Author interview with Capt. Robert Buehn, February 8, 2007.

10. Author interview with Steven Cox, April 4, 2007.

11. Torie Clarke, *Lipstick on a Pig: Winning in the No-Spin Era by Someone Who Knows the Game* (New York: Simon & Schuster, 2006), 79.

12. Author interview with Bob Franken, August 6, 2007.

13. Author interview with Bob Franken, August 6, 2007.

14. Author interview with Bob Franken, August 6, 2007.

15. Clarke, *Lipstick on a Pig*, 81.

16. Author interview with Bob Franken, August 6, 2007.

17. The general name for a riot squad in the military is Emergency Reaction Force. At Guantanamo, it was labeled the Immediate Reaction Force.

18. Author interview with S. Sgt. Robert Farabee, April 22, 2007.

19. Author interview with Carol Rosenberg, March 30, 2008.

20. Sue Anne Pressley, "Detainees Arrive in Cuba Amid Very Tight Security," *Washington Post*, January 12, 2002; Laura Parker, "Detainees in Cuba could be in for long stay," *USA Today*, March 20, 2002.

21. Author interview with S. Sgt. Anthony Gallegos, January 16, 2008.

22. Author interview with Tim Nichols, October 30, 2007.

23. Shafiq Rasul, Asif Iqbal, and Rhuhel Ahmed, *Composite Statement: Detention in Afghanistan and Guantanamo Bay* (New York: Center for Constitutional Rights, 2004), 21. Available at http://ccrjustice.org/files/report_tiptonThree.pdf (accessed on November 12, 2008).

24. Rasul et al., *Composite Statement*, 21.

25. Author interview with W. O. Scott F. Bolman, May 6, 2007.

26. Author interview with Capt. Albert Shimkus, October 12, 2006; author interview with Col. Terry Carrico, April 4, 2007.

27. Rasul et al., *Composite Statement*, 22–23.

28. Author interview with S. Sgt. Robert Farabee, April 22, 2007.

29. Author interview with Capt. Albert Shimkus, October 12, 2006.

30. Author interview with S. Sgt. Anthony Parra, March 2, 2008; Pool Report No. 3, compiled by reporters from Reuters, the *Washington Post*, the *Miami Herald*, and the Associated Press, January 11, 2002.

31. Rasul et al., *Composite Statement*, 24.

32. Rasul et al., *Composite Statement*, 22.

33. Author interview with Capt. Albert Shimkus, October 12, 2006.

34. Author interview with Maj. Marc Coudriet, April 20, 2007.

35. Greg Miller, "Many Held at Guantanamo Not Likely Terrorists," *Los Angeles Times*, December 22, 2002, available at http://www.latimes.com/la-na-gitmo22dec22,0,2294365.story (accessed July 2008).

36. Timothy Nichols to author, August 10, 2008.

37. Author interview with W. O. Scott F. Bolman, May 6, 2007.

38. Leigh Sales, *Detainee #002: The Case of David Hicks* (Melbourne: Melbourne University Press, 2007).

39. Carol Rosenberg, "Congressional Visitors Find Base Jail OK," *Miami Herald*, January 26, 2002.

40. Author interview with Maj. Marc Coudriet, April 20, 2007.

41. Author interview with S. Sgt. Robert Farabee, April 22, 2007.

Chapter 6

1. Daniel LeBlanc, "POW Storm Intensifies, Troops Join U.S. Force," *Globe and Mail* (Canada), January 18, 2002; Marjorie Miller, "Fairness Urged for Detainees in Cuba," *Los Angeles Times*, January 18, 2002; Bruce McDougall and Nada Goodfellow, "Inside Camp Terror & Evil on the Prowl," *Daily Telegraph*, January 19, 2002; Jon Clements, "War

on Terror; Welcome U.S. Style," *Mirror*, January 19, 2002; Marjorie Miller and Carol Rosenberg, "Horror of Camp X-Ray," *Mail on Sunday*, January 20, 2002.

2. Katharine Q. Seelye, "Red Cross Team Will Examine Prisoners from Afghanistan," *New York Times*, January 18, 2002; T. R. Reid, "British Find No Abuse of U.S. Captives at Cuba Base," *Washington Post*, January 22, 2002.

3. Author interview with Maj. Gen. Michael Lehnert, April 19, 2007. See also Torie Clarke, *Lipstick on a Pig: Winning in the No-Spin Era by Someone Who Knows the Game* (New York: Simon & Schuster, 2006), 79–85, for an account of the Pentagon's dismay over the reaction to the release of the photograph.

4. Carol Rosenberg, "Photos Echo Six Years Later," *Miami Herald*, January 11, 2008.

5. Clarke, *Lipstick on a Pig*, 81–82.

6. Author interview with Maj. Gen. Michael Lehnert, November 15, 2006.

7. Author interview with Maj. Tim Nichols, February 19, 2008.

8. John Yoo and Robert J. Delahunty to William H. Taft IV, January 14, 2002, available at http://www.cartoonbank.com/newyorker/slideshows/02YooTaft.pdf (accessed on December 4, 2008).

9. Author interview with David Bowker, July 16, 2008.

10. Author interview with Manuel Supervielle, March 15, 2008; April 16, 2008; August 20, 2008.

11. Taft seemed to understand something of the emotional conflict that Supervielle, his unexpectedly effective ally in the ongoing legal struggle, was experiencing. "Manny, is this your first time back?" he asked. Supervielle nodded, touched by Taft's personal gesture amidst the heated tension of the moment. Author interview with Col. Manuel Supervielle, September 6, 2007.

12. Author interview with Col. Manuel Supervielle, September 6, 2007.

13. Author interview with Capt. Albert Shimkus, March 10, 2008.

14. Author interview with Capt. Samuel Patrick Alford, August 28, 2006.

15. Author interview with Capt. Albert Shimkus, October 12, 2006.

16. Author interview with Capt. Albert Shimkus, October 12, 2006; author interview with Capt. Samuel Patrick Alford, Aug. 28, 2006.

17. Author interview with Capt. Albert Shimkus, October 12, 2006.

18. Author interview with Maj. Gen. Michael Lehnert, July 5, 2006.

19. Seelye, "Red Cross Team Will Examine Prisoners from Afghanistan."

20. Author interview with Capt. Robert and Debra W. Buehn, September 29, 2006.

21. Carol Rosenberg, "Red Cross Inspecting Guantánamo," *Miami Herald*, January 18, 2002.

22. Urs Boegli, "A Few Thoughts on the Relationship between Humanitarian Agencies and the Media," *International Review of the Red Cross*, No. 325 (December 1998), 627–631.

23. Elizabeth Becker, "Red Cross Man in Guantánamo: A 'Busybody,' but not Unwelcome," *New York Times*, February 20, 2002.

24. Author interview with Col. Manuel Supervielle, March 15, 2008.

25. Author interview with Col. Manuel Supervielle, March 15, 2008.

26. Author interview with Lt. Abuhena Saifulislam, February 7, 2008.

27. Author interview with Capt. Albert Shimkus, March 10, 2008.

28. Author interview with Maj. Gen. Michael Lehnert, November 15, 2006.

29. Katharine Q. Seelye, "As Trust Develops, Guards Still Maintain Full Alert," *New York Times*, February 4, 2002; author interview with Capt. Albert Shimkus, March 10, 2008.

30. Author interview with Capt. Albert Shimkus, October 12, 2006; author interview with Terry Carrico, April 4, 2007.

31. Author interview with Maj. Gen. Michael Lehnert, November 15, 2006.

32. Quoted by Capt. Robert and Debra W. Buehn, September 29, 2006.

33. Author interview with Capt. Samuel Patrick Alford, August 28, 2006.

Chapter 7

1. Philip Gourevitch and Errol Morris, "Exposure: The Woman behind the Camera at Abu Ghraib," *New Yorker*, March 24, 2008, 44–57.

2. Author interview with Capt. Samuel Patrick Alford, August 28, 2006.

3. Author interview with Capt. Robert and Debra W. Buehn, September 29, 2006.

4. Christopher Cooper, "Detention Plan: In Guantanamo, Prisoners Languish in Sea of Red Tape," *Wall Street Journal*, January 26, 2005.

5. Sgt. Michael Marshall, Marine Corps interview, March 6, 2002.

6. Sgt. Michael Marshall, Marine Corps interview, March 6, 2002.

7. Author interview with Capt. Robert and Debra W. Buehn, September 29, 2006.

8. Author interview with W. O. Scott F. Bolman, May 6, 2007.

9. Author interview with Maj. Stephen Cox, January 9, 2007.

10. Author interview with Maj. Gen. Michael Lehnert, August 28, 2007.

11. Author interview with Maj. Gen. Michael Lehnert, March 28, 2007; December 5, 2008.

12. Author interview with Maj. Gen. Michael Lehnert, January 4, 2007.

13. Author interview with Maj. Gen. Michael Lehnert, November 15, 2006.

14. Author interview with Col. Terry Carrico, April 4, 2007.

15. Author interview with Maj. Gen. Michael Lehnert, August 19, 2008.

16. Donald Rumsfeld, DOD press conference, January 22, 2002.

17. Donald Rumsfeld, DOD press conference, January 22, 2002.

18. Donald Rumsfeld, DOD press conference, January 22, 2002.

19. Donald Rumsfeld, DOD press conference, January 22, 2002.

20. Donald Rumsfeld, DOD press conference, January 22, 2002.

21. Donald Rumsfeld, DOD press conference, January 22, 2002.

22. "Donald H. Rumsfeld Holds Media Availability En Route to Camp X-Ray," FDCH Political Transcripts (press conference), January 27, 2002.

23. Carol Rosenberg, "Photos Echo Six Years Later," *Miami Herald*, January 11, 2008.

24. Donald Rumsfeld, DOD press conference, January 22, 2002.

25. Author interview with Maj. Gen. Michael Lehnert, January 10, 2007.

26. Karen deYoung, *Soldier: The Life of Colin Powell* (New York: Vintage, 2007), 368–369.

27. Donald Rumsfeld, "Status of Taliban and al Qaeda," memo to Chairman of the Joint Chiefs of Staff, in *The Torture Papers*, eds. Karen J. Greenberg and Joshua L. Dratel (Cambridge: Cambridge UP, 2005), 80.

28. Jay S. Bybee, "Application of Treaties and Laws to al Qaeda and Taliban Detainees," memo to Alberto R. Gonzales and William J. Haynes, January 22, 2002, in *The Torture Papers*, 86.

29. Rowan Scarborough, "Powell Wants Detainees to Be Declared POWs; Memo Shows Differences with White House," *Washington Times*, January 26, 2002.

30. DeYoung, *Soldier*, 369–370; Alberto R. Gonzales, "Decision Re: Application of the Geneva Convention on Prisoners of War to the Conflict with al Qaeda and the Taliban," memo to President George W. Bush, January 25, 2002, in *The Torture Papers*, 118–121.

31. Author interview with David Bowker, February 6, 2008.

32. Donald Rumsfeld, press conference, plane en route to Guantanamo, January 27, 2002.

33. Donald Rumsfeld, DoD news briefing, January 27, 2002.

34. DeYoung, *Soldier*, 369–372.

35. Donald Rumsfeld, DoD news briefing, January 27, 2002.

36. Carol Rosenberg, "Touring Camp X-Ray, Lawmakers Say It's Fine; Members of Congress said International Criticism of Conditions for Afghan War Detainees was Groundless," *Philadelphia Inquirer*, January 26, 2002.

37. Author interview with Maj. Gen. Michael Lehnert, November 15, 2006.

Chapter 8

1. Author interview with Lt. Abuhena Saifulislam, December 1, 2006.

2. Traditionally, immigrants have been allowed to serve in the U.S. armed forces. In fact, a quarter of the Union Army during the Civil War consisted of non-Americans. The tradition has lasted, offering the advantage for immigrants of accelerating the path to citizenship. In the wake of the Iraq War, the numbers of immigrants enlisting and becoming citizens has grown exponentially; there were 750 immigrants in uniform who became U.S. citizens in 2001 and six times as many—4,600—in 2005. Bryan Bender, "Military Considers Recruiting Foreigners," *Boston Globe*, December 26, 2006; and Jeremy Derfner, "Can Non-Citizens Join the Military?" Slate.com, July 7, 2000.

3. Author interview with Abuhena Saifulislam, December 1, 2006.

4. Author interview with Lt. Abuhena Saifulislam, December 1, 2006; author interview with Michael Lehnert, February 7, 2008.

5. Carol Rosenberg, "Camp Guards See Leader Emerging Among Captives," *Miami Herald*, January 21, 2002.

6. Author interview with Major Coudriet, April 20, 2007.

7. Author interview with Carol Rosenberg, April 17, 2008.

8. Author interview with Maj. Gen. Michael Lehnert, June 4, 2008.

9. The first Muslims to arrive as part of the U.S. presence at Guantanamo were interpreters, at which point Lt. Abuhena Saifulislam's role changed and he ministered to them as well as to the detainees. Author interview with Saifulislam, December 1, 2006.

10. Author interview with Lt. Abuhena Saifulislam, December 1, 2006.

11. Jane Sutton, "Muslim Cleric Leads Prayers at Guantanamo Prison," Reuters, January 24, 2002.

12. Author interview with Lt. Abuhena Saifulislam, December 1, 2006.

13. Sutton, "Muslim Cleric Leads Prayers at Guantanamo Prison."

14. Katharine Q. Seelye, "A Nation Challenged: The Detainees; As Trust Develops, Guards Still Maintain Full Alert," *New York Times*, February 4, 2002.

15. Author interview with W. O. Scott F. Bolman, May 6, 2007.

16. Author interview with Shafiq Rasul and Moazzem Begg, February 22, 2007.

17. Carol Rosenberg, "Navy Officer Balances Religious Responsibilities," *Miami Herald*, January 31, 2002.

18. As Tim Nichols described it, "General Lehnert basically said, 'Chaplain, I need you to go and find out what's on their minds.'" Nichols went on, "[Lenhert] needs to get a feel for what was, you know, . . . if the detainees had a legitimate gripe, like someone needed medical attention and wasn't getting it. Or whether they were just unhappy to be there. . . ." Author interview with Tim Nichols, October 30, 2006.

19. Author interview with Maj. Gen. Michael Lehnert, August 11, 2008.

20. Author interview with Lt. Abuhena Saifisulam, December 1, 2006.

21. Author interview with Col. William Meier, August 28, 2006.

22. Author interview with Maj. Gen. Michael Lehnert, November 15, 2006.

23. Author interview with Terry Carrico, April 4, 2007.

24. Future chaplains would encounter an intensified version of this distrust. The cloud of distrust hung heaviest over Chaplain James Yee, a West Point graduate who had been posted to Guantanamo at the end of Dunlavey's time. Yee arrived on November 5, 2002, only to be arrested in September 2003, initially on accusations of espionage, although the actual charge never materialized. Charged later on six counts, including mishandling classified materials, adultery, pornography, and lying to investigators, Yee was cleared of all charges, but not before being subjected to sensory deprivation and held in solitary confinement for 76 days. Notably, Yee was surrounded by suspicions—as Saifulislam had been—about aiding and abetting the enemy.

25. Author interview with Maj. Gen. Michael Lehnert, August 28, 2007.

26. Staff Sergeant Robert Farabee had "lots of respect for Hicks. He had discipline." Author interview with S. Sgt. Robert Farabee, April 22, 2007.

27. Author interview with Shafiq Rasul and Moazzem Begg, February 22, 2007.

28. Author interview with S. Sgt. Anthony Parra, March 2, 2008.

29. Author interview with Lt. Abuhena Saifulislam, December 1, 2006.

30. Author interview with Bob Franken, August 6, 2007.

31. "It was also outstanding to have the Muslim chaplain to be able to do interviews [with the press] on the Muslim faith. It provides some—some insight into—what it means to be a Muslim, what are the issues, what are the tenets, what does the Qur'an [say] on certain issues, you know, all those types of things." Steve Cox, author interview, January 9, 2007.

32. Author interview with Steve Cox, January 9, 2007.

33. Author interview with Bob Franken, August 6, 2007.

34. Sandi Dolbee, "Muslim Chaplain Receives a Warm Welcome in Cuba," *San Diego Union-Tribune*, January 27, 2002.

35. Like Saif, she was given special privileges. Though her relationship to Lehnert was at best cordial and often antagonistic, she had his respect for her concern for the story: she was allowed to stay for the week, while other journalists stayed for several nights and went back home. So, too, she would often show up in the wee hours of the morning in the press room overlooking the airfield. And there, in those nearly dark hours, she saw things others didn't see—such as the arrivals of officers for whom flags would be raised as they landed, giving her a way of investigating who was landing at the base. She learned to read the flags that flew over the airfield when a general arrived. She would check the branch of the service, designated by color, and the rank, designated by the number of stars, and then Google the specific service and rank of the flag officers to try and deduce who might be arriving. More often than not, she was able to figure it out. Author interview with Carol Rosenberg, April 17, 2008.

Chapter 9

1. Author interview with Gen. Galen Jackman, July 21, 2007.

2. Author interview with Maj. Gen. Michael Lehnert, January 4, 2008.

3. Gen. Richard Myers, press conference, February 8, 2002.

4. Carol Rosenberg, "Commanders Reviewing Interrogation Techniques at Camp in Guantanamo," *Miami Herald*, February 9, 2002.

5. Department of the Army, "Intelligence Interrogation," FM 34–52, May 8, 1987, 6–1.

6. Department of the Army, "Intelligence Interrogation," FM 34–52, September 28, 1992, 3–1.

7. Steven M. Kleinman, "The History of MIS-Y: U.S. Strategic Interrogation During World War II" (master's thesis, Joint Military Intelligence College, 2002), 19–20.

8. Department of the Army, "Intelligence Interrogation," 1992, 3–1.

9. Confidential author interview with unnamed military officer, October 12, 2007.

10. Confidential author interview with unnamed military officer, October 12, 2007.

11. Donald Rumsfeld, press briefing, December 18, 2001.

12. Paul Wolfowitz, press briefing, December 18, 2001.

13. Katharine Q. Seelye, "First 'Unlawful Combatants' Seized in Afghanistan Arrive at U.S. Base in Cuba," *New York Times*, January 12, 2002.

14. Donald Rumsfeld, press conference, January 22, 2002.

15. Donald Rumsfeld, press conference, January 22, 2002.

16. Author interview with Gen. Galen Jackman, July 21, 2007.

17. Steven M. Kleinman, "The History of MIS-Y: U.S. Strategic Interrogation During World War II" (master's thesis, Joint Military Intelligence College, 2002), 3.

18. Kleinman, "The History of MIS-Y," 114.

19. Author interview with Maj. Timothy W. Nichols, February 19, 2008.

20. Author interview with Gen. Galen Jackman, July 21, 2007.

21. Report of the Commission to Assess the Ballistic Missile Threat to the United States, Executive Summary (July 15, 1998), 1.

22. Author interview with Maj. Gen. Michael Lehnert, July 5, 2006.

23. Tim Nichols, interview with the Marine Corps, March 8, 2002.

24. Department of the Army, "Intelligence Interrogation," chap. 3.

25. Author interview with David Bowker, February 6, 2008.

26. Memorandum, Colin L. Powell to Alberto Gonzales, in Karen J. Greenberg and Joshua L. Dratel, eds., *The Torture Papers* (Cambridge: Cambridge University Press, 2005), 122–125.

27. Memorandum, George W. Bush for the Vice President et al., February 7, 2002, in Greenberg and Dratel, 134–135.

28. William H. Taft IV, "A View from the Top: American Perspectives on International Law after the Cold War," *Yale Journal of International Law* 31 (Summer 2006): 509.

29. Kleinman, "The History of MIS-Y," 118.

30. Author interview with Stuart Couch; Stuart Couch to author, August 11, 2008.

31. Leigh Sales, *Detainee #002: The Case of David Hicks* (Melbourne: Melbourne University Press, 2007), 72–73.

32. Author interview with Maj. Gen. Michael Lehnert, May 30, 2008.

33. Author interview with Timothy Nichols, June 2008. Nichols's categories regarding intelligence value aptly echoed those of Ambassador Prosper, who had been tasked with making arrangements for the transfer of the detainees, where possible, to their home countries or to third countries. Prosper's three categories focused on the danger posed by the detainees rather than their intelligence value; they were: those who posed the highest threat and would be tried by military commissions, those who constituted a mid-level threat and could possibly be transferred to their home countries, and those who were deemed to be low-level threats and could possibly be released to their home countries.

34. Tom Lasseter, "Day 1: America's Prison for Terrorists Often Held the Wrong Men," McClatchy Washington Bureau, June 15, 2008.

35. Lasseter, "Day 1."

36. Donald Rumsfeld, DOD briefing, January 11, 2002.

Chapter 10

1. Author interview with Pierre-Richard Prosper, July 1, 2008.

2. Katharine Q. Seelye, "A Nation Challenged: The Detainees; As Trust Develops, Guards Still Maintain Full Alert," *New York Times*, February 4, 2002.

3. Seelye, "As Trust Develops."

4. Shafiq Rasul, Asif Iqbal, and Rhuhel Ahmed, *Composite Statement: Detention in Afghanistan and Guantanamo Bay* (New York: Center for Constitutional Rights, 2004), 76.

5. Author interview with Galen Jackman, July 21, 2007.

6. See also U.S. Army, Summarized Witness Statement, Maj. Gen. Michael Dunlavey, "Investigation into FBI Allegations of Detainee Abuse at Guantanamo Bay, Cuba Detention Facility," in Jameel Jaffer and Amrit Singh, *Administration of Torture* (New York: Columbia University Press, 2007), A-21.

7. Phillipe Sands, *Torture Team: Rumsfeld's Memo and the Betrayal of American Values* (New York: Palgrave Macmillan, 2008), 41.

8. Brian Kinal, "New Army General Tops Lottery Odds," *Erie Times-News*, January 29, 1999.

9. James Bamford, *A Pretext for War* (New York: Anchor Books, 2004), 103.

10. Author interview with Alain Grignard, May 24, 2008.

11. Ed Palatella, "Dunlavey Announced Candidacy for Judge," *Erie Times-News*, January 29, 1999.

12. U.S. Army, "Investigation into FBI Allegations of Detainee Abuse," A-21.

13. Philippe Sands, "The Green Light," *Vanity Fair*, May 2008.

14. U.S. Army, "Investigation into FBI Allegations of Detainee Abuse," A-21.

15. Lisa Thompson, "Orders from the Top: Retired General Dunlavey: Guantanamo Mission Came Straight from Bush, Rumsfeld," *Erie Times-News*, November 2, 2007.

16. Author interview with Carol Rosenberg, April 17, 2008.

17. Author interview with unnamed source; author interview with Maj. Gen. Michael Lehnert, August 28, 2007; author interview with Col. Charles Brule, December 14, 2007. In March of 2005, Dunlavey testified that after an initial period as commander of JTF 170, "directions [regarding the chain of command] changed and I got my marching orders from the President of the United States." Jameel Jaffer and Amrit Singh, *Administration of Torture: A Documentary Record from Washington to Abu Ghraib and Beyond* (New York: Columbia University Press, 2007), A-21.

18. Author interview with Maj. Gen. Michael Lehnert, May 30, 2008.

19. Author interview with Maj. Gen. Michael Lehnert, May 30, 2008.

20. Author interview with Maj. Gen. Michael Lehnert, June 4, 2008.

21. Author interview with Tim Nichols, October 30, 2006.

22. Author interview with Maj. Gen. Michael Lehnert, May 30, 2008.

23. Author interview with Maj. Gen. Michael Lehnert, May 30, 2008.

24. Author interview with Maj. Gen. Michael Lehnert, May 30, 2008.

25. Author interview with Lt. Abuhena Saifulislam, December 1, 2006.

26. Author interview with Maj. Gen. Michael Lehnert, January 8, 2008.

27. Author interview with Capt. Albert Shimkus, March 10, 2008.

28. Author interview with Capt. Albert Shimkus, March 10, 2008.

29. Rumsfeld would later sign off on this and other methods of enhanced inter-rogation techniques. William J. Haynes II to Donald Rumsfeld, "Counter-Resistance Techniques," November 27, 2002, in Greenberg and Dratel, *The Torture Papers* (Cambridge: Cambridge University Press, 2005), 237, approved by Secretary Rumsfeld on December 2, 2002.

30. Author interview with Michael Lehnert, June 4, 2008.

31. Author interview with Capt. Samuel Patrick Alford and Col. Wiliam Meier, August 28, 2006.

32. Author interview with Tim Nichols, February 19, 2008.

33. Author interview with Galen Jackman, July 21, 2007.

34. Author interview with Charles Brule, December 14, 2007.

35. Author interview with Migdalia Hettler, February 9, 2007; author interview with Manuel Supervielle, July 29, 2008; author interview with Rick Baccus, March 10, 2008.

36. Author interview with Maj. Gen. Michael Lehnert, May 30, 2008.

37. Department of the Army, "Intelligence Interrogations," FM 34–52, September 28, 1992.

Chapter 11

1. Burn bag chart, in Carol Rosenberg's possession. The blank, khaki-colored can-vas was covered daily with journalistic jottings about the arrival of the detainees and sig-nificant developments at X-Ray. Every now and again over the course of time, a public affairs officer would saunter by, inspect the jottings, and insert politically correct amend-ments, crossing out the word "prisoner," for example, and replacing it with the word "detainee"—an effort at enforcing linguistic conformism that failed utterly because the PAO's correction of the disallowed phraseology was done with a blue pencil that was virtually invisible to the eye. At one point, someone from the military removed the chart. Colonel William Costello, SOUTHCOM'S PAO, salvaged it and brought it to Rosenberg for her to keep. Author interviews with Carol Rosenberg, March 25 and April 17, 2008.

2. Author interview with Tim Nichols, October 30, 2007; author interview with Maj. Gen. Michael Lehnert, January 29, 2007; author interview with Terry Carrico, April 4, 2007. Lehnert related an anecdote from his interaction with the guards, wherein they pro-tested that the Taliban and al Qaeda would not treat Americans so kindly. "You're exactly correct. They would not treat us this way. But your observation was totally irrelevant."

3. Author interview with Maj. Gen. Michael Lehnert, August 4, 2008.

4. Author interview with Shafiq Rasul and Moazzem Begg, February 22, 2007; Shafiq Rasul, Asif Iqbal, and Rhuhel Ahmed, *Composite Statement: Detention in Afghanistan and Guantanamo Bay* (New York: Center for Constitutional Rights, 2004), 37.

5. Author interview with Maj. Gen. Michael Lehnert, January 29, 2007.

6. Author interview with Maj. Gen. Michael Lehnert, June 4, 2008.

7. Michael Lehnert to Peter Chiarelli, in two e-mails of February 1 and February 6, 2002, read to the author in an interview with Robert Buehn on February 6, 2007.

8. According to Lehnert, it was the sign-off of Secretary Rumsfeld rather than that of Congress that was needed for approval of the plan for this stage of construction.

9. Author interview with Carol Rosenberg, March 25, 2008.

10. Murat Kurnaz, *Five Years of My Life: An Innocent Man in Guantanamo* (New York: Palgrave Macmillan, 2008), 148 .

11. Carol Rosenberg, "No More Room at Camp X-Ray, Military Says," *Miami Herald*, February 16, 2002, online ed. Available on Miami Herald Online Archives (accessed on November 12, 2008).

12. Carol Rosenberg, "Wanted in Guantanamo: A Taste of Home for Everyone," *Miami Herald*, February 23, 2002 online ed. Available on Miami Herald Online Archives (accessed on November 12, 2008).

13. Author interview with Capt. Albert Shimkus, March 10, 2008.

14. Rosenberg, "Wanted in Guantanamo."

15. Author interview with Capt. Albert Shimkus, March 10, 2008.

16. Rasul et al., *Composite Statement*, 25, 45.

17. 'Aaidh ibn Abdullah al-Qarni, *Don't Be Sad* (Riyadh: International Islamic Publishing House, 2005). *Don't Be Sad* was originally published in Arabic. It includes quotes from Eastern and Western philosophers in addition to material from Islamic sources.

18. Kurnaz, *Five Years of My Life*, 96; Tom Lasseter, "Guantanamo Inmate Database: Adil Kamel al Wadi," McClatchy Newspapers, June 15, 2008; statement by Tarek Dergoul made available to Human Rights Watch, "Guantanamo Detainee Accounts: Transfer to Guantanamo," *Human Rights Watch* (May 2004, published October 2004); Rasul et al., *Composite Statement*, 18.

19. Carol Rosenberg, "Gurneys Are Used to Transport All Prisoners at Guantanamo," *Miami Herald*, February 7, 2002, online ed. Available on Miami Herald Online Archives (accessed November 12, 2008); author interview with Maj. Gen. Michael Lehnert, May 30, 2008.

20. Kurnaz, *Five Years of My Life*, 148–149.

21. Author interview with Maj. Gen. Michael Lehnert, November 15, 2007.

22. Rasul et al., *Composite Statement*, 39.

23. Rasul et al., *Composite Statement*, 39.

24. Kurnaz, *Five Years of My Life*, 148–150.

25. Rasul et al., *Composite Statement*, 39.

26. Rasul et al., *Composite Statement*, 113; Kurnaz, *Five Years of My Life*, 148–149.

27. Author interview with Maj. Gen. Michael Lehnert, January 29, 2007; author interview with Steve Cox, January 9, 2007.

28. Author interview with Terry Carrico, April 4, 2007.

29. Author interview with Maj. Gen. Michael Lehnert, January 29, 2007.

30. Author interview with Bob Franken, August 6, 2007.

31. Author interview with Steven Cox, January 9, 2007.

32. Carol Rosenberg, "Some Detainees in Cuba Refuse Meals," *Miami Herald*, March 1, 2002. See also burn bag chart, in Carol Rosenberg's possession.

33. Author interview with Capt. Samuel Patrick Alford, August 28, 2006.

34. U.S. Department of Defense, "News Briefing with Secretary of Defense Donald Rumsfeld and Gen. Peter Pace," November 1, 2005.

35. Author interview with Capt. Samuel Patrick Alford, August 28, 2006.

36. Author interview with Capt. Samuel Patrick Alford, August 28, 2006; author interview with Maj. Gen. Michael Lehnert, November 15, 2006.

37. The reported 2,700 caloric intake of the day's food eventually grew to 1,200 calories per meal, according to official government sources, but just when that happened is unclear. Bruce Barton to author, February 2, 2007.

38. Many Muslims fast in the few days preceding Eid-al-Adha, even though it is not required by the Koran.

39. Author interview with Capt. Albert Shimkus, March 10, 2008.

40. Rasul et al., *Composite Statement*, 40–41.

41. Author interview with Maj. Gen. Michael Lehnert, January 29, 2007.

42. Author interview with Maj. Gen. Michael Lehnert, January 29, 2007.

43. Author interview with Steven Cox, January 9, 2007; author interview with Bob Franken, August 6, 2007.

44. Author interview with Maj. Gen. Michael Lehnert, January 29, 2007.

45. Author interview with Maj. Gen. Michael Lehnert, January 29, 2007.

46. Author interview with Carol Rosenberg, April 16, 2008; Carol Rosenberg, burn bag chart.

47. Nizar Sassi and Guy Benhamou, *Prisonnier 325, Camp Delta: De Vénissieux à Guantanamo* (Paris: Editions Denoël, 2006), 128.

48. Kurnaz, *Five Years of My Life*, 150–151.

49. Sassi and Benhamou, *Prisonnier 325*, 128–30.

50. Sassi and Benhamou, *Prisonnier 325*, 128.

51. Sassi and Benhamou, *Prisonnier 325*, 128.

52. Author interview with Maj. Gen. Michael Lehnert, June 4, 2008.

53. Author interview with Maj. Gen. Michael Lehnert, January 29, 2007.

54. Dr. al Alwani was later named as an unindicted co-conspirator in the notorious case of Dr. Sami al-Arian. In 2003, Dr. al-Arian was charged on numerous counts, including conspiracy to provide material support to terrorism. He pleaded guilty to general criminal conspiracy in 2006 and was scheduled to be deported, but was kept in custody for refusing to testify before a federal grand jury in two other terrorism cases.

55. Author interview with Lt. Abuhena Saifulislam, December 1, 2006.

56. Author interview with Shafiq Rasul and Moazzem Begg, February 22, 2007; Rasul et al., *Composite Statement*, 40.

57. Author interview with Lt. Abuhena Saifulislam, December 1, 2006.

58. Tim Golden, "The Battle for Guantanamo," *New York Times*, September 17, 2006, available at http://www.nytimes.com/2006/09/17/magazine/17guantanamo.html (accessed July 2008).

59. The hunger strikes were handled quite differently in subsequent years. A constant at Guantanamo, they were often, though not always, handled with a degree of brutality. Juma al Dosari, Detainee #261, reported that detainees were "strapped in restraint chairs...their feeding tubes inserted and removed so violently that some bled or fainted." General Bantz John Craddock, for example, commanding general of SOUTHCOM in 2006, pointed callously to the generosity of its medical staff for giving the detainees the choice of color for their feeding tubes. Ironically, although Lehnert was stationed at SOUTHCOM at the time, no one approached him for advice on Guantanamo or its hunger strikes. Tom Lasseter, "Guantanamo Inmate Database: Abdul Salam Zaeef," McClatchy Newspapers, June 15, 2008; Kurnaz, *Five Years of My Life*, 150–154, 189–190, 210–215; Eric Schmitt and Tim Golden, "Force-Feeding at Guantanamo Is Now Acknowledged," *New York Times*, February 22, 2006; Tim Golden, "Tough U.S. Steps in Hunger Strike at Camp in Cuba," *New York Times*, February 9, 2006. For a later lenient, but ultimately unsuccessful, approach to the hunger strike, see Tim Golden, "The Battle for Guantanamo," *The New York Times Magazine*, September 17, 2006.

60. Author interview with Maj. Gen. Michael Lehnert, January 29, 2007.

61. Author interview with Shafiq Rasul and Moazzam Begg, February 22, 2007.

62. Author interview with Maj. Gen. Michael Lehnert, January 8, 2008.

63. Author interview with Capt. Samuel Patrick Alford, August 28, 2006.

64. For the most part, Lehnert's attentiveness to the psychological and physical complaints of the detainees had no counterpart during the later hunger strikes. In 2006, Colonel Wade F. Dennis stated that he did not interact with the detainees. He also said that the handful of detainees who continued to wage hunger strikes would get no "special attention...if they want to do that, hook it up," he said, referring to the restraint chair system for force-feeding. "If that's what you want to do, that's your choice." Tim Golden, "Military Taking a Tougher Line with Detainees," *New York Times*, December 16, 2006.

65. Author interview with Galen Jackman, July 21, 2007.

66. Author interview with Terry Carrico, April 4, 2007.

67. Sassi and Benhamou, *Prisonnier 325*, 129.

Chapter 12

1. Author interview with Brig. Gen. Rick Baccus, March 10, 2008.

2. Rick Baccus, *Frontline* interview, PBS, August 27, 2005.

3. Author interview with Brig. Gen. Rick Baccus, March 10, 2008.

4. Author interview with Maj. Gen. Michael Lehnert, August 27, 2007.

5. Author interview with Maj. Gen. Michael Lehnert, June 4, 2008.

6. DOD, "Military Commission Order No. 1," March 21, 2002.

7. Katharine Q. Seelye, "A Nation Challenged: The Trials; Pentagon Says Acquittal Might Not Free Detainees," New York Times, March 22, 2002.

8. Carol Rosenberg, "Guantanamo Prisoners Told About the Tribunals," Miami Herald, 23 March 2002, online ed. Available at Miami Herald Archives (accessed on November 12, 2008).

9. Author interview with Maj. Gen. Michael Lehnert, January 29, 2007.

10. Author interview with Carol Rosenberg, April 16, 2008.

11. Brigadier General Michael Lehnert—January 2002–March 2002; Brigadier General Rick Baccus—March 2002–October 2002; Major General Geoffrey D. Miller—October 2002–March 2004; Army Major General Jay Hood—March 2004–March 2006; Navy Rear Admiral Harry Harris—March 2006–May 2007; Navy Rear Admiral Mark H. Buzby—May 2007–May 2008; Rear Admiral David M. Thomas, Jr.—May 2008.

12. Carol Rosenberg, "Lead U.S. Interrogator Describes Camp X-Ray Captives as Lost Souls or Ideologues," Miami Herald, March 28, 2002.

13. Hollywood Reporter, "Daniels Wrapped in Flag Brouhaha," Chicago Sun-Times, October 30, 2001; Shawn Hubler, "Stirring Public Gesture or Over-the-Top Display?" Los Angeles Times, November 6, 2001; Dan Gilgoff, "Charlie Daniels is Rantin' and Rollin,'" U.S. News & World Report, November 19, 2001.

14. Associated Press, "Frontlines," Marine Corps Times, April 8, 2002.

15. "'Devil Went Down to Gitmo': Charlie Daniels Band Plays Guantanamo," Fox News March 28, 2002, available at http://www.foxnews.com/story/0,2933,48986,00.html (accessed on November 7, 2008).

16. Charlie Daniels, "Poor Ole Al Qaeda," CharlieDaniels.com Soapbox, 2002, available at http://www.charliedaniels.com/soapbox-2002-0244.htm (accessed on November 7, 2008); Charlie Daniels and Band, "From Charlie Daniels and Band after Visiting Guantanamo Bay, Cuba," Sgt. Grit American Courage Newsletter, July 24, 2002, available at http://www.grunt.com/scuttlebutt/newsarchives/2002/jul_24_ac.asp (accessed on November 7, 2008).

17. White House press release, April 2, 2002.

18. Author interview with Capt. Robert Buehn, June 17, 2008; author interview with Capt. Robert and Debra W. Buehn, Sept. 29, 2006.

19. Author interview with Capt. Samuel Patrick Alford, August 28, 2006.

20. Within days of his arrival, an abundance of policy letters appeared, defining one or another aspect of life and business at the camp. "I used to post a lot of disciplinary actions in prominent view where soldiers had to go by and look at them." Scott MacKay, "General: Detainees Handled Humanely under My Watch," The Providence Journal, October 18, 2005.

21. Baccus would have gone further in his restrictive policies. He would have banned liquor from the base, but as Bob Buehn pointed out to him, this would have been unfair to the naval families stationed there.

22. Spc. Frank N. Pellegrini, "Farewell to a Command," *The Wire*, October 11, 2002.

23. "The Torture Question." *Frontline*, PBS, August 27, 2005.

24. Author interview with Brig. Gen. Rick Baccus, March 10, 2008.

25. Author interview with Maj. Gen. Michael Lehnert, July 8, 2008.

Postscript

1. Author interview with Brig. Gen. Rick Baccus, March 10, 2008.

2. Author interview with Capt. Albert Shimkus, March 10, 2008.

3. Author interview with Maj. Gen. Michael Lehnert, March 16, 2008.

4. Author interview with Brig. Gen. Rick Baccus, March 10, 2008.

5. Jay S. Bybee, memorandum for Alberto Gonzales, Counsel to the President, "Standards of Conduct for Interrogation under 18 U.S.C. §§ 2340–2340A," August 1, 2002, in Karen J. Greenberg and Joshua L. Dratel, *The Torture Papers* (Cambridge: Cambridge University Press, 2005), 172–217.

6. Author interview with Charles Brule, December 14, 2007; author interview with Rick Baccus, March 10, 2008.

7. Author interview with Maj. Gen. Galen Jackman, July 21, 2007.

8. The techniques apparently originated with a group convened in Washington that included Haynes, Gonzales, Addington, and others. Philippe Sands, *Torture Team: Rumsfeld's Memo and the Betrayal of American Values* (New York: Palgrave Macmillan, 2008), 45–48.

9. Jerald Phifer, "Memorandum for Commander, Joint Task Force 170," October 11, 2002, in Greenberg and Dratel, *The Torture Papers*, 227–228. For a legal analysis of Geneva and the way these techniques violate the conventions, see Sands, *Torture Team*, 3–6, 220–222.

10. Diane Beaver to Commander JTF 170, "Legal Brief on Proposed Counter-Resistance Strategies," in Greenberg and Dratel, *The Torture Papers*, 229–235.

11. Sands, *Torture Team*, 76–84.

12. Jane Dalton, hearing, Senate Armed Services Committee, "Aggressive Interrogation Techniques toward Detainees in U.S. Custody," June 17, 2008.

13. Author interview with Manuel Supervielle, August 20, 2008.

14. James T. Hill to Chairman of the Joint Chiefs of Staff, October 25, 2002, "Counter-Resistance Techniques," in Greenberg and Dratel, *The Torture Papers*, 223.

15. Sands, *Torture Team*, 42.

16. William J. Haynes to Donald Rumsfeld, November 27, 2002 (approved by Rumsfeld December 2, 2002), "Counter-Resistance Techniques," in Greenberg and Dratel, *The Torture Papers*, 236–237.

17. Janis Karpinski, *One Woman's Army: The Commanding General of Abu Ghraib Tells Her Story* (New York: Hyperion, 2005), 183–205.

18. Errol Morris and Phillip Gourevitch, *Standard Operating Procedure* (New York: Penguin, 2008), 212.

19. Lt. Gen. Ricardo S. Sanchez, *Wiser in Battle: A Soldier's Story* (New York: Harper, 2008), xiii.

20. "The Schlesinger Report, Final Report of the Independent Panel to Review DOD Detention Operations," August 2004, in Greenberg and Dratel, *The Torture Papers*, 911–915.

21. "Tape of Detainee's Distress Released," *Los Angeles Times*, July 16, 2008, online ed., available at http://articles.latimes.com/2008/jul/16/nation/na-gitmo16 (accessed November 7, 2008).

22. Carol J. Williams, "Details on Detainee Suicides Emerging," *Los Angeles Times*, June 12, 2006.

Bibliography

Ball, Howard. *Bush, the Detainees, and the Constitution: The Battle over Presidential Power in the War on Terror.* Lawrence: University Press of Kansas, 2007.

Bamford, James. *The Shadow Factory: The Ultra-Secret NSA from 9/11 to the Eavesdropping on America.* New York: Doubleday, 2008.

Bamford, James. *Body of Secrets: Anatomy of the Ultra-Secret National Security Agency.* New York: Anchor, 2002.

Bamford, James. *The Puzzle Palace: A Report on NSA, America's Most Secret Agency.* New York: Penguin, 1983.

Barnett, Thomas P.M. *The Pentagon's New Map: War and Peace in the Twenty-First Century.* New York: Berkley, 2005.

Bartlett, Robert M. *Trial by Fire and Water: The Medieval Judicial Ordeal.* New York: Oxford University Press, 1986.

Begg, Moazzam. *Enemy Combatant: My Imprisonment at Guantanamo, Bagram, and Kandahar.* New York: The New Press, 2006.

Bennett, Angela. *The Geneva Convention: The Hidden Origins of the Red Cross.* Grand Rapids, MI: Sutton, 2006.

Bergen, Peter L. *Holy War, Inc.: Inside the Secret World of Osama Bin Laden.* New York: Simon & Schuster, 2001.

Berntsen, Gary, and Ralph Pezzullo. *Jawbreaker: The Attack on Bin Laden and Al-Qaeda: A Personal Account by the CIA's Key Field Commander.* New York: Three Rivers Press, 2006.

Bettelheim, Bruno. *Surviving and Other Essays.* New York: Alfred A. Knopf, 1979.

Biguenet, John. *The Torturer's Apprentice: Stories.* New York: HarperCollins, 2002.

Boot, Max. *The Savage Wars of Peace: Small Wars and the Rise of American Power.* New York: Basic Books, 2003.

Boyle, Peter G., ed. *The Eden-Eisenhower Correspondence, 1955–1957.* Chapel Hill: University of North Carolina Press, 2005.

Brooks, Peter. *Troubling Confessions: Speaking Guilt in Law and Literature.* New York: University of Chicago Press, 2001.

Clarke, Torie. *Lipstick on a Pig: Winning in the No-Spin Era by Someone Who Knows the Game.* New York: Free Press, 2006.

Cockburn, Andrew. *Rumsfeld: His Rise, Fall, and Catastrophic Legacy.* New York: Scribner, 2007.

Coll, Steve. *Ghost Wars: The Secret History of the CIA, Afghanistan, and Bin Laden, from the Soviet Invasion to September 10, 2001.* New York: Penguin, 2004.

Conason, Joe. *It Can Happen Here: Authoritarian Peril in the Age of Bush.* New York: Thomas Dunne Books, 2007.

Conover, Ted. *Newjack: Guarding Sing Sing*. New York: Vintage, 2001.

Couch, Dick. *Down Range: Navy SEALs in the War on Terrorism*. New York: Crown, 2005.

Crews, Robert D., and Amin Tarzi, eds. *The Taliban and the Crisis of Afghanistan*. Cambridge, MA: Harvard University Press, 2008.

Curry, Tracy Howard. *Uprising at Guantanamo Bay*. Danbury, CT: iUniverse, 2005.

Danner, Mark. *Torture and Truth: America, Abu Ghraib, and the War on Terror*. New York: New York Review Books, 2004.

DeYoung, Karen. *Soldier: The Life of Colin Powell*. New York: Vintage, 2007.

Drumbl, Mark A. *Atrocity, Punishment, and International Law*. New York: Cambridge University Press, 2007.

Drumheller, Tyler, and Elaine Monaghan. *On the Brink: An Insider's Account of How the White House Compromised American Intelligence*. New York: PublicAffairs, 2007.

Falkoff, Marc, ed. *Poems from Guantanamo: The Detainees Speak*. Iowa City: University of Iowa Press, 2007.

Fesperman, Dan. *The Prisoner of Guantanamo*. New York: Knopf, 2006.

Fick, Nathaniel C. *One Bullet Away: The Making of a Marine Officer*. New York: Mariner Books, 2006.

Francis, Richard. *Judge Sewall's Apology: The Salem Witch Trials and the Forming of the American Conscience*. New York: HarperCollins, 2005.

Gellman, Barton. *Angler: The Cheney Vice Presidency*. New York: Penguin, 2008.

Golden, Tim. "The Battle for Guantánamo." *New York Times Magazine*, Sept. 17, 2006.

Golden, Tim. "Tough U.S. Steps in Hunger Strike at Camp in Cuba." *New York Times*, Feb. 9, 2006.

Golden, Tim, and Don Van Natta Jr. "The Reach of War; U.S. Said to Overstate Value of Guantánamo Detainees." *New York Times*, June 21, 2004.

Golden, Tim, and Eric Schmitt. "Force Feeding at Guantánamo Is Now Acknowledged." *New York Times*, Feb. 22, 2006.

Goldsmith, Jack L., and Eric A. Posner. *Limits of International Law*. New York: Oxford University Press, 2005.

Goldsmith, Jack L. *The Terror Presidency: Law and Judgment Inside the Bush Administration*. Boston: W. W. Norton, 2007.

Goldstein, Brandt. *Storming the Court: How a Band of Law Students Sued the President—And Won*. New York: Scribner, 2005.

Greenberg, Karen J., ed. *The Torture Debate in America*. New York: Cambridge University Press, 2005.

Greenberg, Karen J. and Joshua L. Dratel, eds. *The Torture Papers: The Road to Abu Ghraib*. New York: Cambridge University Press, 2005.

Grey, Stephen. *Ghost Plane: The True Story of the CIA Torture Program*. New York: St. Martin's Press, 2006.

Halper, Stefan, and Jonathan Clarke. *America Alone: The Neo-Conservatives and the Global Order*. New York: Cambridge University Press, 2005.

Harbury, Jennifer K. *Truth, Torture, and the American Way: The History and Consequences of U.S. Involvement in Torture.* New York: Beacon, 2005.

Hedges, Chris. *War Is a Force that Gives Us Meaning.* New York: Anchor, 2003.

Hersh, Seymour M. *Chain of Command: The Road from 9/11 to Abu Ghraib.* New York: HarperCollins, 2004.

Hillman, James. *A Terrible Love of War.* New York: Penguin, 2005.

Hobbs, Joseph P. *Dear General: Eisenhower's Wartime Letters to Marshall.* New York: Johns Hopkins University Press, 1999.

Hoffman, Jon T. *Chesty: The Story of Lieutenant General Lewis B. Puller, USMC.* New York: Random House, 2002.

Huntington, Samuel P. *The Soldier and the State: The Theory and Politics of Civil-Military Relations.* New York: Belknap, 1981.

Ignatieff, Michael. *The Lesser Evil: Political Ethics in an Age of Terror.* Princeton, NJ: Princeton University Press, 2004.

Jaffer, Jameel, and Amrit Singh. *Administration of Torture: A Documentary Record from Washington to Abu Ghraib and Beyond.* New York: Columbia University Press, 2007.

Karpinski, Janis, and Steven Strasser. *One Woman's Army: The Commanding General of Abu Ghraib Tells Her Story.* New York: Miramax Books, 2005.

Khan, Mahvish. *My Guantanamo Diary: The Detainees and the Stories They Told Me.* New York: PublicAffairs, 2008.

Kissinger, Henry A. *Years of Renewal.* New York: Simon & Schuster, 2000.

Kochavi, Arieh J. *Confronting Captivity: Britain and the United States and Their POWs in Nazi Germany.* Chapel Hill: University of North Carolina Press, 2005.

Krulak, Victor H. *First to Fight: An Inside View of the U. S. Marine Corps.* New York: Naval Institute Press, 1999.

Kurnaz, Murat, and Helmut Kuhn. *Five Years of My Life: An Innocent Man in Guantanamo.* Translated by Jefferson Chase. New York: Palgrave Macmillan, 2008.

Lagouranis, Tony, and Allen Mikaelian. *Fear Up Harsh: An Army Interrogator's Dark Journey Through Iraq.* New York: NAL, 2007.

Lelyveld, Joseph. "In Guantanamo." *The New York Review of Books,* Nov. 7, 2002.

Levinson, Sanford, ed. *Torture: A Collection.* New York: Oxford University Press, 2004.

Lichtblau, Eric. *Bush's Law: The Remaking of American Justice.* New York: Pantheon, 2008.

Lincoln, Bruce. *Religion, Empire, and Torture: The Case of Achaemenian Persia, with a Postscript on Abu Ghraib.* New York: University of Chicago Press, 2007.

Mann, James. *Rise of the Vulcans: The History of Bush's War Cabinet.* New York: Penguin, 2004.

Margulies, Joseph. *Guantanamo and the Abuse of Presidential Power.* New York: Simon & Schuster, 2006.

Marvel, William. *Andersonville: The Last Depot.* Chapel Hill: University of North Carolina Press, 2006.

Mason, Theodore K. *Across the Cactus Curtain: The Story of Guantanamo Bay.* New York: Dodd, Mead & Co., 1984.

Mayer, Jane. *The Dark Side: The Inside Story of How the War on Terror Turned into a War on American Ideals.* New York: Doubleday, 2008.

McCoy, Alfred. *A Question of Torture: CIA Interrogation, from the Cold War to the War on Terror.* New York: Metropolitan Books, 2006.

McKelvey, Tara. *Monstering: Inside America's Policy of Secret Interrogations and Torture in the Terror War.* New York: Basic Books, 2008.

McMaster, H. R. *Dereliction of Duty: Johnson, McNamara, the Joint Chiefs of Staff, and the Lies That Led to Vietnam.* New York: HarperCollins, 1998.

Miles, Steven H. *Oath Betrayed: Torture, Medical Complicity, and the War on Terror.* New York: Random House, 2006.

Miller, Greg, and Chris Mackey. *The Interrogators: Task Force 500 and America's Secret War against Al Qaeda.* New York: Back Bay, 2005.

Neiman, Susan. *Evil in Modern Thought: An Alternative History of Philosophy.* Princeton, NJ: Princeton University Press, 2002.

Nenner, Howard. *By Colour of Law: Legal Culture and Constitutional Politics in England, 1660–1689.* Chicago: University of Chicago Press, 1977.

O'Donnell, Pierce. *In Time of War: Hitler's Terrorist Attack on America.* New York: The New Press, 2005.

Overy, Richard. *Interrogations: The Nazi Elite in Allied Hands, 1945.* London: Penguin, 2001.

Pelley, Scott. "Rendition." *60 Minutes.* CBS, Dec. 18, 2005.

Perry, Mark. *Four Stars: The Inside Story of the Forty-Year Battle Between the Joint Chiefs of Staff and America's Civilian Leaders.* Boston: Houghton Mifflin, 1989.

Posner, Richard A. *Countering Terrorism: Blurred Focus, Halting Steps.* New York: Rowman & Littlefield, 2007.

Priest, Dana. *The Mission: Waging War and Keeping Peace with America's Military.* Boston: W. W. Norton, 2003.

Rajiva, Lila. *The Language of Empire: Abu Ghraib and the American Media.* New York: Monthly Review Press, 2005.

Rasul, Shafiq, Asif Iqbal, and Rhuhel Ahmed. *Composite Statement: Detention in Afghanistan and Guantanamo Bay.* New York: Center for Constitutional Rights, July 2004.

Ratner, Michael, Ellen Ray, and Anthony Lewis. *Guantanamo: What the World Should Know.* New York: Chelsea Green, 2004.

Report on Torture and Cruel, Inhuman, and Degrading Treatment of Prisoners at Guantánamo Bay, Cuba. New York: Center for Constitutional Rights, July 2006.

Ricks, Thomas E. *Making the Corps.* New York: Pocket Books, 1998.

Roosevelt, Theodore. *Rough Riders.* Marina del Rey, CA: Aegypan, 2005.

Rose, David. *Guantanamo: The War on Human Rights.* New York: The New Press, 2004.

Roth, Kenneth M., Minky Worden, and Amy D. Bernstein, eds. *Torture: A Human Rights Perspective.* New York: The New Press, 2005.

Saar, Erik, and Viveca Novak. *Inside the Wire: A Military Intelligence Soldier's Eyewitness Account of Life at Guantanamo.* New York: Penguin, 2005.

Sales, Leigh. *Detainee 002: The Case of David Hicks*. New York: Eurospan Group, 2007.

Sanchez, Ricardo S., and Donald T. Phillips. *Wiser in Battle: A Soldier's Story*. New York: HarperCollins, 2008.

Sands, Philippe. *Lawless World: America and the Making and Breaking of Global Rules—From FDR's Atlantic Charter to George W. Bush's Illegal War*. London: Allen Lane, 2005.

Sands, Philippe. *Torture Team: Rumsfeld's Memo and the Betrayal of American Values*. New York: Penguin, 2008.

Sassi, Nizar. *Prisonnier 325, Camp Delta: de Vénissieux à Guantanamo*. Paris: Editions Denoël, 2006.

Scarborough, Rowan. *Rumsfeld's War: The Untold Story of America's Anti-Terrorist Commander*. Boston: Regnery, 2004.

Scarry, Elaine. *The Body in Pain: The Making and Unmaking of the World*. New York: Oxford University Press, 1988.

Scott, John Paul. *Aggression*. Chicago: University of Chicago Press, 1976.

Shephard, Michelle. *Guantanamo's Child: The Untold Story of Omar Khadr*. New York: Wiley, 2008.

Shklar, Judith N. *Ordinary Vices*. New York: Belknap, 1984.

Shulsky, Abram N., and Gary J. Schmitt. *Silent Warfare: Understanding the World of Intelligence*. New York: Potomac Books, 2002.

Simon, Bob. "The Youngest Terrorist." 60 Minutes. CBS. Nov. 18, 2007.

Smith, Clive Stafford. *The Eight O'Clock Ferry to the Windward Side: Seeking Justice in Guantanamo Bay*. New York: Nation Books, 2007.

Sontag, Susan. *Regarding the Pain of Others*. New York: Picador, 2004.

Stone, Geoffrey R. *Perilous Times: Free Speech in Wartime from the Sedition Act of 1798 to the War on Terrorism*. New York: Norton, 2005.

Stover, Eric, and Elena O. Nightingale. *Breaking of Minds and Bodies*. Boston: W. H. Freeman, 1985.

Strauss, David Levi, Charles Stein, et al. *Abu Ghraib: The Politics of Torture*. New York: North Atlantic Books, 2004.

Sykes, Gresham M., and Bruce Western. *The Society of Captives: A Study of a Maximum Security Prison*. Princeton, NJ: Princeton University Press, 2007.

Temple-Raston, Dina. *The Jihad Next Door: The Lackawanna Six and Rough Justice in an Age of Terror*. New York: PublicAffairs, 2007.

U. S. Army Intelligence and Interrogation Handbook: The Official Guide on Prisoner Interrogation. New York: Lyons Press, 2005.

Villa, Dana R. *Politics, Philosophy, Terror—Essays on the Thought of Hannah Arendt*. Princeton, NJ: Princeton University Press, 1999.

Warren, James A. *American Spartans: The U. S. Marines: A Combat History from Iwo Jima to Iraq*. New York: Pocket, 2007.

Wittes, Benjamin. *Law and the Long War: The Future of Justice in the Age of Terror*. New York: Penguin, 2008.

Woodward, Bob. *Bush at War: Inside the Bush White House*. New York: Simon & Schuster, 2002.

Woodward, Bob. *Plan of Attack*. New York: Simon & Schuster, 2004.

Woodward, Bob. *State of Denial: Bush at War, Part III*. New York: Simon & Schuster, 2006.

Woodward, Bob. *The War Within: A Secret White House History*. New York: Simon & Schuster, 2008.

Woulfe, James B. *Into the Crucible: Making Marines for the 21st Century*. New York: Presidio Press, 1999.

Wright, Lawrence. *The Looming Tower: Al Qaeda and the Road to 9/11*. New York: Alfred A. Knopf, 2006.

Yee, James, and Aimee Molloy. *For God and Country: Faith and Patriotism under Fire*. New York: PublicAffairs, 2005.

Yoo, John. *War by Other Means: An Insider's Account of the War on Terror*. New York: Atlantic Monthly Press, 2006.

Zegart, Amy B. *Flawed by Design: The Evolution of the CIA, JCS, and NSC*. Stanford, CA: Stanford University Press, 1999.

Index

Abrams, Elliott, 163
Abu Ghraib, 219
Aburabi, Raed, 99
Addington, David, 7, 46, 94, 122
Afghanistan
  detainees from. *See* Detainees
  International Committee of the Red
    Cross' familiarity with, 58
  Mazar-e Sharif, 2, 4, 116
  Pol-e-Charkhi, 4
  transport of detainees to Guantanamo,
    68–69
Ahmed, Rhuhel, 182
al Qaeda, 2
  denial of prisoner of war status,
    52–53, 156
  escape into Pakistan, 81
  as nonstate actor, 121
al-Alwani, Taha, 192
Alford, Patrick, 103–104, 107,
  115, 186
al-Qahtani, Mohammed, 215
American Samoa, 5
Amnesty International, 58, 80
Aristide, Jean-Bertrand, 14
Armitage, Richard, 2
Ashcroft, John, 45
Ashura, 203
Authorization for Use of Military Force
  Act, 224n7

Baccus, Rick
  Guantanamo command by, 210–212,
    243n11
  Lehnert's briefings with, 200
  memos by, 211
  selection of, 198–199
Bamford, James ("Jim"), 166
Beaver, Diane, 215–216, 218
Begg, Moazzem, 138
Bellinger, John, 163
bin Laden, Osama, 81, 83, 146
Blair, Tony, 87

Bloomfield, Lincoln, 163
Boegli, Urs, 98
Bolman, Scott, 85
Bonard, Paul, 99
Bowker, David, 52, 154
Bravo Block, 78
Buehn, Debra ("Debi"), 11, 39, 77, 108
Buehn, Robert, 1, 33, 159
  as Deputy Commander, 36
  Guantanamo command by, 7–11,
    15–17, 35
  Lehnert and, 36–37, 201, 221
  town meeting with families of
    servicemen and women, 37–38
Buikema, Ronald, 151
Bulkeley Hall Auditorium, 38
Burgess, Ronald, 168, 216
Burn bag chart, 176, 188, 240n1
Burns and Roe, 14
Bush, George W.
  Citadel speech, 29–30
  Military Order, 3
Buzby, Mark H., 243n11
Bybee, Jay, 214

Cambone, Stephen, 168
Camp Alpha, 18
Camp Charles, 18
Camp Delta
  building of, 209
  Camp X-Ray compared to, 210, 212
  description of, 18, 118
  isolation of, 210, 212
  Lehnert's preparations for, 178
  location of, 210
  seeking of approval to build, 178
Camp Freedom, 108
Camp X-Ray
  banning of press from, 77–78
  "cages" at, 18, 80, 100, 123, 180
  Camp Delta compared to, 210, 212
  description of, 18, 34, 69, 118–119
  detainee population at, 180

Camp X-Ray (*continued*)
  environment at, 112, 123, 180
  hunger strikes at. *See* Hunger
    strikes
  interrogations at, 150
  medical staff needed at, 97
  no-talking policy, 129, 152, 211
  prisoners at. *See* Detainees
  visitors to, 90–91
Carrico, Terry, 60–61, 65, 68, 74–75, 79,
    103, 105–106, 111–114, 138, 201
Castro, Fidel, 8
Castro, Raúl, 69
CENTCOM, 1, 59, 62
Central Intelligence Agency
    interrogations, 149
Chain of command, 36
Chaplains. *See also* Saifulislam,
    Abuhena
  description of, 65, 127
  distrust of, 236n23
Charlie Daniels Band, 207–209
Cheney, Dick, 7, 46
Cherry Point, North Carolina, 37
Chertoff, Michael, 44
Civil War (U.S.), 51
Clarke, Torie, 72–73, 89
Cobb, Paul ("Whit"), 93
Comfort items, 183, 185, 193
Corrections team, 61
Costello, William, 71, 184, 204
Coudriet, Marc, 41, 43, 84
Cox, Steve, 71, 80, 115, 140, 182, 184, 204
Craddock, Bantz John, 242n58
Criminal Investigation Task Force, 159,
    196
Cuba
  description of, 8
  refugees from, 15, 225n39
  security concerns, 10
  surveillance by, 18–19
  United States and, relations between,
    10–12
  watchtowers, 18, 34, 74
Cuban Border Brigade, 12

Daily Mail, 87
Dalton, Jane, 63

Daniels, Charlie, 207–209
Dansak, Tom, 137
Dean, Dan, 24
Defense Intelligence Agency, 149
Defense Logistics Agency, 228n8
Delahunty, Robert, 52
Dennis, Wade F., 243
Deployable joint task force, 228n5
Depression, 180–181
Detainees
  abusive behavior against, 82, 116
  adaptations by, 180–181
  addressing of, by Lehnert, 190–192,
    202–205
  alien character of, 139
  anger of, 107
  appearance of, 76, 219
  arrival at Guantanamo, 69, 76, 219
  classification of, 59, 62
  communication, 81–82, 129
  culture of, 83–84
  customs of, 97–98
  danger level of, 160
  detaining authorities and, relationship
    between, 112
  detention in Afghanistan, 4
  English-speaking, 82–83
  food for, 96, 110, 179–180, 193
  gag rule for, 106, 129–130
  guards and, similarities between, 161
  health conditions of, 96–97
  hunger strikes by, 110, 176–177,
    185–189, 192–197
  imam arrives, 128–129
  Individual Service Numbers for, 81
  information-gathering about, 135
  International Committee of the Red
    Cross questioning of, 99–100
  interrogation of, 145–146
  isolation of, 211
  in Kandahar, 4
  lack of information about, 81
  language diversity of, 81–82
  leaders of, 193–194
  legal rights of, 124
  legal status of, 47–48, 52
  Lehnert's view of, 138–139
  life of, 89–90

melancholy of, 179–180
memoirs by, 164
names assigned to, 84
noncompliance by, 184
number of, 43
Office of Legal Counsel memo
    regarding, 52
peer pressure on, 193–194
photographs of, 87–88, 115–116, 124
positive control of, 79
present-day status of, 220
processing of, by Army soldiers,
    78–80
revolts by, 177
riots by, 183
shackling of, 181
sleeping provisions, 100
suicides by, 220
tactical intelligence from, 145
threat associated with, 116
transport of
    from Afghanistan to Guantanamo,
      68–69
    from airfield to Camp X-Ray, 69–70
weighing of, 78, 96, 187
weight gain among, 186–187
Detention
    lack of guidelines for, 42–43
    rationale for, 147–148
Dostum, Abdul Rashid, 4
Dunlavey, Michael
    appointment as intelligence
      commander at Guantanamo,
      166–167
    Army career of, 165
    biographical data, 164–165
    bureaucracy by, 169
    education of, 165
    at INSCOM, 166
    Lehnert and, 171, 173–174
    National Security Agency career,
      165–166
    rank of, 169
    Saifulislam and, 170, 213
    supervision of, 168

Eid al-Adha, 110, 179, 182, 187
European Court of Human Rights, 5

Farabee, Robert, 41
Fasting, 186, 193. *See also* Hunger
    strikes
Feinstein, Dianne, 119, 123
Flanigan, Timothy, 7, 47
Fleet Hospital, 103, 119
Fleischer, Ari, 76
FORSCOM, 60
Franken, Bob, 72–73, 140, 142, 184,
    188, 204
Franks, Tommy, 1, 4
Frontier Brigade, 12

Gag rule, 106, 129–130
Gaudio, Jan, 1, 7, 10–11
Geneva Conventions
    as applied to al Qaeda, 121
    Article 5, 56–57
    Article 17, 154–155
    Civil War violations of, 51
    Common Article 3, 50, 92, 103, 121
    history of, 50–51
    International Committee of the Red
      Cross, 50, 57–59
    in Korean War, 50–51
    Lehnert's review of, 55–56
    Office of Legal Counsel memo
      regarding, 47, 52–55
    photographs as violations of, 88
    Powell on, 155–156
    prisoner of war status under, 52, 57
    Protocol II, 53
    Supervielle's guidelines for, 93–95
    Taft's interpretation of, 53–54, 91–92
    troop training regarding, 105
    in Vietnam War, 51
Gerth, Tom, 11–12
Globe and Mail, 87
Gonzales, Alberto, 2, 7, 44, 51
Guam, 5–6, 15
Guantanamo Bay Detention Facility
    advantages of, 15
    Buehn's command at, 10–11, 35
    challenges associated with, 21, 39–40
    commanders of, 243n11. *See also specific*
      commander
    Cuban employees at, 13
    Cuban surveillance of, 18–19

Guantanamo (*continued*)
　decisions to use, 6, 17–18, 20
　description of, 8
　desolation of, 33–34
　detention facility at, 9, 13–14, 17, 21,
　　40, 59–60
　dual commanders at, 199
　funding of, 225n28
　history of, 14
　hospital capacity at, 16–17
　International Committee of the Red
　　Cross arrival at, 86
　interrogation purposes for, 147–148
　labor force at, 13–14
　landscape of, 32–33
　legacy of, 220–221
　Lehnert's command at. *See* Lehnert,
　　Michael
　life at, 8–9
　media access to, 70–72, 141
　media criticisms of, 163–164
　migrant crisis at, 14–15
　military policing of, 19–20
　Miller's command of, 217
　purpose of, 8, 40, 147
　rebuilding of, 47
　relocation of families to, 38–39
　rotation of command at, 199, 206
　Rumsfeld's visit to, 118–120,
　　122–123
　rushed preparations at, 31–32
　security risk issues, 13
　senators' visit to, 119
　supervision of, 20–21
　supplies delivered to, 8–9
　visitors to, 90–91
Guards
　accountability of, 136
　anonymity requests by, 111, 113–114
　behavior by, 136
　detainees and, similarities
　　between, 161
　fears of, 107
　gag rule for, 106
　Koran abuse by, 182
　living conditions for, 108
　no-talking policy, 129, 152, 211
　safety of, 107

　self-defense by, 107
　shift rotations for, 108
Guter, Donald, 161

Habeas corpus, writ of, 47, 228n14
Haitians, 14–15, 27–28, 225n38
Hajj, 179
Halal food, 96
Hamdan, Salim, 220
Harris, Harry, 243n11
Hayden, Michael, 166
Haynes, William "Jim," 7, 45–46, 51, 63,
　91–92, 94–95, 217–218
Hernández, José Solar, 12
Hettler, Migdalia, 10, 173
Hicks, David, 83, 85–86, 138–139, 220
Hill, James "Tom," 215, 217
Hodgett, Alistair, 195
Hood, Jay, 243n11
Hospitals, 16, 104
Human rights groups, 58–59
Human Rights Watch, 58, 80
Hunger strikes
　description of, 110, 176–177
　handling of, after Lehnert's departure,
　　242n58, 243n63
　Lehnert's handling of, 185–189,
　　192–197
Hutchinson, Kay Bailey, 119, 123

Immediate Reaction Force, 74–75, 91,
　106, 182, 184, 211
Inouye, Daniel, 119, 123
INSCOM, 165, 166
Intelligence gathering
　changes in, 151
　description of, 147
　findings, 161
　lack of, 153
　Nichols's concerns about, 152
　Rumsfeld's failure to sign the execute
　　order for, 150
　by SOUTHCOM, 153
　standard operating procedure for, 153
International Committee of the
　Red Cross
　arrival at Guantanamo, 86, 98
　benefits of, 102–103

Boegli's work with, 98–99
focus of, 65
four-man delegation from, 98–99
Geneva Conventions and, 50, 57–59
interviewing of detainees by, 99–100, 102
invitation to Guantanamo, 62–65,
    92–93
Lehnert's response to, 98–99
medical recommendations provided by,
    101–102
praise by, 143–144
recommendations by, 100–101
welcoming of, 98
Interrogations
    at Camp X-Ray, 150
    Category III techniques, 215–216
    Central Intelligence Agency, 149
    for detention, 160
    environment for, 174
    harsher techniques for, 215–216
    informal, 157
    JTF 170's role in, 157–158
    keys to, 174
    methods of, 172, 214–216
    for military tribunals, 160
    Nichols's concerns about, 152
    organized, 157
    prevention of abuse during, 172
    by SOUTHCOM, 151, 153
    standard operating procedure for, 153
    strategic, 145–146, 158–159
    types of, 145–146
    U.S. historical attempts at, 148
Iqbal, Asif, 83, 164
Iraq, 218–219

Jackman, Galen, 59, 98, 148–149, 159,
    164, 187, 196, 215
Joint Chiefs of Staff, 30–31, 45, 121
Joint Detention Operations Group, 105
Joint Task Force (JTF) 160, 20, 22, 28, 35,
    37, 54, 67, 120, 143, 153, 160, 169,
    173, 175, 177, 182, 206, 213, 218
Joint Task Force (JTF) 170, 157–158, 162,
    173, 175, 213

Kandahar, 4
Karpinski, Janis, 219

Koran
    abuse of, 182
    lack of, 97, 100, 128
Kross, Katherine, 73
Kurnaz, Murat, 179, 181–182
Kvaerner, 14

Land mines, 10–11
Leahy, Patrick, 44
Lehnert, Michael
    addressing of detainees by, 190–192,
        202–205
    advisors to, 36–37
    arrival at Guantanamo, 65–66, 68–69
    Baccus's succession of, 197, 200
    beliefs of, 28–29
    Buehn and, 36–37, 201
    Carrico and, 74–75, 112–114
    command staff with, 32, 64–65
    commanding style of, 114–115
    community outreach efforts by, 27, 65–66
    departure from Guantanamo, 206–207
    description of, 23–24
    detainees as viewed by, 138–139
    Dunlavey and, 171, 173–174
    first visits to Guantanamo, 31–33
    Geneva Conventions review by, 55
    hunger strikes by detainees handled by,
        185–189, 192–197
    Operation Sea Signal, 34, 112
    press and, 204–205
    reflections on Guantanamo, 220–221
    replacement for, 197
    reputation of, 137
    Rumsfeld's discussion with, 119–120
    Saifulislam and, 129–142, 202
    skills of, 26
    sympathy by, 196
    town meeting with families of
        servicemen and women, 66
    U.S. Marine Corps career, 25–26
Leishmaniasis, 101
Levin, Carl, 44–45
Lindh, John Walker, 49, 116

Marine Corps
    description of, 25–26
Marshall, Michael, 108

Martin, Kate, 228n14
Mattis, James, 70
McCalla Airfield, 33
McCoy, Shane, 89
McKay, John, 28
Mecca, 97, 132
Media
    access to Guantanamo, 70–72, 141
    banning from Camp X-Ray, 77–78
    criticisms by, 163
    Lehnert's final meeting with, 205
    Saifulislam's introduction to, 140
Mehl, Christian, 99
Meier, William, 32, 37, 41, 57, 135, 201
Miami Herald, 128–129, 142, 206
Mica, John, 123
Migrants, 14, 34, 226n40
Military commissions, 45, 159
Military Order of November 13, 2001
    Congressional support for, 45
    description of, 3–4, 44, 202–203
    drafting of, 46
Miller, Geoffrey, 217, 243n11
Miller, Tim, 41, 55
Myers, Richard, 68, 144, 217

Nakedness, 97, 100–101
National anthem, 109–110
National Security Agency, 165–166
National Security Council, 123
Natter, Robert J., 17
Naval War College, 16
New York Times, 87, 163, 206
Nichols, Timothy, 32, 74, 85, 90, 151–152,
    160, 170, 173, 191, 238n32
Noel, Monje Malak Abd al-Muta' Ali, 127
No-names request by guards, 111, 113–114
Northern Alliance, 2, 4
No-talking policy, 129, 152, 211

Office of Legal Counsel (OLC), 47, 51, 52,
    54, 93, 121, 122, 154, 156, 157, 214
Operation Enduring Freedom, 161
Operation Sea Signal, 26, 28, 34, 38, 112, 189

Pace, Peter, 31
Pakistan, 81
Panama, 15

Parra, Arthur, 160
Pashto, 81–82
PATRIOT Act, 45, 228n14
Patriotism, 20–21, 35, 208
Peer pressure, 193–194
Philbin, Patrick, 47
Pocket litter, 152
Positive control, 79
Powell, Colin, 3, 45, 94, 121–123, 155–156
Prayer, 97–98, 100, 131–132
Prayer beads, 133, 185
Prayer caps, 192
Prisoner(s). *See* Detainees
Prisoner of war status
    denial of, 52–53, 62, 123, 156
    description of, 52, 57
Prosper, Pierre-Richard, 2–6, 19, 44, 163
Psychiatrists, 172, 213

Quadrennial Defense Review, 30–31, 149

Radio Range, 33, 118, 178, 210
Rasul, Shafiq, 77, 79, 82, 132–133, 191
Red Cross. *See* International Committee of
    the Red Cross
Religious holidays, 110, 179, 182, 187, 203
Rice, Condoleezza, 3
Ridge, Tom, 166
Robinson, Mary, 87
Romig, Thomas J., 159
Roosevelt, Teddy, 8
Rosenberg, Carol, 72, 89, 119, 128, 142,
    168, 204–205, 221
Ros-Lehtinen, Ileana, 85
Rumsfeld, Donald, 6–7, 20, 29–30
    Cheney and, 46
    congressional delegation support
        for, 123
    Lehnert and, 30, 119–120
    living conditions at Guantanamo
        explained by, 115–117
    reactions to photograph of detainees,
        88–89, 115–116
    video teleconference by, 144, 146–147
    visit to Guantanamo, 118–120, 122–123

Saifulislam, Abuhena
    chaplaincy education of, 126–127

detainees' interactions with,
133–134, 171
distrust of, 137, 236n23
Dunlavey and, 170, 213
Guantanamo deployment,
127–128
information-gathering role of, 135,
170–171
introduction to detainees, 132
Lehnert and, 129–142, 202
press meeting with, 140
privileges given to, 135
Sanchez, Ricardo, 219
Sanders, Charles W., 51
Sands, Philippe, 167
Sassi, Nizar, 191
Sensory deprivation, 76
September 11, 2001
patriotism after, 20–21, 35
Shimkus, Albert, 16–17, 33, 37, 79,
102–103, 186, 188, 201, 221
Showering, 100, 102, 135
SOUTHCOM
chain of command at, 172–173
description of, 17, 20
Hill's appointment at, 215
intelligence mission of, 161–162
interrogations by, 151, 153
legal members of, 55
Pace's leadership of, 31
Supervielle's presence at, 55–56
video teleconference by Rumsfeld, 144,
146–147, 151
Speer, Gary, 31, 59, 119, 169, 172, 206
Stafford, Wendy, 55
Stevens, Ted, 119
Supervielle, Manuel
Beaver's memo given to, 216
Geneva Conventions guidelines,
93–95
invitation of ICRC to Guantanamo by,
62–63, 92

Taft, William H. IV
description of, 51–52
response to Office of Legal Counsel
memo, 53–54, 91–92, 121, 153,
156–157

Yoo's visits with, 154
Taliban, 2
denial of prisoner of war status, 52–53,
156
as failed state, 121
Geneva Convention and, 121
Thomas, David M. Jr., 243n11
Tinian, 5
Tora Bora, 81
Torture, mistreatment, and abuse, 76,
79–80, 82, 97, 100, 101, 116, 172,
177–183, 215, 216, 219
Troops
accountability of, 136
anonymity requests by, 111,
113–114
behavior by, 136
demoralization of, 109
detainees and, similarities between,
161
fears of, 107
gag rule for, 106
job responsibilities of, 109
Koran abuse by, 182
living conditions for, 108
no-names request by, 111, 113–114
no-talking policy, 129, 152, 211
resentment by, 108, 110–111
safety of, 107
self-defense by, 107
shift rotations for, 108
Tuberculosis, 96, 107
Tulepan, Randy, 73

Uniform Code of Military Justice, 3, 50
United States
Cuba and, relations between, 10–12
Unity of command, 35–36, 158
Urdu, 81–82, 131
U.S. flag, 109, 205
U.S. House Judiciary Committee,
44, 45
U.S. military
detention efforts by, 21
future direction of, 29
hierarchical nature of, 49
immigrants in, 235n2
Rumsfeld's work with, 29–30

U.S. military (continued)
    streamlining of, 35
    unity of effort in, 35–36
U.S. Senate Appropriations Committee, 119
U.S. Senate Armed Services Committee,
        44–45, 48

Védrine, Hubert, 87

Wake Island, 5, 51
War Council, 46–47, 120

Washington Post, 87, 122
Weddings, 19
Weighing of detainees, 78,
        96, 187
Weight gain, 186–187
White, Thomas, 161
"Wild Bill," 84–85, 160
Wolfowitz, Paul, 49, 147, 167

Yoo, John, 7, 46, 52–53, 91–92, 121,
        154–156, 167, 214